ELEMENTS OF
Literature
THIRD COURSE

D1309561

The Holt Reader
An Interactive WorkText

Instruction in Reading Literature and Informational Materials

Standardized Test Practice

HOLT, RINEHART AND WINSTON

A Harcourt Education Company

Austin • Orlando • Chicago • New York • Toronto • London • San Diego

CREDITS

Supervisory Editors: Juliana Koenig, Fannie Safier

Managing Editor: Mike Topp

Administrative Managing Editor: Michael Neibergall

Senior Product Manager: Don Wulbrecht

Editors: Terence J. Fitzgerald, Carroll Moulton, Sari Wilson

Copyediting Supervisor: Mary Malone

Copyeditors: Elizabeth Dickson, *Senior Copyeditor;* Christine Altgelt, Joel Bourgeois, Emily Force, Julie A. Hill, Julia Thomas Hu, Jennifer Kirkland, Millicent Ondras, Dennis Scharnberg

Project Administration: Elizabeth LaManna

Editorial Support: Bret Isaacs, Brian Kachmar, Mark Koenig, Erik Netcher

Editorial Permissions: David Smith, Carrie Jones

Design: Bruce Bond, *Design Director, Book Design*

Electronic Publishing: Nanda Patel, JoAnn Stringer, *Project Coordinators;* Sally Dewhirst, *Quality Control Team Leader;* Angela Priddy, Barry Bishop, Becky Golden-Harrell, Ellen Rees, *Quality Control;* Juan Baquera, *Electronic Publishing Technology Services Team Leader;* Christopher Lucas, *Team Leader;* Lana Kaupp, Kim Orne, Susan Savkov; *Senior Production Artists;* Ellen Kennedy, Patricia Zepeda, *Production Artists;* Heather Jernt, *Electronic Publishing Supervisor;* Robert Franklin, *Electronic Publishing Director*

Production/Manufacturing: Michael Roche, *Senior Production Coordinator;* Belinda Barbosa Lopez, *Senior Production Coordinator;* Carol Trammel, *Production Manager;* Beth Prevelige, *Senior Production Manager*

Requests for permission to make copies of any part of this work should be mailed to the following address: Permissions Department, Holt, Rinehart and Winston, 10801 N. MoPac Expressway, Building 3, Austin, Texas 78759.

For acknowledgements, see pages 336–37, which are an extension of the copyright page.
Printed in the United States of America

3 4 5   179   03

Contents

PART 3 Standardized Test Practice

Literature

Informational Materials

Skills Table of Contents

Literary Skills

Informational Reading Skills

Vocabulary Skills

To the Student

A Book for You

Imagine this: a book full of stories you want to read and informational articles that are really interesting. Make it a book that actually tells you to write in it, circling, underlining, jotting down responses. Fill it with graphic organizers that encourage you to think a different way. Make it a size that's easy to carry around. That's *The Holt Reader: An Interactive WorkText*—a book created especially for you.

The Holt Reader: An Interactive WorkText is designed to accompany *Elements of Literature*. Like *Elements of Literature*, it's designed to help you interact with the literature and informational materials you read. The chart below shows you what's in your book and how the book is organized.

Part 1 Reading Literature	Part 2 Reading Informational Materials	Part 3 Standardized Test Practice
Literary selections from *Elements of Literature*	Informational texts topically or thematically linked to literary selections	Standardized test practice of literature and informational reading

Learning to Read Literary and Informational Materials

When you read informational materials like a social studies textbook or a newspaper article, you usually read to get the facts. You read mainly to get information that is stated directly on the page. When you read literature, you need to go beyond understanding what the words mean and getting the facts straight. You need to read between the lines of a poem or story to discover the writer's meaning. No matter what kind of reading you do—literary or informational—*The Holt Reader: An Interactive WorkText* will help you practice the skills and strategies you need to become an active and successful reader.

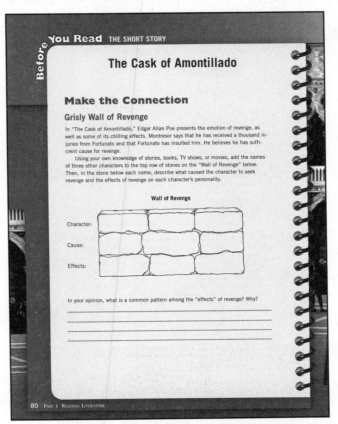

Setting the Stage: Before You Read

In Part 1, the Before-You-Read activity helps you make a personal connection with the selection you are about to read. It helps you sharpen your awareness of what you already know by asking you to think and write about a topic before you read. The more you know about the topic of a text, of course, the easier it is to understand the text. Sometimes this page will provide background information you need to know before you read the text.

Interactive Selections from
Elements of Literature

The literary selections in Part 1 are many of the same selections that appear in *Elements of Literature*, Third Course. The selections are reprinted in a single column and in larger type to give you the room you need to mark up the text.

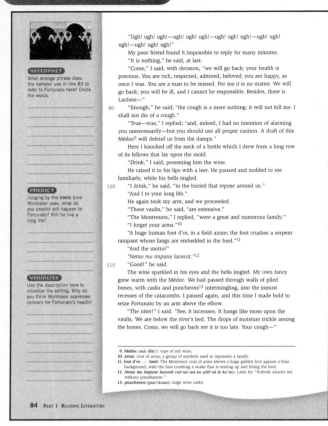

INTERPRET
What strange phrase does the narrator use in line 83 to refer to Fortunato here? Circle the words.

"Ugh! ugh! ugh!—ugh! ugh! ugh!—ugh! ugh! ugh!—ugh! ugh! ugh!—ugh! ugh! ugh! ugh!"

My poor friend found it impossible to reply for many minutes.

"It is nothing," he said, at last.

"Come," I said, with decision, "we will go back; your health is precious. You are rich, respected, admired, beloved; you are happy, as once I was. You are a man to be missed. For me it is no matter. We will go back; you will be ill, and I cannot be responsible. Besides, there is Luchesi—"

90 "Enough," he said; "the cough is a mere nothing; it will not kill me. I shall not die of a cough."

"True—true," I replied; "and, indeed, I had no intention of alarming you unnecessarily—but you should use all proper caution. A draft of this Médoc[9] will defend us from the damps."

Here I knocked off the neck of a bottle which I drew from a long row of its fellows that lay upon the mold.

"Drink," I said, presenting him the wine.

He raised it to his lips with a leer. He paused and nodded to me familiarly, while his bells jingled.

PREDICT
Judging by the ironic tone Montresor uses, what do you predict will happen to Fortunato? Will he live a long life?

100 "I drink," he said, "to the buried that repose around us."

"And I to your long life."

He again took my arm, and we proceeded.

"These vaults," he said, "are extensive."

"The Montresors," I replied, "were a great and numerous family."

"I forget your arms."[10]

"A huge human foot d'or, in a field azure; the foot crushes a serpent rampant whose fangs are embedded in the heel."[11]

"And the motto?"

"*Nemo me impune lacessit.*"[12]

110 "Good!" he said.

VISUALIZE
Use the description here to visualize the setting. Why do you think Montresor expresses concern for Fortunato's health?

The wine sparkled in his eyes and the bells jingled. My own fancy grew warm with the Médoc. We had passed through walls of piled bones, with casks and puncheons[13] intermingling, into the inmost recesses of the catacombs. I paused again, and this time I made bold to seize Fortunato by an arm above the elbow.

"The niter!" I said. "See, it increases. It hangs like moss upon the vaults. We are below the river's bed. The drops of moisture trickle among the bones. Come, we will go back ere it is too late. Your cough—"

---

9. **Médoc** (mā-dōk'): type of red wine.
10. **arms**: coat of arms, a group of symbols used to represent a family.
11. **foot d'or . . . heel**: The Montresor coat of arms shows a huge golden foot against a blue background, with the foot crushing a snake that is rearing up and biting the heel.
12. *Nemo me impune lacessit* (nā'mō mā im-p̄oo'nā lä-ke'sit): Latin for "Nobody attacks me without punishment."
13. **puncheons** (pun'chənz): large wine casks.

"It is nothing," he said; "let us go on. But first, another draft of the 120 Médoc."

I broke and reached him a flagon of de Grâve.[14] He emptied it at a breath. His eyes flashed with a fierce light. He laughed and threw the bottle upward with a gesticulation I did not understand.

I looked at him in surprise. He repeated the movement—a grotesque one.

"You do not comprehend?" he said.

"Not I," I replied.

"Then you are not of the brotherhood."

"How?"

130 "You are not of the Masons."[15]

"Yes, yes," I said, "yes, yes."

"You? Impossible! A Mason?"

"A mason," I replied.

"A sign," he said.

"It is this," I answered, producing a trowel from beneath the folds of my roquelaure.

"You jest," he exclaimed, recoiling a few paces. "But let us proceed to the amontillado."

"Be it so," I said, replacing the tool beneath the cloak and again 140 offering him my arm. He leaned upon it heavily. We continued our route in search of the amontillado. We passed through a range of low arches, descended, passed on, and, descending again, arrived at a deep crypt in which the foulness of the air caused our flambeaux rather to glow than flame.

At the most remote end of the crypt there appeared another less spacious. Its walls had been lined with human remains, piled to the vault overhead, in the fashion of the great catacombs of Paris. Three sides of this interior crypt were still ornamented in this manner. From the fourth the bones had been thrown down and lay promiscuously[16] upon 150 the earth, forming at one point a mound of some size. Within the wall thus exposed by the displacing of the bones, we perceived a still interior recess, in depth about four feet, in width three, in height six or seven. It seemed to have been constructed for no especial use within itself, but formed merely the interval between two of the colossal supports of the roof of the catacombs and was backed by one of their circumscribing walls of solid granite.

WORDS TO OWN
recoiling (rĭ-koil'ĭn)
v. used as *adj.*: moving backward, as if in horror.

IDENTIFY
Underline two details in this passage (lines 145–156) that help to create an ominous atmosphere, or mood.

---

14. **flagon of de Grâve**: narrow-necked bottle with a handle and sometimes a lid, containing a wine from the Graves region of France.
15. **Masons** (mā'sənz): Freemasons, a secret society of people who believe in brotherhood, giving to the poor, and helping one another. Members use secret signs and gestures to recognize one another.
16. **promiscuously** (prŏ-mĭs'kyōō-əs-lē): randomly; in a disorganized way.

Strategies to Guide Your Reading: Side Notes

Notes in the side column accompany each selection. They guide your interaction with the text and help you unlock meaning. Many notes ask you to circle or underline in the text itself. Others provide lines on which you can write. Here are the kinds of notes you will work with as you read the selections: identify, retell, infer, predict, interpret, evaluate, visualize, and build fluency.

Identify asks you to find information (like the name of a character or a description of the setting) that is stated directly in the text. You will often be asked to circle or underline the information in the text.

Retell asks you to restate or explain in your own words something that appears in the text.

Infer asks you to make an **inference,** or an educated guess. You make inferences on the basis of clues writers give you and on experiences from your own life. When you make an inference, you read between the lines to figure out what the writer suggests but does not say directly.

Predict asks you to figure out what will happen next. Making predictions as you read helps you think about and understand what you are reading. To make predictions, look for clues that the writer gives you. Connect those clues with other things you've read, as well as your own experience. You'll probably find yourself adjusting predictions as you read.

Interpret asks you to explain the meaning of something. When you make an interpretation of a character, for example, you look at what the character says or does, and then you think about what the character's words and actions mean. You ask yourself why the character said those words and did those things. Your answer is the interpretation. Interpretations help you get at the main idea of a selection, the discovery about life you take away from it.

Evaluate asks you to form opinions about what you read. For example, you might see the following note at the end of a story: "How satisfying is the ending of this story? Give two reasons for your answer."

Visualize asks you to picture the characters, settings, and events being described in a selection. As you read, look for details that help you make a mental picture. Think of visualizing as making your own mental movie of a selection.

Build Fluency asks you to read a poem or passages from a story. It lets you practice phrasing, expression, and reading in meaningful chunks. Sometimes hearing text read aloud makes the text easier to understand.

Words to Own lists words for you to learn and own. These words are underlined in the selection, letting you see the words in context. The words are defined for you right there in the side column.

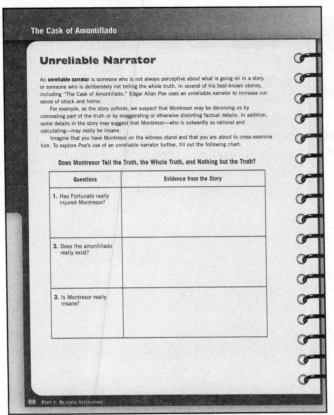

The Cask of Amontillado

Unreliable Narrator

An **unreliable narrator** is someone who is not always perceptive about what is going on in a story, or someone who is deliberately not telling the whole truth. In several of his best-known stories, including "The Cask of Amontillado," Edgar Allan Poe uses an unreliable narrator to increase our sense of shock and horror.

For example, as the story unfolds, we suspect that Montresor may be deceiving us by concealing part of the truth or by exaggerating or otherwise distorting factual details. In addition, some details in the story may suggest that Montresor—who is outwardly so rational and calculating—may really be insane.

Imagine that you have Montresor on the witness stand and that you are about to cross-examine him. To explore Poe's use of an unreliable narrator further, fill out the following chart.

Does Montresor Tell the Truth, the Whole Truth, and Nothing but the Truth?

Questions	Evidence from the Story
1. Has Fortunato really injured Montresor?	
2. Does the amontillado really exist?	
3. Is Montresor really insane?	

88   PART 1 READING LITERATURE

After You Read: Graphic Organizers

After each selection, **graphic organizers** give you a visual way to organize, interpret, and understand the reading or literary focus of the selection. You might be asked to chart the main events of the plot or complete a cause-and-effect chain.

In addition, you will find graphic organizers for use with different genres. These appear under the head **Graphic Organizers for Reading Strategies.**

The Cask of Amontillado

Vocabulary: How to Own a Word

Synonyms and Antonyms

Below are ten word pairs. For each numbered pair, write **S** in the blank if the second word in the pair is a synonym of the Word to Own. Write **A** if the word is an antonym. You may need a dictionary or a thesaurus for this activity.

Word Bank
precluded
impunity
retribution
immolation
connoisseurship
impose upon
recoiling
endeavored
obstinate
succession

_____ 1. impose upon : burden
_____ 2. retribution : retaliation
_____ 3. endeavored : avoided
_____ 4. obstinate : tenacious
_____ 5. immolation : creation
_____ 6. impunity : exemption
_____ 7. succession : precedence
_____ 8. precluded : included
_____ 9. recoiling : repulsing
_____ 10. connoisseurship : apprenticeship

THE CASK OF AMONTILLADO   89

After You Read: Vocabulary: How to Own a Word

Vocabulary: How to Own a Word worksheets at the end of literary selections check your knowledge of the Words to Own and develop skills for vocabulary building.

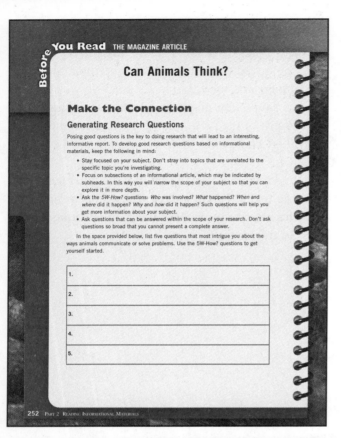

Focus on Skills: Before You Read

The Before-You-Read page in Part 2 teaches skills and strategies you'll need to read informational materials like textbooks, newspaper and magazine articles, and instructional manuals. You'll learn how to recognize text structure, find the main idea, and determine an author's perspective or point of view on these Before-You-Read pages.

Interactive Informational Texts

The informational texts in Part 2 are linked by theme or by topic to the literature selections that appear in *Elements of Literature,* Third Course, and *The Holt Reader: An Interactive WorkText,* Third Course. The informational selections are printed in a single column and in larger type to give you the room you need to mark up the text.

WORDS TO OWN
balmy (bäm′ē) *adj.*: mild; pleasant.

INFER
Why might the keepers at Omaha Zoo have assumed that Fu Manchu's first escape was the result of human error?

_____

IDENTIFY
Underline the detail in the second paragraph that suggests Fu Manchu possesses high-level problem-solving skills.

_____

EVALUATE
Based on your prior knowledge and what you've read so far, write your own answer to the question in lines 37–38.

_____

The first time Fu Manchu broke out, zookeepers chalked it up to human error. On a balmy day, the orangutans at the Omaha Zoo had been playing in their big outdoor enclosure. Not long thereafter, shocked keepers looked up and saw Fu and his family hanging out in some trees near the elephant barn. Later investigation revealed that the door that connects the furnace room to the orangutan enclosure was open. Head keeper Jerry Stones chewed out his staff, and the incident was forgotten. But the next time the weather was nice, Fu Manchu escaped again. Fuming, Stones recalls, "I was getting ready to fire someone."

10 The next nice day, alerted by keepers desperate to keep their jobs, Stones finally managed to catch Fu Manchu in the act. First, the young ape climbed down some air-vent louvers into a dry moat. Then, taking hold of the bottom of the furnace door, he used brute force to pull it back just far enough to slide a wire into the gap, slip a latch, and pop the door open. The next day, Stones noticed something shiny sticking out of Fu's mouth. It was the wire lock pick, bent to fit between his lip and gum and stowed there between escapes.

Fu Manchu's jailbreaks made headlines in 1968, but his clever tricks didn't make a big impression on the scientists who specialize in looking
20 for signs of higher mental processes in animals. At the time, much of the action in animal intelligence was focused on efforts to teach apes to use human languages. No researcher cared much about ape escape artists.

And neither did I. In 1970, I began following studies of animal intelligence, particularly the early reports of chimpanzees who learned how to use human words. The big breakthrough in these experiments came when two psychologists,[1] R. Allen and Beatrice Gardner, realized their chimps were having trouble forming wordlike sounds and decided to teach a young female named Washoe sign language instead. Washoe eventually learned more than 130 words from the language of the deaf
30 called American Sign Language.

Washoe's success spurred more language studies and created such ape celebrities as Koko the gorilla and Chantek the orangutan. The work also set off a fierce debate in scientific circles about the nature of animal intelligence—one that continues to this day. Indeed, it has been easier to defeat communism than to get scientists to agree on what Washoe meant three decades ago when she saw a swan on a pond and made the signs for "water bird." Was she inventing a phrase to describe waterfowl, or merely generating signs vaguely associated with the scene in front of her?

I began to wonder whether there might be better windows on animal
40 minds than experiments designed to teach them human signs and symbols. When I heard about Fu Manchu, I realized what to me now seems obvious: If animals can think, they will probably do their best thinking when it serves their purposes, not when some scientist asks them to.

1. **psychologists** (sī-kŏl′ə-jĭsts) *n.*: specialists who study the mind and emotions.

Can Animals Think?

Generating Research Questions Chart

Try using a *KWL* chart to begin researching a specific aspect of animal intelligence. After you read "Can Animals Think?" list what you already know about the topic in the *K* column. In the *W* column, list the questions you have—what you want to learn. You can use the five questions about animal intelligence that you posed before you read the article or change them based on what you learned from the article. When you've finished your research, complete column *L* by telling what you've learned. Which question yielded the best research results and why?

K	W	L

Strategies to Guide Your Reading: Side Notes

As in Part 1, **notes** in the side column accompany each selection. They guide your interaction with the text and help you unlock meaning. Many notes ask you to circle or underline in the text itself. Others provide lines on which you can write. Here are the kinds of notes you will work with as you read the informational materials in Part 2: identify, retell, infer, predict, interpret, evaluate, visualize, and build fluency. See page xii for an explanation of each note.

After You Read: Graphic Organizers

After each selection, a **graphic organizer** gives you a visual way to organize, interpret, and understand the selection. These organizers focus on the strategy introduced on the Before-You-Read page. You might be asked to collect supporting details that point to a main idea or to complete a comparison chart.

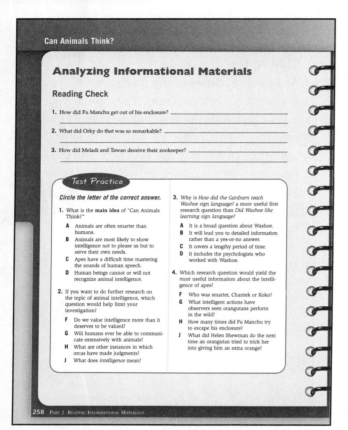

Can Animals Think?

Analyzing Informational Materials

Reading Check

1. How did Fu Manchu get out of his enclosure? _____

2. What did Orky do that was so remarkable? _____

3. How did Meladi and Tawan deceive their zookeeper? _____

Test Practice

Circle the letter of the correct answer.

1. What is the **main idea** of "Can Animals Think?"

   A Animals are often smarter than humans.

   B Animals are most likely to show intelligence not to please us but to serve their own needs.

   C Apes have a difficult time mastering the sounds of human speech.

   D Human beings cannot or will not recognize animal intelligence.

2. If you want to do further research on the topic of animal intelligence, which question would help limit your investigation?

   F Do we value intelligence more than it deserves to be valued?

   G Will humans ever be able to communicate extensively with animals?

   H What are other instances in which orcas have made judgments?

   J What does *intelligence* mean?

3. Why is *How did the Gardners teach Washoe sign language?* a more useful first research question than *Did Washoe like learning sign language?*

   A It is a broad question about Washoe.

   B It will lead you to detailed information rather than a yes-or-no answer.

   C It covers a lengthy period of time.

   D It includes the psychologists who worked with Washoe.

4. Which research question would yield the *most* useful information about the intelligence of apes?

   F Who was smarter, Chantek or Koko?

   G What intelligent actions have observers seen orangutans perform in the wild?

   H How many times did Fu Manchu try to escape his enclosure?

   J What did Helen Shewman do the next time an orangutan tried to trick her into giving him an extra orange?

258 PART 2 READING INFORMATIONAL MATERIALS

After You Read: Reading Check and Test Practice

Reading Check and Test Practice worksheets at the end of informational selections check your understanding of the selection with multiple-choice questions. The multiple-choice questions are similar to the ones you'll answer on state and national standardized tests.

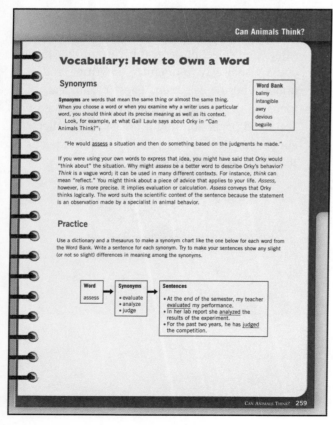

Can Animals Think?

Vocabulary: How to Own a Word

Synonyms

Synonyms are words that mean the same thing or almost the same thing. When you choose a word or when you examine why a writer uses a particular word, you should think about its precise meaning as well as its context.

Look, for example, at what Gail Laule says about Orky in "Can Animals Think?":

"He would <u>assess</u> a situation and then do something based on the judgments he made."

Word Bank
balmy
intangible
awry
devious
beguile

If you were using your own words to express that idea, you might have said that Orky would "think about" the situation. Why might *assess* be a better word to describe Orky's behavior? *Think* is a vague word; it can be used in many different contexts. For instance, *think* can mean "reflect." You might think about a piece of advice that applies to your life. *Assess,* however, is more precise. It implies evaluation or calculation. *Assess* conveys that Orky thinks logically. The word suits the scientific context of the sentence because the statement is an observation made by a specialist in animal behavior.

Practice

Use a dictionary and a thesaurus to make a synonym chart like the one below for each word from the Word Bank. Write a sentence for each synonym. Try to make your sentences show any slight (or not so slight) differences in meaning among the synonyms.

Word	Synonyms	Sentences
assess	• evaluate • analyze • judge	• At the end of the semester, my teacher <u>evaluated</u> my performance. • In her lab report she <u>analyzed</u> the results of the experiment. • For the past two years, he has <u>judged</u> the competition.

CAN ANIMALS THINK? 259

After You Read: Vocabulary: How to Own a Word

When informational texts in Part 2 have Words to Own, you will practice your understanding of the words in exercises like the one shown here.

STANDARDIZED TEST PRACTICE — INFORMATIONAL MATERIALS

DIRECTIONS

The following passage is from the true story of a year the writer spent observing a fifth-grade classroom in Holyoke, Massachusetts. Read the passage carefully. Then, read each item, and circle the letter of the best response.

from Among Schoolchildren
Tracy Kidder

Mrs. Zajac wasn't born yesterday. She knows you didn't do your best work on this paper, Clarence. Don't you remember Mrs. Zajac saying that if you didn't do your best, she'd make you do it over? As for you, Claude, God forbid that you should ever need brain surgery. But Mrs. Zajac hopes that if you do, the doctor won't open up your head and walk off saying he's almost done, as you just said when Mrs. Zajac asked you for your penmanship, which, by the way, looks like you did it and ran. Felipe, the reason you have hiccups is, your mouth is always open and the wind rushes in. You're in fifth grade now. So, Felipe, put a lock on it. Zip it up. Then go get a drink of water. Mrs. Zajac means business, Robert. The sooner you realize she never said everybody in the room has to do the work except for Robert, the sooner you'll get along with her. And . . . Clarence. Mrs. Zajac knows you didn't try. You don't just hand in junk to Mrs. Zajac. She's been teaching an awful lot of years. She didn't fall off the turnip cart yesterday. She told you she was an old-lady teacher.

She was thirty-four. She wore a white skirt and yellow sweater and a thin gold necklace, which she held in her fingers, as if holding her own reins, while waiting for children to answer. Her hair was black with a hint of Irish red.

It was cut short to the tops of her ears, and swept back like a pair of folded wings. She had a delicately cleft chin, and she was short—the children's chairs would have fit her. Although her voice sounded conversational, it had projection.[1] She had never acted. She had found this voice in classrooms.

Mrs. Zajac seemed to have a frightening amount of energy. She strode across the room, her arms swinging high and her hands in small fists. Taking her stand in front of the green chalkboard, discussing the rules with her new class, she repeated sentences, and her lips held the shapes of certain words, such as "homework," after she had said them. Her hands kept very busy. They sliced the air and made karate chops to mark off boundaries. They extended straight out like a traffic cop's, halting illegal maneuvers yet to be perpetrated. When they rested momentarily on her hips, her hands looked as if they were in holsters. She told the children, "One thing Mrs. Zajac expects from each of you is that you do your best." She said, "Mrs. Zajac gives homework. I'm sure you've all heard. The old meanie gives homework." Mrs. Zajac. It was in part a role. She worked her way into it every September.

At home on late summer days like these, Chris Zajac wore shorts or blue jeans. Although there was no dress code for teachers here at Kelly School, she always went to work in skirts or dresses. She dressed as if she were applying for a job, and hoped in the back of her mind that someday, heading for job interviews, her students would remember her example. Outside

1. projection (prŏ-jĕk´shən): carrying power.

school, she wept easily over small and large catastrophes and at sentimental movies, but she never cried in front of students, except once a few years ago when the news came over the intercom that the Space Shuttle had exploded and Christa McAuliffe had died—and then she saw in her students' faces that the sight of Mrs. Zajac crying had frightened them, and she made herself stop and then explained.

At home, Chris laughed at the antics of her infant daughter and egged the child on. She and her first-grade son would sneak up to the radio when her husband wasn't looking and change the station from classical to rock-and-roll music. "You're regressing,[2] Chris," her husband would say. But especially on the first few days of school, she didn't let her students get away with much. She was not amused when, for instance,

2. regressing: here, acting childish.

on the first day, two of the boys started dueling with their rulers. On nights before the school year started, Chris used to have bad dreams: her principal would come to observe her, and her students would choose that moment to climb up on their desks . . . or they would simply wander out the door. But a child in her classroom would never know that Mrs. Zajac had the slightest doubt that students would obey her.

The first day, after going over all the school rules, Chris spoke to them about effort. "If you put your name on a paper, you should be proud of it," she said. "You should think, 'This is the best I can do and I'm proud of it and I want to hand this in.'" Then she asked, "If it isn't your best, what's Mrs. Zajac going to do?"

Many voices, most of them female, answered softly in unison, "Make us do it over."

"Make you do it over," Chris repeated. It sounded like a chant.

---

1. Which of the following descriptions of Mrs. Zajac's movements does **not** use figurative language?
   - A Making karate chops to mark off boundaries
   - B Extending her hands as if to halt illegal maneuvers
   - C Swinging her arms, with her hands in small fists
   - D Placing her hands on her hips as if her hands were in holsters

2. Tracy Kidder's tone, or attitude, toward Mrs. Zajac could be described as —
   - F amused
   - G scornful
   - H pitying
   - J admiring

3. Which of the following details about Mrs. Zajac is the most subjective?
   - A She wore a skirt and sweater.
   - B She had a frightening amount of energy.
   - C She wore a gold necklace.
   - D She had black hair.

4. Who is speaking in the first paragraph?
   - F Tracy Kidder
   - G A student
   - H Mrs. Zajac
   - J The principal

5. Mrs. Zajac tries to set a good example for her students by —
   - A wearing a skirt or dress to class every day
   - B being easy on the students the first day
   - C showing all emotions in front of her students
   - D letting them know her dreams

The last part of this book gives you practice in reading and responding to the kinds of literary and informational selections you read in Parts 1 and 2. The selections and multiple-choice questions are similar to the ones you'll see on state and national standardized tests.

PART 1 READING LITERATURE

The Sniper

Make the Connection

Setting the Scene

The **setting** of a short story is the time and place of the action. "The Sniper," for example, is set in Dublin, Ireland, in the 1920s. During that time, there was a civil war in Ireland. On one side, the Republicans wanted all of Ireland to become a republic, totally free of British rule. On the other side, the Free Staters wanted the British to continue to rule six counties in the northern province of Ulster. Like all civil wars, this one tore families apart. The setting is important to the main conflict in O'Flaherty's story, and it also contributes to the story's mood or emotional effect.

How do you set the scene when *you* tell a story? Think of a recent experience that you would like to relate to a small group of friends or family members. Write a title for your story on the chart below. Then, write the details of setting you would use for your tale.

Story Title: ———————————————————

Place/Location: ———————————————————

Time of Year: ———————————————————

Time of Day: ———————————————————

Other Background Details: ———————————————————

———————————————————

Main Events: ———————————————————

———————————————————

THE SNIPER

Liam O'Flaherty

IDENTIFY

Re-read the opening paragraph. In what month does the story take place? Underline the sentence that tells you. What city is the **setting**? Circle the correct answer.

INFER

What inference can you make about the sniper's **character,** based on lines 8–12? Write your conclusion.

_____

_____

_____

_____

_____

_____

_____

PREDICT

What do you think may happen to the sniper? Write a prediction.

_____

_____

_____

_____

_____

INTERPRET

What is the "gray monster" in line 37? Circle the answer.

_____

_____

_____

_____

_____

_____

_____

The long June twilight faded into night. Dublin lay enveloped in darkness but for the dim light of the moon that shone through fleecy clouds, casting a pale light as of approaching dawn over the streets and the dark waters of the Liffey.[1] Around the beleaguered Four Courts[2] the heavy guns roared. Here and there through the city, machine guns and rifles broke the silence of the night, spasmodically, like dogs barking on lone farms. Republicans and Free Staters were waging civil war.

On a rooftop near O'Connell Bridge, a Republican sniper lay watching. Beside him lay his rifle and over his shoulders was slung a
10 pair of field glasses. His face was the face of a student, thin and ascetic,[3] but his eyes had the cold gleam of the fanatic. They were deep and thoughtful, the eyes of a man who is used to looking at death.

He was eating a sandwich hungrily. He had eaten nothing since morning. He had been too excited to eat. He finished the sandwich, and, taking a flask of whiskey from his pocket, he took a short draft. Then he returned the flask to his pocket. He paused for a moment, considering whether he should risk a smoke. It was dangerous. The flash might be seen in the darkness, and there were enemies watching. He decided to take the risk.
20 Placing a cigarette between his lips, he struck a match, inhaled the smoke hurriedly, and put out the light. Almost immediately, a bullet flattened itself against the parapet[4] of the roof. The sniper took another whiff and put out the cigarette. Then he swore softly and crawled away to the left.

Cautiously he raised himself and peered over the parapet. There was a flash and a bullet whizzed over his head. He dropped immediately. He had seen the flash. It came from the opposite side of the street.

He rolled over the roof to a chimney stack in the rear and slowly drew himself up behind it, until his eyes were level with the top of the
30 parapet. There was nothing to be seen—just the dim outline of the opposite housetop against the blue sky. His enemy was under cover.

Just then an armored car came across the bridge and advanced slowly up the street. It stopped on the opposite side of the street, fifty yards ahead. The sniper could hear the dull panting of the motor. His heart beat faster. It was an enemy car. He wanted to fire, but he knew it was useless. His bullets would never pierce the steel that covered the gray monster.

Then round the corner of a side street came an old woman, her head covered by a tattered shawl. She began to talk to the man in the turret of
40 the car. She was pointing to the roof where the sniper lay. An informer.

---

1. **Liffey:** river that runs through Dublin.
2. **beleaguered** (bē·lē′gərd) **Four Courts:** government buildings in Dublin that were surrounded and under attack.
3. **ascetic** (ə·set′ik): extremely self-disciplined and severe.
4. **parapet** (par′ə·pet′): low wall or railing.

The turret opened. A man's head and shoulders appeared, looking toward the sniper. The sniper raised his rifle and fired. The head fell heavily on the turret wall. The woman darted toward the side street. The sniper fired again. The woman whirled round and fell with a shriek into the gutter.

Suddenly from the opposite roof a shot rang out and the sniper dropped his rifle with a curse. The rifle clattered to the roof. The sniper thought the noise would wake the dead. He stooped to pick the rifle up. He couldn't lift it. His forearm was dead. "I'm hit," he muttered.

50   Dropping flat onto the roof, he crawled back to the parapet. With his left hand he felt the injured right forearm. The blood was oozing through the sleeve of his coat. There was no pain—just a deadened sensation, as if the arm had been cut off.

Quickly he drew his knife from his pocket, opened it on the breastwork[5] of the parapet, and ripped open the sleeve. There was a small hole where the bullet had entered. On the other side there was no hole. The bullet had lodged in the bone. It must have fractured it. He bent the arm below the wound. The arm bent back easily. He ground his teeth to overcome the pain.

60   Then taking out his field dressing, he ripped open the packet with his knife. He broke the neck of the iodine bottle and let the bitter fluid drip into the wound. A paroxysm[6] of pain swept through him. He placed the cotton wadding over the wound and wrapped the dressing over it. He tied the ends with his teeth.

Then he lay still against the parapet, and, closing his eyes, he made an effort of will to overcome the pain.

In the street beneath all was still. The armored car had retired speedily over the bridge, with the machine gunner's head hanging lifeless over the turret. The woman's corpse lay still in the gutter.

70   The sniper lay still for a long time nursing his wounded arm and planning escape. Morning must not find him wounded on the roof. The enemy on the opposite roof covered his escape. He must kill that enemy and he could not use his rifle. He had only a revolver to do it. Then he thought of a plan.

Taking off his cap, he placed it over the muzzle of his rifle. Then he pushed the rifle slowly upward over the parapet, until the cap was visible from the opposite side of the street. Almost immediately there was a report, and a bullet pierced the center of the cap. The sniper slanted the rifle forward. The cap slipped down into the street. Then,

80   catching the rifle in the middle, the sniper dropped his left hand over the roof and let it hang, lifelessly. After a few moments he let the rifle drop to the street. Then he sank to the roof, dragging his hand with him.

---

5. **breastwork:** low wall put up as a military defense.
6. **paroxysm** (par'əks·iz'əm): sudden attack; fit.

RETELL
Summarize the events narrated in lines 46–49.

_____

_____

_____

_____

_____

_____

_____

_____

INFER
What can you infer about the sniper's **character,** based on the steps he takes to treat his wound?

_____

_____

_____

_____

_____

PREDICT
What do you think the sniper's plan might be?

_____

_____

_____

_____

_____

_____

_____

_____

Crawling quickly to the left, he peered up at the corner of the roof. His ruse had succeeded. The other sniper, seeing the cap and rifle fall, thought that he had killed his man. He was now standing before a row of chimney pots, looking across, with his head clearly silhouetted against the western sky.

The Republican sniper smiled and lifted his revolver above the edge of the parapet. The distance was about fifty yards—a hard shot in the dim light, and his right arm was paining him like a thousand devils. He took a steady aim. His hand trembled with eagerness. Pressing his lips together, he took a deep breath through his nostrils and fired. He was almost deafened with the report and his arm shook with the recoil.

Then when the smoke cleared he peered across and uttered a cry of joy. His enemy had been hit. He was reeling over the parapet in his death agony. He struggled to keep his feet, but he was slowly falling forward, as if in a dream. The rifle fell from his grasp, hit the parapet, fell over, bounded off the pole of a barber's shop beneath, and then clattered on the pavement.

Then the dying man on the roof crumpled up and fell forward. The body turned over and over in space and hit the ground with a dull thud. Then it lay still.

The sniper looked at his enemy falling and he shuddered. The lust of battle died in him. He became bitten by remorse. The sweat stood out in beads on his forehead. Weakened by his wound and the long summer day of fasting and watching on the roof, he revolted from the sight of the shattered mass of his dead enemy. His teeth chattered, he began to gibber to himself, cursing the war, cursing himself, cursing everybody.

He looked at the smoking revolver in his hand, and with an oath he hurled it to the roof at his feet. The revolver went off with the concussion and the bullet whizzed past the sniper's head. He was frightened back to his senses by the shock. His nerves steadied. The cloud of fear scattered from his mind and he laughed.

Taking the whiskey flask from his pocket, he emptied it at a draft. He felt reckless under the influence of the spirit. He decided to leave the roof now and look for his company commander, to report. Everywhere around was quiet. There was not much danger in going through the streets. He picked up his revolver and put it in his pocket. Then he crawled down through the skylight to the house underneath.

When the sniper reached the laneway on the street level, he felt a sudden curiosity as to the identity of the enemy sniper whom he had killed. He decided that he was a good shot, whoever he was. He wondered did he know him. Perhaps he had been in his own company before the split in the army. He decided to risk going over to have a look at him. He peered around the corner into O'Connell Street. In the upper part of the street there was heavy firing, but around here all was quiet.

The sniper darted across the street. A machine gun tore up the ground around him with a hail of bullets, but he escaped. He threw himself face downward beside the corpse. The machine gun stopped.

130   Then the sniper turned over the dead body and looked into his brother's face.

INFER

What does this ending imply about the writer's attitude toward the civil war?

_____

_____

_____

_____

_____

_____

_____

_____

_____

_____

_____

_____

_____

_____

_____

_____

_____

_____

_____

_____

_____

_____

Setting

A story's **setting** is the time and place of the events. Fill in the chart below to explain the connections between details of setting and other elements in the story.

Details of Setting	Story Elements
Dublin in 1920s ➡	**Conflict:** _____
	_____
	_____
	_____
	_____
	_____
Rooftop at night ➡	**Atmosphere:** _____
	_____
	_____
	_____
	_____
	_____
Irish civil war ➡	**Climax/Surprise Ending:** ___
	_____
	_____
	_____
	_____
	_____

Vocabulary: How to Own a Word

Academic Vocabulary

METAPHOR   A comparison of two unlike things without the use of a direct word of comparison such as *like* or *as: Juliet is the sun.*

SIMILE   A comparison of two unlike things using a specific word of comparison, such as *like, as,* or *resembles: Juliet is like the sun. Juliet is as beautiful as the sun. Juliet resembles the sun.*

Metaphors and similes are called **figures of speech** or **figurative language.** Identify each figure of speech underlined in the following sentences by circling the correct term. Then, write down what is compared to what.

1. Machine guns and rifles broke the silence of the night, <u>like dogs barking on lone farms</u>.

   ❑ Metaphor   ❑ Simile

   _____ compared with _____

2. After he saw his enemy's body hit the ground, the sniper became <u>bitten by remorse</u>.

   ❑ Metaphor   ❑ Simile

   _____ compared with _____

3. The sniper's wounded right arm was paining him <u>like a thousand devils</u>.

   ❑ Metaphor   ❑ Simile

   _____ compared with _____

4. As the sniper darted across the street, a machine gun <u>tore up the ground</u> around him.

   ❑ Metaphor   ❑ Simile

   _____ compared with _____

The Most Dangerous Game

Make the Connection

The Thrill of the Chase

A **conflict** is a clash or struggle of some kind. The most basic type of conflict in a story pits one person against someone or something else. In stories, movies, and television shows, this conflict often unfolds in the form of a tense chase or pursuit. The suspense, or feeling of uncertainty about the outcome, is a major reason most of us enjoy "the thrill of the chase."

Explore ideas about the chase by filling in the chart below. First, read the two lists and draw arrows to connect the hunters (pursuers) with the correct hunted (pursued). Then, use the lines provided to rank the top five skills or characteristics that a person or animal needs in order to carry out a successful chase. Be prepared to explain your rankings.

Hunter/Pursuer	Hunted/Pursued
detective	deer
hound	small fish
shark	criminal
tiger	fox
villain	hero/heroine

Skills/Abilities

generosity	stamina	intelligence
loyalty	cunning	strength
agility	eloquence	determination
organization	moderation	patience

1. _____
2. _____
3. _____
4. _____
5. _____

Richard Connell

The Most Dangerous Game

IDENTIFY

Which two **characters** take part in the opening dialogue? Circle their names.

WORDS TO OWN

palpable (pal′pə·bəl) *adj.:* easily felt or touched.

_____

_____

_____

_____

_____

_____

_____

_____

_____

_____

_____

IDENTIFY

According to Rainsford, which two classes make up the world? Underline the answer.

_____

_____

_____

IDENTIFY

What effect does passing the island have on the crew and on Whitney?

_____

_____

_____

_____

_____

_____

"**O**ff there to the right—somewhere—is a large island," said Whitney. "It's rather a mystery—"

"What island is it?" Rainsford asked.

"The old charts call it Ship-Trap Island," Whitney replied. "A suggestive name, isn't it? Sailors have a curious dread of the place. I don't know why. Some superstition—"

"Can't see it," remarked Rainsford, trying to peer through the dank tropical night that was <u>palpable</u> as it pressed its thick warm blackness in upon the yacht.

10 "You've good eyes," said Whitney, with a laugh, "and I've seen you pick off a moose moving in the brown fall bush at four hundred yards, but even you can't see four miles or so through a moonless Caribbean night."

"Nor four yards," admitted Rainsford. "Ugh! It's like moist black velvet."

"It will be light in Rio," promised Whitney. "We should make it in a few days. I hope the jaguar guns have come from Purdey's.[1] We should have some good hunting up the Amazon. Great sport, hunting."

"The best sport in the world," agreed Rainsford.

20 "For the hunter," amended Whitney. "Not for the jaguar."

"Don't talk rot, Whitney," said Rainsford. "You're a big-game hunter, not a philosopher. Who cares how a jaguar feels?"

"Perhaps the jaguar does," observed Whitney.

"Bah! They've no understanding."

"Even so, I rather think they understand one thing—fear. The fear of pain and the fear of death."

"Nonsense," laughed Rainsford. "This hot weather is making you soft, Whitney. Be a realist. The world is made up of two classes—the hunters and the huntees. Luckily, you and I are the hunters. Do you

30 think we've passed that island yet?"

"I can't tell in the dark. I hope so."

"Why?" asked Rainsford.

"The place has a reputation—a bad one."

"Cannibals?" suggested Rainsford.

"Hardly. Even cannibals wouldn't live in such a Godforsaken place. But it's gotten into sailor lore, somehow. Didn't you notice that the crew's nerves seemed a bit jumpy today?"

"They were a bit strange, now you mention it. Even Captain Nielsen—"

40 "Yes, even that tough-minded old Swede, who'd go up to the devil himself and ask him for a light. Those fishy blue eyes held a look I never saw there before. All I could get out of him was: 'This place has an evil name among seafaring men, sir.' Then he said to me, very gravely: 'Don't

---

1. **Purdey's:** British manufacturer of hunting equipment.

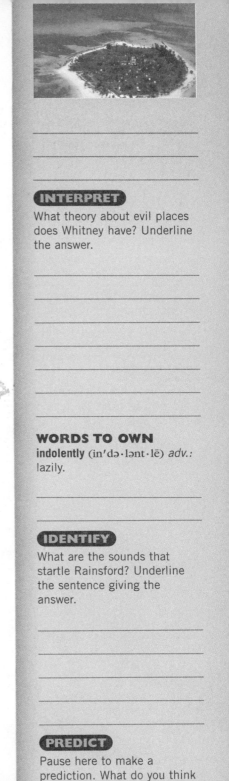

you feel anything?'—as if the air about us was actually poisonous. Now, you mustn't laugh when I tell you this—I did feel something like a sudden chill.

"There was no breeze. The sea was as flat as a plate-glass window. We were drawing near the island then. What I felt was a—a mental chill; a sort of sudden dread."

50 "Pure imagination," said Rainsford. "One superstitious sailor can taint the whole ship's company with his fear."

"Maybe. But sometimes I think sailors have an extra sense that tells them when they are in danger. Sometimes I think evil is a tangible thing—with wavelengths, just as sound and light have. An evil place can, so to speak, broadcast vibrations of evil. Anyhow, I'm glad we're getting out of this zone. Well, I think I'll turn in now, Rainsford."

"I'm not sleepy," said Rainsford. "I'm going to smoke another pipe on the afterdeck."

"Good night, then, Rainsford. See you at breakfast."

60 "Right. Good night, Whitney."

There was no sound in the night as Rainsford sat there but the muffled throb of the engine that drove the yacht swiftly through the darkness, and the swish and ripple of the wash of the propeller.

Rainsford, reclining in a steamer chair, <u>indolently</u> puffed on his favorite brier.[2] The sensuous drowsiness of the night was on him. "It's so dark," he thought, "that I could sleep without closing my eyes; the night would be my eyelids—"

An abrupt sound startled him. Off to the right he heard it, and his ears, expert in such matters, could not be mistaken. Again he heard the
70 sound, and again. Somewhere, off in the blackness, someone had fired a gun three times.

Rainsford sprang up and moved quickly to the rail, mystified. He strained his eyes in the direction from which the reports had come, but it was like trying to see through a blanket. He leaped upon the rail and balanced himself there, to get greater elevation; his pipe, striking a rope, was knocked from his mouth. He lunged for it; a short, hoarse cry came from his lips as he realized he had reached too far and had lost his balance. The cry was pinched off short as the blood-warm waters of the Caribbean Sea closed over his head.

80 He struggled up to the surface and tried to cry out, but the wash from the speeding yacht slapped him in the face and the salt water in his open mouth made him gag and strangle. Desperately he struck out with strong strokes after the receding lights of the yacht, but he stopped before he had swum fifty feet. A certain coolheadedness had come to him; it was not the first time he had been in a tight place. There was a

---

2. **brier** (brī'ər): tobacco pipe made from the root of a brier bush or tree.

INTERPRET

What theory about evil places does Whitney have? Underline the answer.

WORDS TO OWN

indolently (in′də·lənt·lē) *adv.*: lazily.

IDENTIFY

What are the sounds that startle Rainsford? Underline the sentence giving the answer.

PREDICT

Pause here to make a prediction. What do you think will happen now to Rainsford?

INTERPRET

Why does Rainsford stop
following the yacht?

_____

_____

_____

_____

_____

_____

_____

INTERPRET

How do you think Rainsford
feels when he hears the sea
breaking on the shore?

_____

_____

_____

_____

_____

_____

_____

_____

_____

INFER

List the character traits that
Rainsford's thoughts in lines
119–121 reveal.

_____

_____

_____

_____

_____

_____

_____

chance that his cries could be heard by someone aboard the yacht, but
that chance was slender and grew more slender as the yacht raced on.
He wrestled himself out of his clothes and shouted with all his power.
The lights of the yacht became faint and ever-vanishing fireflies; then
90 they were blotted out entirely by the night.

Rainsford remembered the shots. They had come from the right, and
doggedly he swam in that direction, swimming with slow, deliberate
strokes, conserving his strength. For a seemingly endless time he fought
the sea. He began to count his strokes; he could do possibly a hundred
more and then—

Rainsford heard a sound. It came out of the darkness, a high
screaming sound, the sound of an animal in an extremity of anguish
and terror.

He did not recognize the animal that made the sound; he did not try
100 to; with fresh vitality he swam toward the sound. He heard it again; then
it was cut short by another noise, crisp, staccato.

"Pistol shot," muttered Rainsford, swimming on.

Ten minutes of determined effort brought another sound to his
ears—the most welcome he had ever heard—the muttering and growling
of the sea breaking on a rocky shore. He was almost on the rocks before
he saw them; on a night less calm he would have been shattered against
them. With his remaining strength he dragged himself from the swirling
waters. Jagged crags appeared to jut into the opaqueness.[3]

He forced himself upward, hand over hand. Gasping, his hands raw,
110 he reached a flat place at the top. Dense jungle came down to the very
edge of the cliffs. What perils that tangle of trees and underbrush might
hold for him did not concern Rainsford just then. All he knew was that
he was safe from his enemy, the sea, and that utter weariness was on
him. He flung himself down at the jungle edge and tumbled headlong
into the deepest sleep of his life.

When he opened his eyes he knew from the position of the sun that
it was late in the afternoon. Sleep had given him new vigor; a sharp
hunger was picking at him. He looked about him, almost cheerfully.

"Where there are pistol shots, there are men. Where there are men,
120 there is food," he thought. But what kind of men, he wondered, in so
forbidding a place? An unbroken front of snarled and ragged jungle
fringed the shore.

He saw no sign of a trail through the closely knit web of weeds and
trees; it was easier to go along the shore, and Rainsford floundered along
by the water. Not far from where he had landed, he stopped.

Some wounded thing, by the evidence a large animal, had thrashed
about in the underbrush; the jungle weeds were crushed down and the

---

3. opaqueness (ō·pāk′nis): here, darkness. Something opaque does not let light pass through.
Milk is an opaque liquid; water is not.

moss was lacerated; one patch of weeds was stained crimson. A small, glittering object not far away caught Rainsford's eye and he picked it up.

130 It was an empty cartridge.

"A twenty-two," he remarked. "That's odd. It must have been a fairly large animal too. The hunter had his nerve with him to tackle it with a light gun. It's clear that the brute put up a fight. I suppose the first three shots I heard was when the hunter flushed his quarry[4] and wounded it. The last shot was when he trailed it here and finished it."

He examined the ground closely and found what he had hoped to find—the print of hunting boots. They pointed along the cliff in the direction he had been going. Eagerly he hurried along, now slipping on a rotten log or a loose stone, but making headway; night was beginning to

140 settle down on the island.

Bleak darkness was blacking out the sea and jungle when Rainsford sighted the lights. He came upon them as he turned a crook in the coastline, and his first thought was that he had come upon a village, for there were many lights. But as he forged along he saw to his great astonishment that all the lights were in one enormous building—a lofty structure with pointed towers plunging upward into the gloom. His eyes made out the shadowy outlines of a palatial château;[5] it was set on a high bluff, and on three sides of it cliffs dived down to where the sea licked greedy lips in the shadows.

150 "Mirage," thought Rainsford. But it was no mirage, he found, when he opened the tall spiked iron gate. The stone steps were real enough; the massive door with a leering gargoyle for a knocker was real enough; yet about it all hung an air of unreality.

He lifted the knocker, and it creaked up stiffly, as if it had never before been used. He let it fall, and it startled him with its booming loudness. He thought he heard steps within; the door remained closed. Again Rainsford lifted the heavy knocker and let it fall. The door opened then, opened as suddenly as if it were on a spring, and Rainsford stood blinking in the river of glaring gold light that poured out. The first thing

160 Rainsford's eyes discerned was the largest man Rainsford had ever seen—a gigantic creature, solidly made and blackbearded to the waist. In his hand the man held a long-barreled revolver, and he was pointing it straight at Rainsford's heart.

Out of the snarl of beard two small eyes regarded Rainsford.

"Don't be alarmed," said Rainsford, with a smile which he hoped was disarming. "I'm no robber. I fell off a yacht. My name is Sanger Rainsford of New York City."

The menacing look in the eyes did not change. The revolver pointed as rigidly as if the giant were a statue. He gave no sign that he

---

4. **flushed his quarry:** drove the animal he was hunting out of its shelter or hiding place.
5. **château** (sha·tō′): large country house.

INFER

What is "odd" about the situation, according to Rainsford?

_____

_____

_____

_____

_____

_____

_____

INTERPRET

Why do you think that Rainsford assumes at first that the château is a mirage?

_____

_____

_____

_____

_____

_____

WORDS TO OWN

disarming (dis·ärm′iŋ) *adj.:* removing or lessening suspicions or fears.

_____

_____

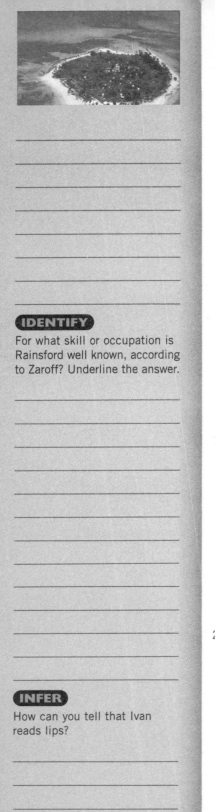

IDENTIFY

For what skill or occupation is Rainsford well known, according to Zaroff? Underline the answer.

INFER

How can you tell that Ivan reads lips?

170 understood Rainsford's words or that he had even heard them. He was dressed in uniform, a black uniform trimmed with gray astrakhan.[6]

"I'm Sanger Rainsford of New York," Rainsford began again. "I fell off a yacht. I am hungry."

The man's only answer was to raise with his thumb the hammer of his revolver. Then Rainsford saw the man's free hand go to his forehead in a military salute, and he saw him click his heels together and stand at attention. Another man was coming down the broad marble steps, an erect, slender man in evening clothes. He advanced to Rainsford and held out his hand.

180 In a cultivated voice marked by a slight accent that gave it added precision and deliberateness, he said: "It is a very great pleasure and honor to welcome Mr. Sanger Rainsford, the celebrated hunter, to my home."

Automatically Rainsford shook the man's hand.

"I've read your book about hunting snow leopards in Tibet, you see," explained the man. "I am General Zaroff."

Rainsford's first impression was that the man was singularly handsome; his second was that there was an original, almost bizarre quality about the general's face. He was a tall man past middle age, for 190 his hair was a vivid white; but his thick eyebrows and pointed military moustache were as black as the night from which Rainsford had come. His eyes, too, were black and very bright. He had high cheekbones, a sharp-cut nose, a spare, dark face, the face of a man used to giving orders, the face of an aristocrat. Turning to the giant in uniform, the general made a sign. The giant put away his pistol, saluted, withdrew.

"Ivan is an incredibly strong fellow," remarked the general, "but he has the misfortune to be deaf and dumb. A simple fellow, but, I'm afraid, like all his race, a bit of a savage."

"Is he Russian?"

200 "He is a Cossack,"[7] said the general, and his smile showed red lips and pointed teeth. "So am I."

"Come," he said, "we shouldn't be chatting here. We can talk later. Now you want clothes, food, rest. You shall have them. This is a most restful spot."

Ivan had reappeared, and the general spoke to him with lips that moved but gave forth no sound.

"Follow Ivan, if you please, Mr. Rainsford," said the general.

"I was about to have my dinner when you came. I'll wait for you. You'll find that my clothes will fit you, I think."

---

6. **astrakhan** (as′trə·kən): curly fur of very young lambs.
7. **Cossack** (käs′ak′): member of a group from Ukraine, many of whom served as horsemen to the Russian czars and were famed for their fierceness in battle.

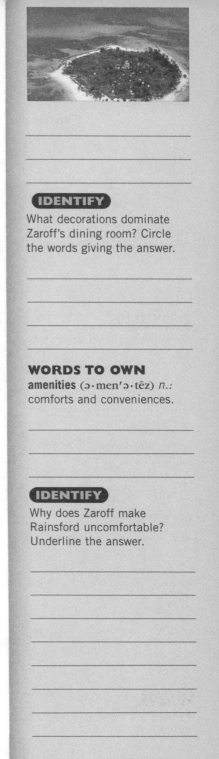

210   It was to a huge, beam-ceilinged bedroom with a canopied bed big enough for six men that Rainsford followed the silent giant. Ivan laid out an evening suit, and Rainsford, as he put it on, noticed that it came from a London tailor who ordinarily cut and sewed for none below the rank of duke.

    The dining room to which Ivan conducted him was in many ways remarkable. There was a medieval magnificence about it; it suggested a baronial hall of feudal times, with its oaken panels, its high ceiling, its vast refectory table[8] where two-score men could sit down to eat. About the hall were the mounted heads of many animals—lions, tigers,
220 elephants, moose, bears; larger or more perfect specimens Rainsford had never seen. At the great table the general was sitting, alone.

    "You'll have a cocktail, Mr. Rainsford," he suggested. The cocktail was surpassingly good; and, Rainsford noted, the table appointments were of the finest—the linen, the crystal, the silver, the china.

    They were eating borscht, the rich red soup with sour cream so dear to Russian palates. Half apologetically General Zaroff said: "We do our best to preserve the amenities of civilization here. Please forgive any lapses. We are well off the beaten track, you know. Do you think the champagne has suffered from its long ocean trip?"
230   "Not in the least," declared Rainsford. He was finding the general a most thoughtful and affable host, a true cosmopolite.[9] But there was one small trait of the general's that made Rainsford uncomfortable. Whenever he looked up from his plate he found the general studying him, appraising him narrowly.

    "Perhaps," said General Zaroff, "you were surprised that I recognized your name. You see, I read all books on hunting published in English, French, and Russian. I have but one passion in my life, Mr. Rainsford, and it is the hunt."

    "You have some wonderful heads here," said Rainsford as he ate a
240 particularly well-cooked filet mignon. "That Cape buffalo is the largest I ever saw."

    "Oh, that fellow. Yes, he was a monster."

    "Did he charge you?"

    "Hurled me against a tree," said the general. "Fractured my skull. But I got the brute."

    "I've always thought," said Rainsford, "that the Cape buffalo is the most dangerous of all big game."

    For a moment the general did not reply; he was smiling his curious red-lipped smile. Then he said slowly: "No. You are wrong, sir. The Cape
250 buffalo is not the most dangerous big game." He sipped his wine. "Here

---

8. **refectory table:** long, narrow table, like the tables used in a monastery or college dining hall.
9. **cosmopolite** (käz·mäp′ə·līt′): knowledgeable citizen of the world.

IDENTIFY
What decorations dominate Zaroff's dining room? Circle the words giving the answer.

WORDS TO OWN
amenities (ə·men′ə·tēz) *n.:* comforts and conveniences.

IDENTIFY
Why does Zaroff make Rainsford uncomfortable? Underline the answer.

IDENTIFY

What seems to be Zaroff's most important goal in life? Circle the words giving the answer.

RETELL

Summarize the facts Zaroff reveals about his youth.

WORDS TO OWN

imprudent (im·prood′′nt) adj.: unwise.

in my preserve on this island," he said in the same slow tone, "I hunt more dangerous game."

Rainsford expressed his surprise. "Is there big game on this island?"

The general nodded. "The biggest."

"Really?"

"Oh, it isn't here naturally, of course. I have to stock the island."

"What have you imported, general?" Rainsford asked. "Tigers?"

The general smiled. "No," he said. "Hunting tigers ceased to interest me some years ago. I exhausted their possibilities, you see. No thrill left 260 in tigers, no real danger. I live for danger, Mr. Rainsford."

The general took from his pocket a gold cigarette case and offered his guest a long black cigarette with a silver tip; it was perfumed and gave off a smell like incense.

"We will have some capital hunting, you and I," said the general. "I shall be most glad to have your society."

"But what game—" began Rainsford.

"I'll tell you," said the general. "You will be amused, I know. I think I may say, in all modesty, that I have done a rare thing. I have invented a new sensation. May I pour you another glass of port, Mr. Rainsford?"

270 "Thank you, general."

The general filled both glasses and said: "God makes some men poets. Some He makes kings, some beggars. Me He made a hunter. My hand was made for the trigger, my father said. He was a very rich man, with a quarter of a million acres in the Crimea,[10] and he was an ardent sportsman. When I was only five years old, he gave me a little gun, specially made in Moscow for me, to shoot sparrows with. When I shot some of his prize turkeys with it, he did not punish me; he complimented me on my marksmanship. I killed my first bear in the Caucasus[11] when I was ten. My whole life has been one prolonged hunt. 280 I went into the army—it was expected of noblemen's sons—and for a time commanded a division of Cossack cavalry, but my real interest was always the hunt. I have hunted every kind of game in every land. It would be impossible for me to tell you how many animals I have killed."

The general puffed at his cigarette.

"After the debacle in Russia[12] I left the country, for it was imprudent for an officer of the czar to stay there. Many noble Russians lost everything. I, luckily, had invested heavily in American securities, so I shall never have to open a tearoom in Monte Carlo[13] or drive a taxi in

---

10. **Crimea** (krī·mē′ə): peninsula in Ukraine jutting out into the Black Sea.
11. **Caucasus** (kô′kə·səs): mountainous region between southeastern Europe and western Asia.
12. **debacle** (di·bä′kəl) **in Russia:** A debacle is an overwhelming defeat. Zaroff is referring to the Russian Revolution of 1917, in which the czar was overthrown.
13. **Monte Carlo** (mänt′ə kär′lō): gambling resort in Monaco, a country on the Mediterranean Sea.

Paris. Naturally, I continued to hunt—grizzlies in your Rockies, crocodiles in the Ganges,[14] rhinoceroses in East Africa. It was in Africa that the Cape buffalo hit me and laid me up for six months. As soon as I recovered I started for the Amazon to hunt jaguars, for I had heard they were unusually cunning. They weren't." The Cossack sighed. "They were no match at all for a hunter with his wits about him and a high-powered rifle. I was bitterly disappointed. I was lying in my tent with a splitting headache one night when a terrible thought pushed its way into my mind. Hunting was beginning to bore me! And hunting, remember, had been my life. I have heard that in America businessmen often go to pieces when they give up the business that has been their life."

"Yes, that's so," said Rainsford.

The general smiled. "I had no wish to go to pieces," he said. "I must do something. Now, mine is an analytical mind, Mr. Rainsford. Doubtless that is why I enjoy the problems of the chase."

"No doubt, General Zaroff."

"So," continued the general, "I asked myself why the hunt no longer fascinated me. You are much younger than I am, Mr. Rainsford, and have not hunted as much, but you perhaps can guess the answer."

"What was it?"

"Simply this: Hunting had ceased to be what you call a sporting proposition. It had become too easy. I always got my quarry. Always. There is no greater bore than perfection."

The general lit a fresh cigarette.

"No animal had a chance with me anymore. That is no boast; it is a mathematical certainty. The animal had nothing but his legs and his instinct. Instinct is no match for reason. When I thought of this, it was a tragic moment for me, I can tell you."

Rainsford leaned across the table, absorbed in what his host was saying.

"It came to me as an inspiration what I must do," the general went on.

"And that was?"

The general smiled the quiet smile of one who has faced an obstacle and surmounted it with success. "I had to invent a new animal to hunt," he said.

"A new animal? You're joking."

"Not at all," said the general. "I never joke about hunting. I needed a new animal. I found one. So I bought this island, built this house, and here I do my hunting. The island is perfect for my purposes—there are jungles with a maze of trails in them, hills, swamps—"

"But the animal, General Zaroff?"

"Oh," said the general, "it supplies me with the most exciting

_____
14. **Ganges** (gan'jēz): river in northern India and Bangladesh.

INFER

How does Rainsford interpret Zaroff's use of the word *invent*?

BUILD FLUENCY

Read this passage aloud. Use different tones of voice for Zaroff and Rainsford. Try to capture the mood of tension at this point in the story.

_____

_____

_____

_____

_____

_____

_____

_____

_____

_____

_____

_____

_____

_____

_____

_____

WORDS TO OWN
scruples (skr$\overline{oo}$′pəlz) _n._: feelings of doubt or guilt about a suggested action.

INTERPRET

What does this speech show about Zaroff's **character**?

_____

_____

_____

_____

_____

_____

_____

hunting in the world. No other hunting compares with it for an instant. Every day I hunt, and I never grow bored now, for I have a quarry with which I can match my wits."

Rainsford's bewilderment showed in his face.

"I wanted the ideal animal to hunt," explained the general. "So I said: 'What are the attributes of an ideal quarry?' And the answer was, of course: 'It must have courage, cunning, and, above all, it must be able to reason.'"

340 "But no animal can reason," objected Rainsford.

"My dear fellow," said the general, "there is one that can."

"But you can't mean—" gasped Rainsford.

"And why not?"

"I can't believe you are serious, General Zaroff. This is a grisly joke."

"Why should I not be serious? I am speaking of hunting."

"Hunting? Good God, General Zaroff, what you speak of is murder."

The general laughed with entire good nature. He regarded Rainsford quizzically. "I refuse to believe that so modern and civilized a young man as you seem to be harbors romantic ideas about the value of human

350 life. Surely your experiences in the war—"

"Did not make me condone coldblooded murder," finished Rainsford stiffly.

Laughter shook the general. "How extraordinarily droll you are!" he said. "One does not expect nowadays to find a young man of the educated class, even in America, with such a naive, and, if I may say so, mid-Victorian point of view. It's like finding a snuffbox in a limousine. Ah, well, doubtless you had Puritan ancestors. So many Americans appear to have had. I'll wager you'll forget your notions when you go hunting with me. You've a genuine new thrill in store for you, Mr.

360 Rainsford."

"Thank you, I'm a hunter, not a murderer."

"Dear me," said the general, quite unruffled, "again that unpleasant word. But I think I can show you that your scruples are quite ill-founded."

"Yes?"

"Life is for the strong, to be lived by the strong, and if need be, taken by the strong. The weak of the world were put here to give the strong pleasure. I am strong. Why should I not use my gift? If I wish to hunt, why should I not? I hunt the scum of the earth—sailors from tramp

370 ships—lascars,[15] blacks, Chinese, whites, mongrels—a thoroughbred horse or hound is worth more than a score of them."

"But they are men," said Rainsford hotly.

"Precisely," said the general. "That is why I use them. It gives me pleasure. They can reason, after a fashion. So they are dangerous."

---

15. **lascars** (las′kərz): East Indian sailors employed on European ships.

"But where do you get them?"

The general's left eyelid fluttered down in a wink. "This island is called Ship-Trap," he answered. "Sometimes an angry god of the high seas sends them to me. Sometimes, when Providence is not so kind, I help Providence a bit. Come to the window with me."

380 Rainsford went to the window and looked out toward the sea.

"Watch! Out there!" exclaimed the general, pointing into the night. Rainsford's eyes saw only blackness, and then, as the general pressed a button, far out to sea Rainsford saw the flash of lights.

The general chuckled. "They indicate a channel," he said, "where there's none; giant rocks with razor edges crouch like a sea monster with wide-open jaws. They can crush a ship as easily as I crush this nut." He dropped a walnut on the hardwood floor and brought his heel grinding down on it. "Oh, yes," he said, casually, as if in answer to a question,

"I have electricity. We try to be civilized here."

390 "Civilized? And you shoot down men?"

A trace of anger was in the general's black eyes, but it was there for but a second, and he said, in his most pleasant manner: "Dear me, what a righteous young man you are! I assure you I do not do the thing you suggest. That would be barbarous. I treat these visitors with every consideration. They get plenty of good food and exercise. They get into splendid physical condition. You shall see for yourself tomorrow."

"What do you mean?"

"We'll visit my training school," smiled the general. "It's in the cellar. I have about a dozen pupils down there now. They're from the Spanish

400 bark *San Lucar* that had the bad luck to go on the rocks out there. A very inferior lot, I regret to say. Poor specimens and more accustomed to the deck than to the jungle."

He raised his hand, and Ivan, who served as waiter, brought thick Turkish coffee. Rainsford, with an effort, held his tongue in check.

"It's a game, you see," pursued the general blandly. "I suggest to one of them that we go hunting. I give him a supply of food and an excellent hunting knife. I give him three hours' start. I am to follow, armed only with a pistol of the smallest caliber and range. If my quarry eludes me for three whole days, he wins the game. If I find him"—the general

410 smiled—"he loses."

"Suppose he refuses to be hunted?"

"Oh," said the general, "I give him his option, of course. He need not play that game if he doesn't wish to. If he does not wish to hunt, I turn him over to Ivan. Ivan once had the honor of serving as official knouter[16] to the Great White Czar, and he has his own ideas of sport. Invariably, Mr. Rainsford, invariably they choose the hunt."

"And if they win?"

---

16. knouter (nout′ər): person who beats criminals with a knout, a kind of leather whip.

INTERPRET

Tell what is **ironic** about Zaroff's use of the word *civilized*.

INTERPRET

How does the detail about Zaroff's humming (line 434) affect the **mood** at this point in the story?

WORDS TO OWN
solicitously (sə·lis′ə·təs·lē) *adv.*: in a concerned manner.

WORDS TO OWN
opiate (ō′pē·it) *n.*: anything that tends to soothe or calm someone. An opiate may also be a medicine containing opium or a related drug used to relieve pain.

INFER

What **internal conflict** does Rainsford experience in lines 447–458?

The smile on the general's face widened. "To date I have not lost," he said.

420   Then he added, hastily: "I don't wish you to think me a braggart, Mr. Rainsford. Many of them afford only the most elementary sort of problem. Occasionally I strike a tartar.[17] One almost did win. I eventually had to use the dogs."

"The dogs?"

"This way, please. I'll show you."

The general steered Rainsford to a window. The lights from the windows sent a flickering illumination that made grotesque patterns on the courtyard below, and Rainsford could see moving about there a dozen or so huge black shapes; as they turned toward him, their eyes 430 glittered greenly.

"A rather good lot, I think," observed the general. "They are let out at seven every night. If anyone should try to get into my house—or out of it—something extremely regrettable would occur to him." He hummed a snatch of song from the Folies-Bergère.[18]

"And now," said the general, "I want to show you my new collection of heads. Will you come with me to the library?"

"I hope," said Rainsford, "that you will excuse me tonight, General Zaroff. I'm really not feeling at all well."

"Ah, indeed?" the general inquired solicitously. "Well, I suppose 440 that's only natural, after your long swim. You need a good, restful night's sleep. Tomorrow you'll feel like a new man, I'll wager. Then we'll hunt, eh? I've one rather promising prospect—"

Rainsford was hurrying from the room.

"Sorry you can't go with me tonight," called the general. "I expect rather fair sport—a big, strong black. He looks resourceful— Well, good night, Mr. Rainsford; I hope you have a good night's rest."

The bed was good and the pajamas of the softest silk, and he was tired in every fiber of his being, but nevertheless Rainsford could not quiet his brain with the opiate of sleep. He lay, eyes wide open. Once 450 he thought he heard stealthy steps in the corridor outside his room. He sought to throw open the door; it would not open. He went to the window and looked out. His room was high up in one of the towers. The lights of the château were out now, and it was dark and silent, but there was a fragment of sallow moon, and by its wan light he could see, dimly, the courtyard; there, weaving in and out in the pattern of shadow, were black, noiseless forms; the hounds heard him at the window and looked up, expectantly, with their green eyes. Rainsford went back to the bed and lay down. By many methods he tried to put himself to sleep. He had

---

17. **strike a tartar:** get more than one bargained for. A tartar is a violent, unmanageable person.
18. **Folies-Bergère** (fô′lē ber·zher′): famous nightclub in Paris.

achieved a doze when, just as morning began to come, he heard, far off
460 in the jungle, the faint report of a pistol.

General Zaroff did not appear until luncheon. He was dressed
faultlessly in the tweeds of a country squire. He was solicitous about the
state of Rainsford's health.

"As for me," sighed the general, "I do not feel so well. I am worried,
Mr. Rainsford. Last night I detected traces of my old complaint."

To Rainsford's questioning glance the general said: "Ennui.
Boredom."

Then, taking a second helping of crêpes suzette,[19] the general
explained: "The hunting was not good last night. The fellow lost his
470 head. He made a straight trail that offered no problems at all. That's the
trouble with these sailors; they have dull brains to begin with, and they
do not know how to get about in the woods. They do excessively stupid
and obvious things. It's most annoying. Will you have another glass of
Chablis, Mr. Rainsford?"

"General," said Rainsford firmly, "I wish to leave this island at once."

The general raised his thickets of eyebrows; he seemed hurt. "But,
my dear fellow," the general protested, "you've only just come. You've
had no hunting—"

"I wish to go today," said Rainsford. He saw the dead black eyes
480 of the general on him, studying him. General Zaroff's face suddenly
brightened.

He filled Rainsford's glass with venerable Chablis from a dusty
bottle.

"Tonight," said the general, "we will hunt—you and I."

Rainsford shook his head. "No, general," he said. "I will not hunt."

The general shrugged his shoulders and delicately ate a hothouse
grape. "As you wish, my friend," he said. "The choice rests entirely with
you. But may I not venture to suggest that you will find my idea of sport
more diverting than Ivan's?"
490 He nodded toward the corner where the giant stood, scowling, his
thick arms crossed on his hogshead of chest.

"You don't mean—" cried Rainsford.

"My dear fellow," said the general, "have I not told you I always
mean what I say about hunting? This is really an inspiration. I drink to
a foeman worthy of my steel—at last."

The general raised his glass, but Rainsford sat staring at him.

"You'll find this game worth playing," the general said
enthusiastically. "Your brain against mine. Your woodcraft against mine.
Your strength and stamina against mine. Outdoor chess! And the stake is
500 not without value, eh?"

---

19. **crêpes suzette** (krăp soo·zet′): thin pancakes folded in a hot orange-flavored sauce and
served in flaming brandy.

PREDICT

What **external conflict** do you
think will dominate the rest of
the story? How do you think
this conflict will be **resolved**?

IDENTIFY

According to Zaroff, why should Rainsford avoid Death Swamp? Underline the words giving the answer.

WORDS TO OWN

deplorable (dē·plôr′ə·bəl) *adj.:* regrettable; very bad.

IDENTIFY

What is the island compared to in this passage? To what is the ocean compared? Circle the answers.

"And if I win—" began Rainsford huskily.

"I'll cheerfully acknowledge myself defeated if I do not find you by midnight of the third day," said General Zaroff. "My sloop will place you on the mainland near a town."

The general read what Rainsford was thinking.

"Oh, you can trust me," said the Cossack. "I will give you my word as a gentleman and a sportsman. Of course you, in turn, must agree to say nothing of your visit here."

"I'll agree to nothing of the kind," said Rainsford.

510   "Oh," said the general, "in that case— But why discuss that now? Three days hence we can discuss it over a bottle of Veuve Clicquot,[20] unless—"

The general sipped his wine.

Then a businesslike air animated him. "Ivan," he said to Rainsford, "will supply you with hunting clothes, food, a knife. I suggest you wear moccasins; they leave a poorer trail. I suggest too that you avoid the big swamp in the southeast corner of the island. We call it Death Swamp. There's quicksand there. One foolish fellow tried it. The deplorable part of it was that Lazarus followed him. You can imagine my feelings, Mr.

520 Rainsford. I loved Lazarus; he was the finest hound in my pack. Well, I must beg you to excuse me now. I always take a siesta after lunch. You'll hardly have time for a nap, I fear. You'll want to start, no doubt. I shall not follow till dusk. Hunting at night is so much more exciting than by day, don't you think? Au revoir, Mr. Rainsford, au revoir."

General Zaroff, with a deep, courtly bow, strolled from the room.

From another door came Ivan. Under one arm he carried khaki hunting clothes, a haversack of food, a leather sheath containing a long-bladed hunting knife; his right hand rested on a cocked revolver thrust in the crimson sash about his waist . . .

530 Rainsford had fought his way through the bush for two hours. "I must keep my nerve. I must keep my nerve," he said through tight teeth.

He had not been entirely clearheaded when the château gates snapped shut behind him. His whole idea at first was to put distance between himself and General Zaroff, and, to this end, he had plunged along, spurred on by the sharp rowels[21] of something very like panic. Now he had got a grip on himself, had stopped, and was taking stock of himself and the situation.

He saw that straight flight was futile; inevitably it would bring him face to face with the sea. He was in a picture with a frame of water, and

540 his operations, clearly, must take place within that frame.

---

20. Veuve Clicquot (võv klē·kô′): brand of fine champagne.
21. rowels (rou′əlz): small wheels with spurs that horseback riders wear on their heels.

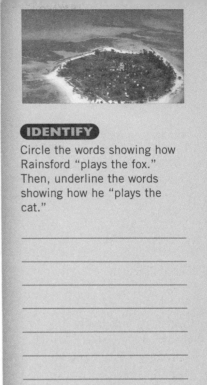

"I'll give him a trail to follow," muttered Rainsford, and he struck off from the rude paths he had been following into the trackless wilderness. He executed a series of intricate loops; he doubled on his trail again and again, recalling all the lore of the fox hunt and all the dodges of the fox. Night found him leg-weary, with hands and face lashed by the branches, on a thickly wooded ridge. He knew it would be insane to blunder on through the dark, even if he had the strength. His need for rest was imperative and he thought: "I have played the fox; now I must play the cat of the fable." A big tree with a thick trunk and outspread branches

550 was nearby, and taking care to leave not the slightest mark, he climbed up into the crotch and stretching out on one of the broad limbs, after a fashion, rested. Rest brought him new confidence and almost a feeling of security. Even so zealous a hunter as General Zaroff could not trace him there, he told himself; only the devil himself could follow that complicated trail through the jungle after dark. But, perhaps, the general was a devil—

An apprehensive night crawled slowly by like a wounded snake, and sleep did not visit Rainsford, although the silence of a dead world was on the jungle. Toward morning, when a dingy gray was varnishing the

560 sky, the cry of some startled bird focused Rainsford's attention in that direction. Something was coming through the bush, coming slowly, carefully, coming by the same winding way Rainsford had come. He flattened himself down on the limb, and through a screen of leaves almost as thick as tapestry, he watched. The thing that was approaching was a man.

It was General Zaroff. He made his way along with his eyes fixed in utmost concentration on the ground before him. He paused, almost beneath the tree, dropped to his knees and studied the ground. Rainsford's impulse was to hurl himself down like a panther, but he

570 saw the general's right hand held something metallic—a small automatic pistol.

The hunter shook his head several times, as if he were puzzled. Then he straightened up and took from his case one of his black cigarettes; its pungent incenselike smoke floated up to Rainsford's nostrils.

Rainsford held his breath. The general's eyes had left the ground and were traveling inch by inch up the tree. Rainsford froze there, every muscle tensed for a spring. But the sharp eyes of the hunter stopped before they reached the limb where Rainsford lay; a smile spread over

580 his brown face. Very deliberately he blew a smoke ring into the air; then he turned his back on the tree and walked carelessly away, back along the trail he had come. The swish of the underbrush against his hunting boots grew fainter and fainter.

Then pent-up air burst hotly from Rainsford's lungs. His first thought made him feel sick and numb. The general could follow a trail through

IDENTIFY

Circle the words showing how Rainsford "plays the fox." Then, underline the words showing how he "plays the cat."

_____

_____

_____

_____

_____

_____

_____

_____

INFER

Tell how Zaroff has managed to follow Rainsford.

_____

_____

_____

_____

_____

INTERPRET

Underline the clue in this passage suggesting that Zaroff knows where Rainsford is hiding.

_____

_____

_____

INTERPRET

How does the realization that Zaroff is merely toying with him affect Rainsford?

_____
_____
_____
_____
_____

WORDS TO OWN

precariously (prē·ker′ē·əs·lē) *adv.:* unsteadily; in an unstable manner.

_____
_____

IDENTIFY

These two paragraphs (lines 604–620) contain animal imagery that emphasizes the inhuman nature of the contest. Circle four animals that are mentioned.

_____
_____
_____
_____
_____
_____
_____
_____
_____
_____
_____
_____
_____

the woods at night; he could follow an extremely difficult trail; he must have uncanny powers; only by the merest chance had the Cossack failed to see his quarry.

Rainsford's second thought was even more terrible. It sent a shudder 590 of cold horror through his whole being. Why had the general smiled? Why had he turned back?

Rainsford did not want to believe what his reason told him was true, but the truth was as evident as the sun that had by now pushed through the morning mists. The general was playing with him! The general was saving him for another day's sport! The Cossack was the cat; he was the mouse. Then it was that Rainsford knew the full meaning of terror.

"I will not lose my nerve. I will not."

He slid down from the tree and struck off again into the woods. His face was set and he forced the machinery of his mind to function. Three 600 hundred yards from his hiding place he stopped where a huge dead tree leaned precariously on a smaller living one. Throwing off his sack of food, Rainsford took his knife from its sheath and began to work with all his energy.

The job was finished at last, and he threw himself down behind a fallen log a hundred feet away. He did not have to wait long. The cat was coming again to play with the mouse.

Following the trail with the sureness of a bloodhound came General Zaroff. Nothing escaped those searching black eyes, no crushed blade of grass, no bent twig, no mark, no matter how faint, in the moss. So 610 intent was the Cossack on his stalking that he was upon the thing Rainsford had made before he saw it. His foot touched the protruding bough that was the trigger. Even as he touched it, the general sensed his danger and leaped back with the agility of an ape. But he was not quite quick enough; the dead tree, delicately adjusted to rest on the cut living one, crashed down and struck the general a glancing blow on the shoulder as it fell; but for his alertness, he must have been smashed beneath it. He staggered, but he did not fall; nor did he drop his revolver. He stood there, rubbing his injured shoulder, and Rainsford, with fear again gripping his heart, heard the general's mocking laugh ring through 620 the jungle.

"Rainsford," called the general, "if you are within the sound of my voice, as I suppose you are, let me congratulate you. Not many men know how to make a Malay mancatcher. Luckily for me, I too have hunted in Malacca.[22] You are proving interesting, Mr. Rainsford. I am going now to have my wound dressed; it's only a slight one. But I shall be back. I shall be back."

When the general, nursing his bruised shoulder, had gone, Rainsford took up his flight again. It was flight now, a desperate, hopeless flight,

---

22. **Malacca** (mə·lak′ə): state in what is now the nation of Malaysia in southeastern Asia.

that carried him on for some hours. Dusk came, then darkness, and still
630 he pressed on. The ground grew softer under his moccasins; the
vegetation grew ranker, denser; insects bit him savagely. Then, as he
stepped forward, his foot sank into the ooze. He tried to wrench it back,
but the muck sucked viciously at his foot as if it were a giant leech. With
a violent effort, he tore loose. He knew where he was now. Death
Swamp and its quicksand.

His hands were tight closed as if his nerve were something tangible
that someone in the darkness was trying to tear from his grip. The
softness of the earth had given him an idea. He stepped back from the
quicksand a dozen feet or so, and, like some huge prehistoric beaver, he
640 began to dig.

Rainsford had dug himself in in France,[23] when a second's delay
meant death. That had been a placid pastime compared to his digging
now. The pit grew deeper; when it was above his shoulders, he climbed
out and from some hard saplings cut stakes and sharpened them to a
fine point. These stakes he planted in the bottom of the pit with the
points sticking up. With flying fingers he wove a rough carpet of weeds
and branches and with it he covered the mouth of the pit. Then, wet
with sweat and aching with tiredness, he crouched behind the stump of
a lightning-charred tree.

650 He knew his pursuer was coming; he heard the padding sound of
feet on the soft earth, and the night breeze brought him the perfume of
the general's cigarette. It seemed to Rainsford that the general was
coming with unusual swiftness; he was not feeling his way along, foot
by foot. Rainsford, crouching there, could not see the general, nor could
he see the pit. He lived a year in a minute. Then he felt an impulse to
cry aloud with joy, for he heard the sharp crackle of the breaking
branches as the cover of the pit gave way; he heard the sharp scream of
pain as the pointed stakes found their mark. He leaped up from his place
of concealment. Then he cowered back. Three feet from the pit a man
660 was standing, with an electric torch in his hand.

"You've done well, Rainsford," the voice of the general called. "Your
Burmese tiger pit has claimed one of my best dogs. Again you score.
I think, Mr. Rainsford, I'll see what you can do against my whole pack.
I'm going home for a rest now. Thank you for a most amusing evening."

At daybreak Rainsford, lying near the swamp, was awakened by the
sound that made him know that he had new things to learn about fear.
It was a distant sound, faint and wavering, but he knew it. It was the
baying of a pack of hounds.

Rainsford knew he could do one of two things. He could stay where
670 he was and wait. That was suicide. He could flee. That was postponing

---

23. **dug himself in in France:** dug a hole for shelter from gunfire during World War I (1914–1918).

INTERPRET

Why does Rainsford's awareness of his location add to the **suspense** here?

_____

_____

_____

_____

_____

_____

_____

_____

_____

_____

_____

_____

_____

_____

EVALUATE

Is Zaroff a true sportsman? Explain.

_____

_____

_____

_____

_____

IDENTIFY

What two choices does Rainsford now have? Circle the words giving the answer.

EVALUATE

Is Connell's use of short
sentences in lines 697–702
effective? Tell why or why not.

IDENTIFY

What two "slight annoyances"
bother Zaroff at dinner? Circle
the words giving the answer.

the inevitable. For a moment he stood there, thinking. An idea that held a wild chance came to him, and, tightening his belt, he headed away from the swamp.

The baying of the hounds drew nearer, then still nearer, nearer, ever nearer. On a ridge Rainsford climbed a tree. Down a watercourse, not a quarter of a mile away, he could see the bush moving. Straining his eyes, he saw the lean figure of General Zaroff; just ahead of him Rainsford made out another figure whose wide shoulders surged through the tall jungle weeds. It was the giant Ivan, and he seemed pulled forward by 680 some unseen force. Rainsford knew that Ivan must be holding the pack in leash.

They would be on him any minute now. His mind worked frantically. He thought of a native trick he had learned in Uganda. He slid down the tree. He caught hold of a springy young sapling and to it he fastened his hunting knife, with the blade pointing down the trail; with a bit of wild grapevine he tied back the sapling. Then he ran for his life. The hounds raised their voices as they hit the fresh scent. Rainsford knew now how an animal at bay feels.

He had to stop to get his breath. The baying of the hounds stopped 690 abruptly, and Rainsford's heart stopped too. They must have reached the knife.

He shinnied excitedly up a tree and looked back. His pursuers had stopped. But the hope that was in Rainsford's brain when he climbed died, for he saw in the shallow valley that General Zaroff was still on his feet. But Ivan was not. The knife, driven by the recoil of the springing tree, had not wholly failed.

"Nerve, nerve, nerve!" he panted, as he dashed along. A blue gap showed between the trees dead ahead. Ever nearer drew the hounds. Rainsford forced himself on toward that gap. He reached it. It was the 700 shore of the sea. Across a cove he could see the gloomy gray stone of the château. Twenty feet below him the sea rumbled and hissed. Rainsford hesitated. He heard the hounds. Then he leaped far out into the sea. . . .

When the general and his pack reached the place by the sea, the Cossack stopped. For some minutes he stood regarding the blue-green expanse of water. He shrugged his shoulders. Then he sat down, took a drink of brandy from a silver flask, lit a perfumed cigarette, and hummed a bit from *Madama Butterfly*.

General Zaroff had an exceedingly good dinner in his great paneled dining hall that evening. With it he had a bottle of Pol Roger[24] and half 710 a bottle of Chambertin.[25] Two slight annoyances kept him from perfect enjoyment. One was the thought that it would be difficult to replace

---

24. **Pol Roger** (pôl *rô*·zhā′): brand of champagne.
25. **Chambertin** (shä*n*′ber·ta*n*′): red burgundy wine.

Ivan; the other was that his quarry had escaped him; of course the American hadn't played the game—so thought the general as he tasted his after-dinner liqueur. In his library he read, to soothe himself, from the works of Marcus Aurelius.[26] At ten he went up to his bedroom. He was deliciously tired, he said to himself as he locked himself in. There was a little moonlight, so before turning on his light, he went to the window and looked down at the courtyard. He could see the great hounds, and he called: "Better luck another time," to them. Then he

720 switched on the light.

A man, who had been hiding in the curtains of the bed, was standing there.

"Rainsford!" screamed the general. "How in God's name did you get here?"

"Swam," said Rainsford. "I found it quicker than walking through the jungle."

The general sucked in his breath and smiled. "I congratulate you," he said. "You have won the game."

Rainsford did not smile. "I am still a beast at bay," he said, in a low,

730 hoarse voice. "Get ready, General Zaroff."

The general made one of his deepest bows. "I see," he said. "Splendid! One of us is to furnish a repast for the hounds. The other will sleep in this very excellent bed. On guard, Rainsford. . . ."

He had never slept in a better bed, Rainsford decided.

INTERPRET

Explain the significance of the statement, "I am still a beast at bay."

INFER

What is the **resolution** of the story's main **conflict**? How do you know?

---

26. **Marcus Aurelius** (mär′kəs ô·rē′lē·əs): emperor of Rome from A.D. 161 to 180, who wrote about the philosophy of Stoicism, which held that people should make themselves indifferent to both pain and pleasure.

Conflict

A **conflict** is a struggle of some kind. If a person is struggling against something outside himself or herself, the conflict is **external.** If the person is fighting to control some inner problem—such as fear, anger, or disappointment—the conflict is **internal.**

Each quotation below refers to an external or internal conflict in the story. Fill in the chart by briefly describing the conflict and identifying it as external or internal. Then, tell how the conflict is resolved.

Story Passage	Nature of Conflict	How Conflict Is Resolved
1. For a seemingly endless time he fought the sea. He began to count his strokes. . . .		
2. "Hunting tigers ceased to interest me some years ago. I exhausted their possibilities, you see. No thrill left in tigers, no real danger."		
3. The bed was good and the pajamas of the softest silk, and he was tired in every fiber of his being, but nevertheless Rainsford could not quiet his brain with the opiate of sleep.		
4. The Cossack was the cat; he was the mouse. Then it was that Rainsford knew the full meaning of terror.		
5. Rainsford did not smile. "I am still a beast at bay," he said, in a low, hoarse voice. "Get ready, General Zaroff."		

Vocabulary: How to Own a Word

Suffix

A **suffix** is a word part added to the end of a root or base word. A suffix changes a word's meaning and its function as a part of speech. Use a dictionary to complete the chart below. Find the root or base of each Word to Own in the left-hand column of the chart. Then, give the definition and part of speech of the Word to Own's root or base, the Word to Own's suffix and the definition of that suffix, the definition of the Word to Own, and the Word to Own's part of speech. Some parts of the chart have been filled in for you.

Word Bank
indolently
disarming
solicitously
deplorable
precariously

Word to Own	Root or Base Word and Definition	Root or Base Word's Part of Speech	Word to Own's Suffix & Definition of Suffix	Word to Own's Definition	Word to Own's Part of Speech
indolently	indolent—lazy	adjective	–ly—in a manner	lazily	adverb
disarming			–ing—an act or instance of		
solicitously	solicitous—showing concern	adjective			
deplorable				regrettable	
precariously		adjective			

The Interlopers

Make the Connection

What's in a Feud?

A **feud** is a violent dispute or quarrel, especially one between families or clans. Most arguments can be settled through a process of discussion or compromise. Feuds occur when neither side will compromise or give up its hatred for the other. Feuds are quite different from rivalries or healthy competitions, such as in political debates or sports events.

Besides Saki's story "The Interlopers," literary examples of feuds include the warring families in Shakespeare's *Romeo and Juliet* and the Grangerford and the Shepherdson clans in Mark Twain's *Adventures of Huckleberry Finn.* Unfortunately, feuds in real life today involve whole regions of the world that have been locked in conflict for generations.

On the chart below, write examples of feuds that have torn families or even countries apart. Add a few brief comments for each example you include. [Hint: One entry on your chart might relate to the first story in this book, Liam O'Flaherty's "The Sniper."]

Feuds	Comments
_____ vs. _____	_____
	_____
	_____
_____ vs. _____	_____
	_____
	_____
_____ vs. _____	_____
	_____
	_____

Saki

The Interlopers

WORDS TO OWN
precipitous (prē·sip′ə·təs) *adj.:*
very steep.
acquiesced (ak′wē·est′) *v.*
(used with *in*): accepted;
complied with.

IDENTIFY

What is the main **conflict** in this story? Underline the words giving the answer.

IDENTIFY

Why does Ulrich suspect that thieves are present on his land this evening? Underline the words giving the answer.

WORDS TO OWN
marauders (mə·rôd′·ərz) *n.:*
people who roam in search of loot.

INTERPRET

What factors make this meeting **suspenseful**? List them.

In a forest of mixed growth somewhere on the eastern spurs of the Carpathians, a man stood one winter night watching and listening, as though he waited for some beast of the woods to come within the range of his vision and, later, of his rifle. But the game for whose presence he kept so keen an outlook was none that figured in the sportsman's calendar as lawful and proper for the chase; Ulrich von Gradwitz patrolled the dark forest in quest of a human enemy.

The forest lands of Gradwitz were of wide extent and well stocked with game; the narrow strip of precipitous woodland that lay on its
10 outskirt was not remarkable for the game it harbored or the shooting it afforded, but it was the most jealously guarded of all its owner's territorial possessions. A famous lawsuit, in the days of his grandfather, had wrested it from the illegal possession of a neighboring family of petty landowners; the dispossessed party had never acquiesced in the judgment of the courts, and a long series of poaching affrays[1] and similar scandals had embittered the relationships between the families for three generations. The neighbor feud had grown into a personal one since Ulrich had come to be head of his family; if there was a man in the world whom he detested and wished ill to, it was Georg Znaeym, the
20 inheritor of the quarrel and the tireless game snatcher and raider of the disputed border forest. The feud might, perhaps, have died down or been compromised if the personal ill will of the two men had not stood in the way; as boys they had thirsted for one another's blood, as men each prayed that misfortune might fall on the other, and this wind-scourged winter night Ulrich had banded together his foresters to watch the dark forest, not in quest of four-footed quarry, but to keep a lookout for the prowling thieves whom he suspected of being afoot from across the land boundary. The roebuck,[2] which usually kept in the sheltered hollows during a storm wind, were running like driven things tonight, and there
30 was movement and unrest among the creatures that were wont to sleep through the dark hours. Assuredly there was a disturbing element in the forest, and Ulrich could guess the quarter from whence it came.

He strayed away by himself from the watchers whom he had placed in ambush on the crest of the hill and wandered far down the steep slopes amid the wild tangle of undergrowth, peering through the tree trunks and listening through the whistling and skirling[3] of the wind and the restless beating of the branches for sight or sound of the marauders. If only on this wild night, in this dark, lone spot, he might come across Georg Znaeym, man to man, with none to witness—that was the wish
40 that was uppermost in his thoughts. And as he stepped round the trunk of a huge beech he came face to face with the man he sought.

---

1. **affrays** (ə·frāz′): noisy quarrels; brawls.
2. **roebuck:** roe deer, small deer that live in Europe and Asia.
3. **skirling:** shrill, piercing sound.

The two enemies stood glaring at one another for a long silent moment. Each had a rifle in his hand, each had hate in his heart and murder uppermost in his mind. The chance had come to give full play to the passions of a lifetime. But a man who has been brought up under the code of a restraining civilization cannot easily nerve himself to shoot down his neighbor in cold blood and without a word spoken, except for an offense against his hearth and honor. And before the moment of hesitation had given way to action, a deed of Nature's own violence
50 overwhelmed them both. A fierce shriek of the storm had been answered by a splitting crash over their heads, and ere they could leap aside, a mass of falling beech tree had thundered down on them. Ulrich von Gradwitz found himself stretched on the ground, one arm numb beneath him and the other held almost as helplessly in a tight tangle of forked branches, while both legs were pinned beneath the fallen mass. His heavy shooting boots had saved his feet from being crushed to pieces, but if his fractures were not as serious as they might have been, at least it was evident that he could not move from his present position till someone came to release him. The descending twigs had slashed the
60 skin of his face, and he had to wink away some drops of blood from his eyelashes before he could take in a general view of the disaster. At his side, so near that under ordinary circumstances he could almost have touched him, lay Georg Znaeym, alive and struggling, but obviously as helplessly pinioned[4] down as himself. All round them lay a thick-strewn wreckage of splintered branches and broken twigs.

Relief at being alive and exasperation at his captive plight brought a strange medley of pious thank offerings and sharp curses to Ulrich's lips. Georg, who was nearly blinded with the blood which trickled across his eyes, stopped his struggling for a moment to listen, and then gave a
70 short, snarling laugh.

"So you're not killed, as you ought to be, but you're caught, anyway," he cried, "caught fast. Ho, what a jest, Ulrich von Gradwitz snared in his stolen forest. There's real justice for you!"

And he laughed again, mockingly and savagely.

"I'm caught in my own forest land," retorted Ulrich. "When my men come to release us, you will wish, perhaps, that you were in a better plight than caught poaching on a neighbor's land, shame on you."

Georg was silent for a moment; then he answered quietly:

"Are you sure that your men will find much to release? I have men,
80 too, in the forest tonight, close behind me, and *they* will be here first and do the releasing. When they drag me out from under these branches, it won't need much clumsiness on their part to roll this mass of trunk right

---

4. **pinioned:** pinned, as if chained or tied up.

INTERPRET

How do lines 94–97 reveal the **irony** of the two men's predictions to each other?

IDENTIFY

Underline the phrase in this passage that hints at a change in Ulrich's attitude.

WORDS TO OWN

languor (laṇ'gər) *n.:* weakness; weariness.

IDENTIFY

Underline the two places at which Ulrich refers to Georg as his "neighbor."

over on the top of you. Your men will find you dead under a fallen beech tree. For form's sake I shall send my condolences to your family."

"It is a useful hint," said Ulrich fiercely. "My men had orders to follow in ten minutes' time, seven of which must have gone by already, and when they get me out—I will remember the hint. Only as you will have met your death poaching on my lands, I don't think I can decently send any message of condolence to your family."

90   "Good," snarled Georg, "good. We fight this quarrel out to the death, you and I and our foresters, with no cursed interlopers to come between us. Death and damnation to you, Ulrich von Gradwitz."

"The same to you, Georg Znaeym, forest thief, game snatcher."

Both men spoke with the bitterness of possible defeat before them, for each knew that it might be long before his men would seek him out or find him; it was a bare matter of chance which party would arrive first on the scene.

Both had now given up the useless struggle to free themselves from the mass of wood that held them down; Ulrich limited his endeavors to

100 an effort to bring his one partially free arm near enough to his outer coat pocket to draw out his wine flask. Even when he had accomplished that operation, it was long before he could manage the unscrewing of the stopper or get any of the liquid down his throat. But what a heaven-sent draft[5] it seemed! It was an open winter,[6] and little snow had fallen as yet, hence the captives suffered less from the cold than might have been the case at that season of the year; nevertheless, the wine was warming and reviving to the wounded man, and he looked across with something like a throb of pity to where his enemy lay, just keeping the groans of pain and weariness from crossing his lips.

110 "Could you reach this flask if I threw it over to you?" asked Ulrich suddenly. "There is good wine in it, and one may as well be as comfortable as one can. Let us drink, even if tonight one of us dies."

"No, I can scarcely see anything; there is so much blood caked round my eyes," said Georg; "and in any case I don't drink wine with an enemy."

Ulrich was silent for a few minutes and lay listening to the weary screeching of the wind. An idea was slowly forming and growing in his brain, an idea that gained strength every time that he looked across at the man who was fighting so grimly against pain and exhaustion. In the

120 pain and <u>languor</u> that Ulrich himself was feeling, the old fierce hatred seemed to be dying down.

"Neighbor," he said presently, "do as you please if your men come first. It was a fair compact. But as for me, I've changed my mind. If my men are the first to come, you shall be the first to be helped, as though

---

5. **draft:** drink.
6. **open winter:** mild winter.

you were my guest. We have quarreled like devils all our lives over this
stupid strip of forest, where the trees can't even stand upright in a breath
of wind. Lying here tonight, thinking, I've come to think we've been
rather fools; there are better things in life than getting the better of a
boundary dispute. Neighbor, if you will help me to bury the old quarrel,
130 I—I will ask you to be my friend."

Georg Znaeym was silent for so long that Ulrich thought perhaps
he had fainted with the pain of his injuries. Then he spoke slowly and
in jerks.

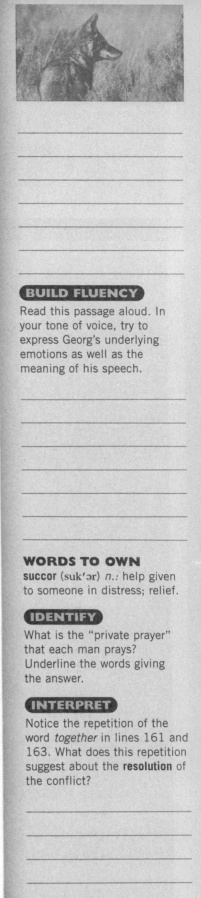

"How the whole region would stare and gabble if we rode into the
market square together. No one living can remember seeing a Znaeym
and a von Gradwitz talking to one another in friendship. And what
peace there would be among the forester folk if we ended our feud
tonight. And if we choose to make peace among our people, there is
none other to interfere, no interlopers from outside. . . . You would come
140 and keep the Sylvester night[7] beneath my roof, and I would come and
feast on some high day at your castle. . . . I would never fire a shot on
your land, save when you invited me as a guest; and you should come
and shoot with me down in the marshes where the wildfowl are. In all
the countryside there are none that could hinder if we willed to make
peace. I never thought to have wanted to do other than hate you all my
life, but I think I have changed my mind about things too, this last half-
hour. And you offered me your wine flask. . . . Ulrich von Gradwitz, I
will be your friend."

For a space both men were silent, turning over in their minds the
150 wonderful changes that this dramatic reconciliation would bring about.
In the cold, gloomy forest, with the wind tearing in fitful gusts through
the naked branches and whistling round the tree trunks, they lay and
waited for the help that would now bring release and <u>succor</u> to both
parties. And each prayed a private prayer that his men might be the first
to arrive, so that he might be the first to show honorable attention to the
enemy that had become a friend.

Presently, as the wind dropped for a moment, Ulrich broke the silence.

"Let's shout for help," he said; "in this lull our voices may carry a
little way."

160 "They won't carry far through the trees and undergrowth," said
Georg, "but we can try. Together, then."

The two raised their voices in a prolonged hunting call.

"Together again," said Ulrich a few minutes later, after listening in
vain for an answering halloo.

"I heard something that time, I think," said Ulrich.

---

7. **Sylvester night:** feast day honoring Saint Sylvester (Pope Sylvester I, d. 335), observed on
December 31.

BUILD FLUENCY

Read this passage aloud. In
your tone of voice, try to
express Georg's underlying
emotions as well as the
meaning of his speech.

WORDS TO OWN

succor (suk′ər) *n.:* help given
to someone in distress; relief.

IDENTIFY

What is the "private prayer"
that each man prays?
Underline the words giving
the answer.

INTERPRET

Notice the repetition of the
word *together* in lines 161 and
163. What does this repetition
suggest about the **resolution**
of the conflict?

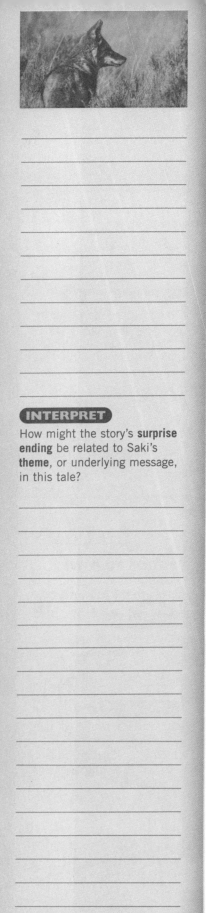

INTERPRET

How might the story's **surprise ending** be related to Saki's **theme**, or underlying message, in this tale?

"I heard nothing but the pestilential[8] wind," said Georg hoarsely.

There was silence again for some minutes, and then Ulrich gave a joyful cry.

"I can see figures coming through the wood. They are following in 170 the way I came down the hillside."

Both men raised their voices in as loud a shout as they could muster.

"They hear us! They've stopped. Now they see us. They're running down the hill toward us," cried Ulrich.

"How many of them are there?" asked Georg.

"I can't see distinctly," said Ulrich; "nine or ten."

"Then they are yours," said Georg; "I had only seven out with me."

"They are making all the speed they can, brave lads," said Ulrich gladly.

"Are they your men?" asked Georg. "Are they your men?" he repeated 180 impatiently, as Ulrich did not answer.

"No," said Ulrich with a laugh, the idiotic chattering laugh of a man unstrung with hideous fear.

"Who are they?" asked Georg quickly, straining his eyes to see what the other would gladly not have seen.

"*Wolves.*"

---

8. **pestilential:** Strictly speaking, *pestilential* means "deadly; causing disease; harmful." Here, Georg uses the word to mean "cursed."

Surprise Ending

A **surprise ending** resolves a story's conflict in a totally unexpected—yet logical—way. A surprise ending may be a powerful way of suggesting an author's **theme**, or underlying message about human nature and people's behavior.

Fill out the following graphic organizer in order to explore the surprise ending of "The Interlopers."

EXPLAIN

Why did the ending surprise you?

_____

_____

_____

_____

_____

_____

SPECULATE

What do you think happens to the men in the end?

_____

_____

_____

_____

_____

ANALYZE

How is the ending related to the story's theme or message?

_____

_____

_____

_____

_____

Vocabulary: How to Own a Word

Synonyms

Word Bank
precipitous
acquiesced
marauder
languor
succor

For each of the sentences below, choose the word that is a synonym of the italicized Word to Own. Write the letter of the synonym on the line provided.

_____ 1. Ulrich von Gradwitz's land lay on the edge of the Carpathians, a mountain range with *precipitous* rock walls.

      a. attractive   **b.** sheer   **c.** heavy

_____ 2. The Znaeym family had never *acquiesced* in the courts' decision about the land.

      a. concurred   **b.** participated   **c.** bothered

_____ 3. Ulrich von Gradwitz was willing to shoot any *marauders* hunting game in his forest.

      a. residents   **b.** raiders   **c.** murderers

_____ 4. Suffering under the weight of the tree, von Gradwitz felt a growing *languor* come over his limbs.

      a. inhibition   **b.** hatred   **c.** weariness

_____ 5. The two men waited for their followers to arrive and give them *succor*.

      a. aid   **b.** refreshment   **c.** applause

Selection: _____

Plot Outline

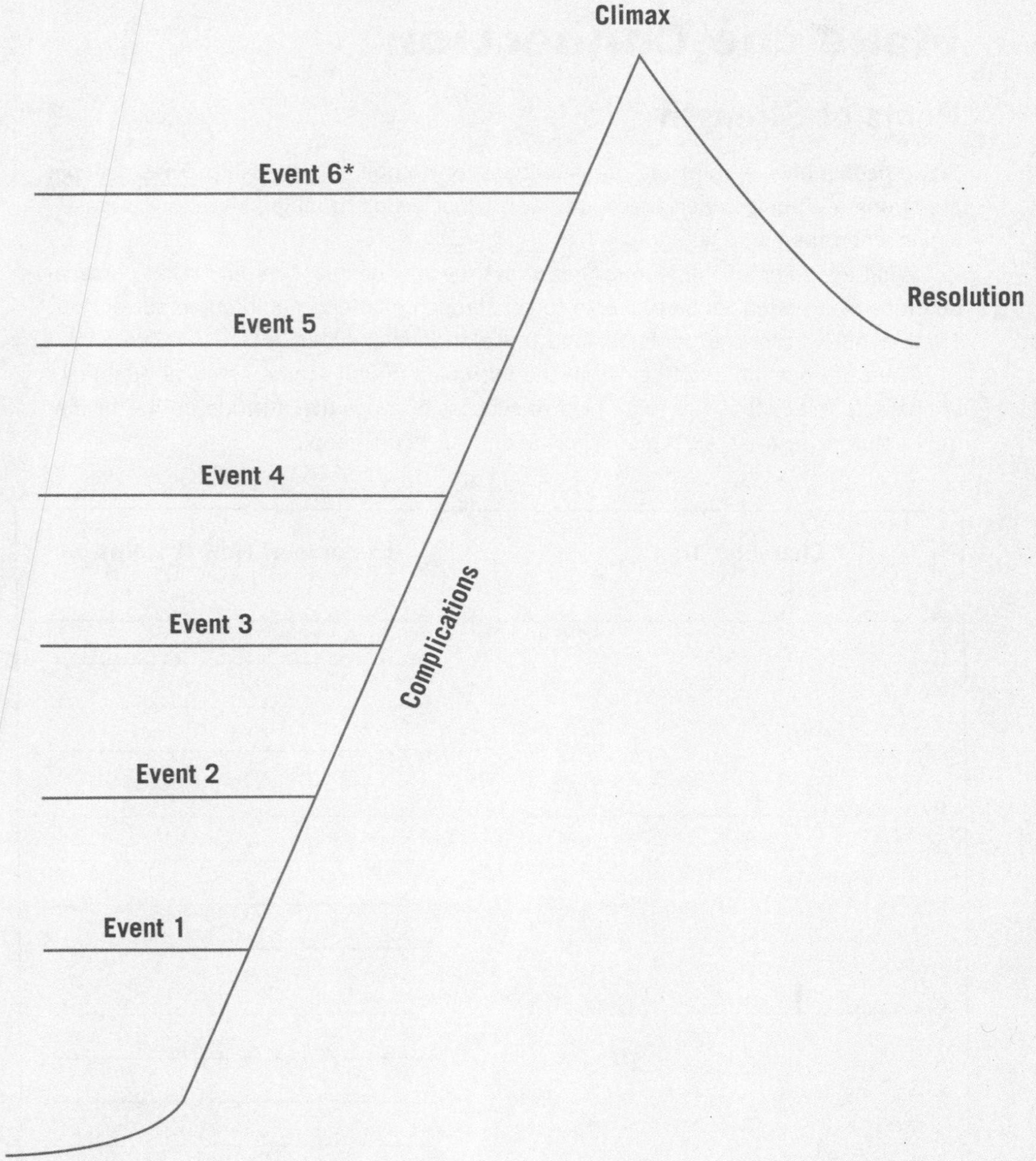

Climax

Event 6*

Event 5

Resolution

Event 4

Complications

Event 3

Event 2

Event 1

Basic Situation and Conflict

_____

*Number of events will vary

Thank You, M'am

Make the Connection

Roots of Strength

Some people have a spirit that pushes them to triumph over hardship. These people are strong and tough when times are hard. Other people, though, surrender or go wrong when the going gets tough.

What are some of the factors that affect the way people turn out? What personal qualities or experiences help people to get through challenges and come out on top? Think about your own experiences and those of people you know.

Then, fill out the chart below. In the left column, write three personal qualities or character traits that you think lead to success or a positive attitude in life. In the right column, write an example of how each trait helps people.

Character Trait	Example of How It Helps
a. _____	_____
	_____
	_____
	_____
b. _____	_____
	_____
	_____
	_____
c. _____	_____
	_____
	_____
	_____

Langston Hughes

THANK YOU, M'AM

IDENTIFY

Circle the words that identify the two **characters** in the story. Then, write the cause of the **conflict** between these characters.

_____

_____

_____

_____

_____

_____

INFER

What do the woman's words and actions here suggest about her **character**? List some adjectives.

_____

_____

_____

_____

_____

_____

INFER

What does the boy's answer in line 30 suggest about the circumstances of his home life?

_____

_____

_____

_____

_____

_____

_____

_____

She was a large woman with a large purse that had everything in it but hammer and nails. It had a long strap and she carried it slung across her shoulder. It was about eleven o'clock at night, and she was walking alone, when a boy ran up behind her and tried to snatch her purse. The strap broke with the single tug the boy gave it from behind. But the boy's weight and the weight of the purse combined caused him to lose his balance so, instead of taking off full blast as he had hoped, the boy fell on his back on the sidewalk and his legs flew up. The large woman simply turned around and kicked him right square in his blue-jeaned

10 sitter. Then she reached down, picked the boy up by his shirt front, and shook him until his teeth rattled.

After that the woman said, "Pick up my pocketbook, boy, and give it here."

She still held him. But she bent down enough to permit him to stoop and pick up her purse. Then she said, "Now ain't you ashamed of yourself?"

Firmly gripped by his shirt front, the boy said, "Yes'm."

The woman said, "What did you want to do it for?"

The boy said, "I didn't aim to."

20 She said, "You a lie!"

By that time two or three people passed, stopped, turned to look, and some stood watching.

"If I turn you loose, will you run?" asked the woman.

"Yes'm," said the boy.

"Then I won't turn you loose," said the woman. She did not release him.

"Lady, I'm sorry," whispered the boy.

"Um-hum! And your face is dirty. I got a great mind to wash your face for you. Ain't you got nobody home to tell you to wash your face?"

30 "No'm," said the boy.

"Then it will get washed this evening," said the large woman starting up the street, dragging the frightened boy behind her.

He looked as if he were fourteen or fifteen, frail and willow-wild, in tennis shoes and blue jeans.

The woman said, "You ought to be my son. I would teach you right from wrong. Least I can do right now is to wash your face. Are you hungry?"

"No'm," said the being-dragged boy. "I just want you to turn me loose."

"Was I bothering _you_ when I turned that corner?" asked the woman.

40 "No'm."

"But you put yourself in contact with _me,_" said the woman. "If you think that that contact is not going to last awhile, you got another thought coming. When I get through with you, sir, you are going to remember Mrs. Luella Bates Washington Jones."

Sweat popped out on the boy's face and he began to struggle. Mrs. Jones stopped, jerked him around in front of her, put a half nelson about his neck, and continued to drag him up the street. When she got to her door, she dragged the boy inside, down a hall, and into a large kitchenette-furnished room at the rear of the house. She switched on the light and
50   left the door open. The boy could hear other roomers laughing and talking in the large house. Some of their doors were open, too, so he knew he and the woman were not alone. The woman still had him by the neck in the middle of her room.

She said, "What is your name?"

"Roger," answered the boy.

"Then, Roger, you go to that sink and wash your face," said the woman, whereupon she turned him loose—at last. Roger looked at the door—looked at the woman—looked at the door—*and went to the sink.*

"Let the water run until it gets warm," she said. "Here's a clean
60   towel."

"You gonna take me to jail?" asked the boy, bending over the sink.

"Not with that face, I would not take you nowhere," said the woman. "Here I am trying to get home to cook me a bite to eat and you snatch my pocketbook! Maybe you ain't been to your supper either, late as it be. Have you?"

"There's nobody home at my house," said the boy.

"Then we'll eat," said the woman. "I believe you're hungry—or been hungry—to try to snatch my pocketbook."

"I wanted a pair of blue suede shoes," said the boy.

70   "Well, you didn't have to snatch *my* pocketbook to get some suede shoes," said Mrs. Luella Bates Washington Jones. "You could of asked me."

"M'am?"

The water dripping from his face, the boy looked at her. There was a long pause. A very long pause. After he had dried his face and, not knowing what else to do, dried it again, the boy turned around, wondering what next. The door was open. He could make a dash for it down the hall. He could run, run, run, run, *run*!

The woman was sitting on the daybed. After a while she said, "I were young once and I wanted things I could not get."

80   There was another long pause. The boy's mouth opened. Then he frowned, but not knowing he frowned.

> The woman said, "Um-hum! You thought I was going to say *but,* didn't you? You thought I was going to say, *but I didn't snatch people's pocketbooks.* Well, I wasn't going to say that." Pause. Silence. "I have done things, too, which I would not tell you, son—neither tell God, if He didn't already know. Everybody's got something in common. So you set down while I fix us something to eat. You might run that comb through your hair so you will look presentable."

VISUALIZE

Visualize the scene. Then, write why you think Hughes uses italics to emphasize the boy's action in *and went to the sink.*

_____

_____

_____

_____

_____

_____

_____

_____

PREDICT

Do you think Roger will run? Tell why or why not.

_____

_____

_____

BUILD FLUENCY

Read this passage aloud, using a suitable tone of voice, emphasis, and pace.

INTERPRET

Briefly describe Roger's **internal conflict** at this point in the story.

_____
_____
_____
_____
_____
_____
_____
_____
_____
_____
_____
_____

INFER

Why do you think Mrs. Jones gives Roger the money to buy the shoes?

_____
_____
_____
_____
_____
_____
_____

EVALUATE

Do you find the end of the story satisfying? Tell why or why not.

_____
_____
_____
_____
_____
_____

90 In another corner of the room behind a screen was a gas plate and an icebox. Mrs. Jones got up and went behind the screen. The woman did not watch the boy to see if he was going to run now, nor did she watch her purse which she left behind her on the daybed. But the boy took care to sit on the far side of the room where he thought she could easily see him out of the corner of her eye, if she wanted to. He did not trust the woman *not* to trust him. And he did not want to be mistrusted now.

"Do you need somebody to go the store," asked the boy, "maybe to get some milk or something?"

"Don't believe I do," said the woman, "unless you just want sweet
100 milk yourself. I was going to make cocoa out of this canned milk I got here."

"That will be fine," said the boy.

She heated some lima beans and ham she had in the icebox, made the cocoa, and set the table. The woman did not ask the boy anything about where he lived, or his folks, or anything else that would embarrass him. Instead, as they ate, she told him about her job in a hotel beauty shop that stayed open late, what the work was like, and how all kinds of women came in and out, blondes, redheads, and Spanish. Then she cut him a half of her ten-cent cake.

110 "Eat some more, son," she said.

When they were finished eating she got up and said, "Now, here, take this ten dollars and buy yourself some blue suede shoes. And next time, do not make the mistake of latching onto *my* pocketbook *nor nobody else's*—because shoes come by devilish like that will burn your feet. I got to get my rest now. But from here on in, son, I hope you will behave yourself."

She led him down the hall to the front door and opened it. "Good night! Behave yourself, boy!" she said, looking out into the street.

The boy wanted to say something other than "Thank you, m'am" to
120 Mrs. Luella Bates Washington Jones, but although his lips moved, he couldn't even say that as he turned at the foot of the barren stoop and looked up at the large woman in the door. Then she shut the door.

Character

Characters who are challenged or under stress often reveal a lot about their personalities. What can you infer about Mrs. Jones and Roger from the ways they react to this encounter? Fill in a chart like the one below to explore your ideas. The last column is where you will write your inference.

Character	Cause of Stress	Reactions	What Reactions Reveal
Mrs. Jones	_____	_____	_____
	_____	_____	_____
	_____	_____	_____
Roger	_____	_____	_____
	_____	_____	_____
	_____	_____	_____

Harrison Bergeron

Make the Connection

What If . . . ?

Kurt Vonnegut's story "Harrison Bergeron" takes place in the year 2081. Ever since science fiction started to become popular during the nineteenth century, a favorite topic for writers has been to speculate about the future.

Below are three "what if" questions about the future. On the lines provided, write your thoughts about these questions. Jot down everything that comes to mind. Then, when you have finished reading the story, review your notes. See how your writing applies to Vonnegut's tale.

1. WHAT IF a powerful government were able to make everyone equal to everyone else?

_____

_____

_____

2. WHAT IF all competition were removed from society?

_____

_____

_____

3. WHAT IF the technology of the future became so advanced that it could read people's thoughts?

_____

_____

_____

Kurt Vonnegut

Harrison Bergeron

2 0 8 1

IDENTIFY

According to the opening paragraph, what is the chief characteristic of life in the year 2081? Circle the words giving the answer.

_____

_____

INFER

What is the target of the author's **satire** here?

_____

_____

_____

_____

_____

_____

_____

_____

_____

_____

IDENTIFY

Why does the transmitter in George's ear emit another noise? Underline the words giving the answer.

_____

_____

_____

_____

_____

_____

The year was 2081, and everybody was finally equal. They weren't only equal before God and the law. They were equal every which way. Nobody was smarter than anybody else. Nobody was better looking than anybody else. Nobody was stronger or quicker than anybody else. All this equality was due to the 211th, 212th, and 213th Amendments to the Constitution, and to the unceasing vigilance of agents of the United States Handicapper General.

Some things about living still weren't quite right, though. April, for instance, still drove people crazy by not being springtime. And it was in
10 that clammy month that the H-G men took George and Hazel Bergeron's fourteen-year-old son, Harrison, away.

It was tragic, all right, but George and Hazel couldn't think about it very hard. Hazel had a perfectly average intelligence, which meant she couldn't think about anything except in short bursts. And George, while his intelligence was way above normal, had a little mental handicap radio in his ear. He was required by law to wear it at all times. It was tuned to a government transmitter. Every twenty seconds or so, the transmitter would send out some sharp noise to keep people like George from taking unfair advantage of their brains.
20 George and Hazel were watching television. There were tears on Hazel's cheeks, but she'd forgotten for the moment what they were about.

On the television screen were ballerinas.

A buzzer sounded in George's head. His thoughts fled in panic, like bandits from a burglar alarm.

"That was a real pretty dance, that dance they just did," said Hazel.

"Huh?" said George.

"That dance—it was nice," said Hazel.

"Yup," said George. He tried to think a little about the ballerinas. They weren't really very good—no better than anybody else would have
30 been, anyway. They were burdened with sash weights and bags of birdshot, and their faces were masked, so that no one, seeing a free and graceful gesture or a pretty face, would feel like something the cat drug in. George was toying with the vague notion that maybe dancers shouldn't be handicapped. But he didn't get very far with it before another noise in his ear radio scattered his thoughts.

George winced. So did two out of the eight ballerinas.

Hazel saw him wince. Having no mental handicap herself, she had to ask George what the latest sound had been.

"Sounded like somebody hitting a milk bottle with a ball-peen
40 hammer,"[1] said George.

"I'd think it would be real interesting, hearing all the different sounds," said Hazel, a little envious. "All the things they think up."

"Um," said George.

_____

1. **ball-peen hammer:** hammer with a ball-shaped head.

"Only, if I was Handicapper General, you know what I would do?" said Hazel. Hazel, as a matter of fact, bore a strong resemblance to the Handicapper General, a woman named Diana Moon Glampers. "If I was Diana Moon Glampers," said Hazel, "I'd have chimes on Sunday—just chimes. Kind of in honor of religion."

"I could think, if it was just chimes," said George.

50   "Well—maybe make 'em real loud," said Hazel. "I think I'd make a good Handicapper General."

"Good as anybody else," said George.

"Who knows better'n I do what normal is?" said Hazel.

"Right," said George. He began to think glimmeringly about his abnormal son who was now in jail, about Harrison, but a twenty-one-gun salute in his head stopped that.

"Boy!" said Hazel, "that was a doozy, wasn't it?"

It was such a doozy that George was white and trembling, and tears stood on the rims of his red eyes. Two of the eight ballerinas had collapsed

60   to the studio floor and were holding their temples.

"All of a sudden you look so tired," said Hazel. "Why don't you stretch out on the sofa, so's you can rest your handicap bag on the pillows, honeybunch." She was referring to the forty-seven pounds of birdshot in a canvas bag which was padlocked around George's neck. "Go on and rest the bag for a little while," she said. "I don't care if you're not equal to me for a while."

George weighed the bag with his hands. "I don't mind it," he said. "I don't notice it anymore. It's just a part of me."

"You been so tired lately—kind of wore out," said Hazel. "If there

70   was just some way we could make a little hole in the bottom of the bag, and just take out a few of them lead balls. Just a few."

"Two years in prison and two thousand dollars fine for every ball I took out," said George. "I don't call that a bargain."

"If you could just take a few out when you came home from work," said Hazel. "I mean—you don't compete with anybody around here. You just set around."

"If I tried to get away with it," said George, "then other people'd get away with it—and pretty soon we'd be right back to the Dark Ages again, with everybody competing against everybody else. You wouldn't

80   like that, would you?"

"I'd hate it," said Hazel.

"There you are," said George. "The minute people start cheating on laws, what do you think happens to society?"

If Hazel hadn't been able to come up with an answer to this question, George couldn't have supplied one. A siren was going off in his head.

"Reckon it'd fall all apart," said Hazel.

"What would?" said George blankly.

"Society," said Hazel uncertainly. "Wasn't that what you just said?"

INTERPRET

What is **ironic** about George and Hazel's conversation here?

_____

_____

_____

_____

_____

_____

BUILD FLUENCY

Read this passage aloud. In your tone of voice, be sure to differentiate between the narrative portion and the dialogue.

_____

_____

_____

IDENTIFY

How does the government enforce the law? Underline the words that identify the stiff punishments.

_____

_____

_____

_____

_____

_____

_____

_____

_____

"Who knows?" said George.

90   The television program was suddenly interrupted for a news bulletin. It wasn't clear at first as to what the bulletin was about, since the announcer, like all announcers, had a serious speech impediment. For about half a minute, and in a state of high excitement, the announcer tried to say, "Ladies and gentlemen—"

He finally gave up, handed the bulletin to a ballerina to read.

"That's all right—" Hazel said of the announcer, "he tried. That's the big thing. He tried to do the best he could with what God gave him. He should get a nice raise for trying so hard."

"Ladies and gentlemen—" said the ballerina, reading the bulletin.

100 She must have been extraordinarily beautiful, because the mask she wore was hideous. And it was easy to see that she was the strongest and most graceful of all the dancers, for her handicap bags were as big as those worn by two-hundred-pound men.

And she had to apologize at once for her voice, which was a very unfair voice for a woman to use. Her voice was a warm, luminous, timeless melody. "Excuse me—" she said, and she began again, making her voice absolutely uncompetitive.

"Harrison Bergeron, age fourteen," she said in a grackle squawk,[2] "has just escaped from jail, where he was held on suspicion of plotting
110 to overthrow the government. He is a genius and an athlete, is under-handicapped, and should be regarded as extremely dangerous."

A police photograph of Harrison Bergeron was flashed on the screen—upside down, then sideways, upside down again, then right side up. The picture showed the full length of Harrison against a background calibrated[3] in feet and inches. He was exactly seven feet tall.

The rest of Harrison's appearance was Halloween and hardware. Nobody had ever borne heavier handicaps. He had outgrown <u>hindrances</u> faster than the H-G men could think them up. Instead of a little ear radio for a mental handicap, he wore a tremendous pair of earphones, and
120 spectacles with thick wavy lenses. The spectacles were intended not only to make him half blind, but to give him whanging headaches besides.

Scrap metal was hung all over him. Ordinarily, there was a certain <u>symmetry</u>, a military neatness to the handicaps issued to strong people, but Harrison looked like a walking junkyard. In the race of life, Harrison carried three hundred pounds.

And to offset his good looks, the H-G men required that he wear at all times a red rubber ball for a nose, keep his eyebrows shaved off, and cover his even white teeth with black caps at snaggletooth random.

"If you see this boy," said the ballerina, "do not—I repeat, do not—
130 try to reason with him."

---

2. **grackle squawk:** loud, harsh cry, like that of a grackle (blackbird).
3. **calibrated** (kal′ə·brāt′id): marked with measurements.

There was the shriek of a door being torn from its hinges.

Screams and barking cries of <u>consternation</u> came from the television set. The photograph of Harrison Bergeron on the screen jumped again and again, as though dancing to the tune of an earthquake.

George Bergeron correctly identified the earthquake, and well he might have—for many was the time his own home had danced to the same crashing tune. "My God—" said George, "that must be Harrison!"

The realization was blasted from his mind instantly by the sound of an automobile collision in his head.

140　　When George could open his eyes again, the photograph of Harrison was gone. A living, breathing Harrison filled the screen.

Clanking, clownish, and huge, Harrison stood in the center of the studio. The knob of the uprooted studio door was still in his hand. Ballerinas, technicians, musicians, and announcers <u>cowered</u> on their knees before him, expecting to die.

"I am the Emperor!" cried Harrison. "Do you hear? I am the Emperor! Everybody must do what I say at once!" He stamped his foot and the studio shook.

"Even as I stand here—" he bellowed, "crippled, hobbled, sickened—
150 I am a greater ruler than any man who ever lived! Now watch me become what I *can* become!"

Harrison tore the straps of his handicap harness like wet tissue paper, tore straps guaranteed to support five thousand pounds.

Harrison's scrap-iron handicaps crashed to the floor.

Harrison thrust his thumbs under the bar of the padlock that secured his head harness. The bar snapped like celery. Harrison smashed his headphones and spectacles against the wall.

He flung away his rubber-ball nose, revealed a man that would have awed Thor, the god of thunder.

160　　"I shall now select my Empress!" he said, looking down on the people. "Let the first woman who dares rise to her feet claim her mate and her throne!"

A moment passed, and then a ballerina arose, swaying like a willow.

Harrison plucked the mental handicap from her ear, snapped off her physical handicaps with marvelous delicacy. Last of all, he removed her mask.

She was blindingly beautiful.

"Now—" said Harrison, taking her hand, "shall we show the people the meaning of the word *dance?* Music!" he commanded.

170　　The musicians scrambled back into their chairs, and Harrison stripped them of their handicaps, too. "Play your best," he told them, "and I'll make you barons and dukes and earls."

The music began. It was normal at first—cheap, silly, false. But Harrison snatched two musicians from their chairs, waved them like

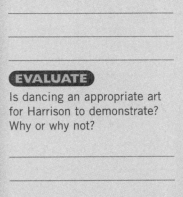

WORDS TO OWN

synchronizing (siŋ′krə·nī′ziŋ) *v.:* causing to occur at the same rate or time.

IDENTIFY

The **climax** of a story is its turning point or moment of greatest emotional tension. What is the **climax** of this story? Underline the words giving the answer.

EVALUATE

What do you think of the story's ending? Is it effective, or would you have written the ending differently? Explain your answer.

batons as he sang the music as he wanted it played. He slammed them back into their chairs.

The music began again and was much improved.

Harrison and his Empress merely listened to the music for a while—listened gravely, as though <u>synchronizing</u> their heartbeats with it.

180   They shifted their weights to their toes.

Harrison placed his big hands on the girl's tiny waist, letting her sense the weightlessness that would soon be hers.

And then, in an explosion of joy and grace, into the air they sprang!

Not only were the laws of the land abandoned, but the law of gravity and the laws of motion as well.

They reeled, whirled, swiveled, flounced, capered, gamboled, and spun.

They leaped like deer on the moon.

The studio ceiling was thirty feet high, but each leap brought the dancers nearer to it.

190   It became their obvious intention to kiss the ceiling.

They kissed it.

And then, neutralizing gravity with love and pure will, they remained suspended in air inches below the ceiling, and they kissed each other for a long, long time.

It was then that Diana Moon Glampers, the Handicapper General, came into the studio with a double-barreled ten-gauge shotgun. She fired twice, and the Emperor and the Empress were dead before they hit the floor.

Diana Moon Glampers loaded the gun again. She aimed it at the musicians and told them they had ten seconds to get their handicaps 200 back on.

It was then that the Bergerons' television tube burned out.

Hazel turned to comment about the blackout to George. But George had gone out into the kitchen for a can of beer.

George came back in with the beer, paused while a handicap signal shook him up. And then he sat down again. "You been crying?" he said to Hazel.

"Yup," she said.

"What about?" he said.

"I forget," she said. "Something real sad on television."

210   "What was it?" he said.

"It's all kind of mixed up in my mind," said Hazel.

"Forget sad things," said George.

"I always do," said Hazel.

"That's my girl," said George. He winced. There was the sound of a riveting-gun in his head.

"Gee—I could tell that one was a doozy," said Hazel.

"You can say that again," said George.

"Gee—" said Hazel, "I could tell that one was a doozy."

Satire

In a **satire,** a writer uses exaggeration, irony, and absurdity to ridicule or mock some weakness in individuals or society. A satirist hopes that the reader's laughter is the first step in bringing about change.

To explore Vonnegut's use of satire in "Harrison Bergeron," fill out the chart below. Under each target of satire, list specific story details that emphasize the author's theme or message.

Targets of Satire	
Erasing differences among individuals	**Absolute control of people**
Abolishing the value of merit and quality	**Excessive reliance on technology**

Vocabulary: How to Own a Word

Etymologies

Word Bank
consternation
symmetry
hindrances
synchronizing
cowered

Etymology refers to where a word comes from—its origins in earlier languages. By becoming familiar with a word's etymology, you can increase your vocabulary power.

For example, you may be unfamiliar with the word *hideous.* Yet, when you discover that the Old French root *hisde* means "fright," the contemporary meaning of *hideous*—"horrible to see, hear; very ugly or revolting"—makes more sense. Harrison is required to make his perfect teeth look hideous. If his teeth are horrible looking, they might frighten others.

Match each word in the Word Bank with its correct etymology by writing the Word to Own on the line provided. You may need a dictionary to help you with this exercise.

_____ **1.** From the Old English word *hindrian,* meaning "to keep or hold back"

_____ **2.** From the Old Norse base *kura,* meaning "to squat"

_____ **3.** From the classical Greek words *syn,* meaning "together," and *chronos,* meaning "time"

_____ **4.** From the Latin word *consternare,* meaning "to terrify"

_____ **5.** From the classical Greek words *syn,* meaning "together," and *metron,* meaning "a measure"

Selection: _____

Story Map

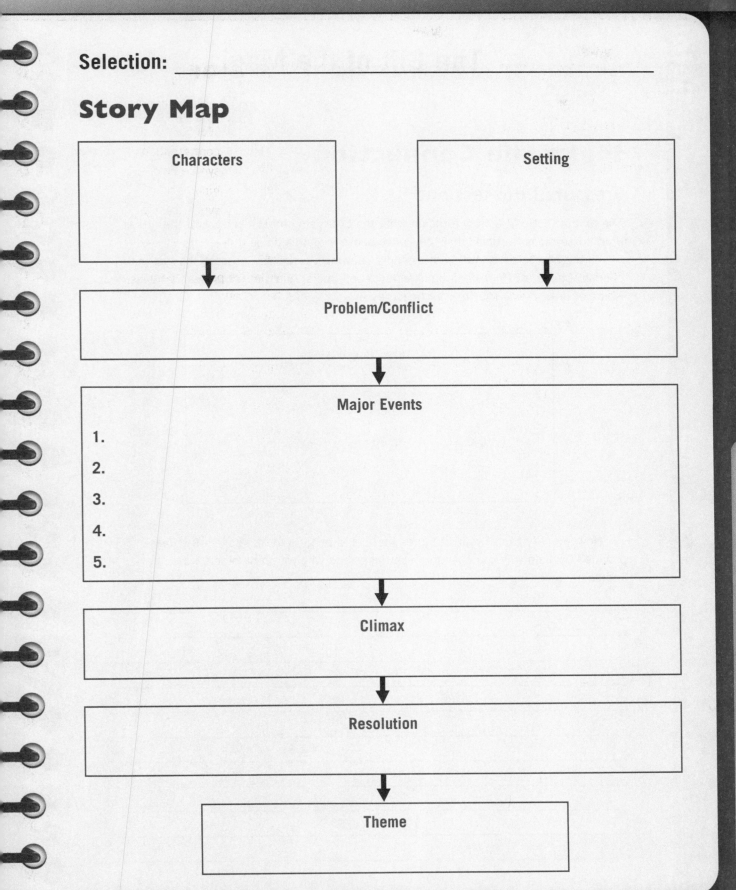

Characters

Setting

Problem/Conflict

Major Events

1.

2.

3.

4.

5.

Climax

Resolution

Theme

The Gift of the Magi

Make the Connection

Treasured Possessions

The plot of O. Henry's story turns on what the two main characters do with their treasured possessions—articles that they value above everything else they own.

In the box below, show—with symbols, drawings, or words—possessions that you cherish. Cherished things can be objects, people, pets, qualities, activities, or ideals. Name or draw them. They're *your* treasures.

> **Treasured Possessions**

Now, identify two of your treasures that could be gifts for others. On the lines provided, explain why you cherish these things and why you think others would appreciate receiving them as gifts.

_____

_____

_____

_____

_____

_____

_____

_____

_____

_____

_____

O. Henry

The Gift of the Magi

IDENTIFY

What **character** is introduced in the first paragraph? Circle the person's name.

WORDS TO OWN

instigates (in′stə·gāts′) *v.:* gives rise to. *Instigates* is generally used to mean "provokes or urges on to some action."

IDENTIFY

Circle four details that tell you that James and Della are poor.

One dollar and eighty-seven cents. That was all. And sixty cents of it was in pennies. Pennies saved one and two at a time by bulldozing the grocer and the vegetable man and the butcher until one's cheeks burned with the silent imputation of parsimony[1] that such close dealing implied. Three times Della counted it. One dollar and eighty-seven cents. And the next day would be Christmas.

There was clearly nothing to do but flop down on the shabby little couch and howl. So Della did it. Which instigates the moral reflection that life is made up of sobs, sniffles, and smiles, with sniffles predominating.

10 While the mistress of the home is gradually subsiding from the first stage to the second, take a look at the home. A furnished flat[2] at $8 per week. It did not exactly beggar description, but it certainly had that word on the lookout for the mendicancy squad.[3]

In the vestibule[4] below was a letter box into which no letter would go, and an electric button from which no mortal finger could coax a ring. Also appertaining[5] thereunto was a card bearing the name "Mr. James Dillingham Young."

The "Dillingham" had been flung to the breeze during a former period of prosperity when its possessor was being paid $30 per week. 20 Now, when the income was shrunk to $20, the letters of "Dillingham" looked blurred, as though they were thinking seriously of contracting to a modest and unassuming *D*. But whenever Mr. James Dillingham Young came home and reached his flat above, he was called Jim and greatly hugged by Mrs. James Dillingham Young, already introduced to you as Della. Which is all very good.

Della finished her cry and attended to her cheeks with the powder rag. She stood by the window and looked out dully at a gray cat walking a gray fence in a gray back yard. Tomorrow would be Christmas Day and she had only $1.87 with which to buy Jim a present. She had been 30 saving every penny she could for months, with this result. Twenty dollars a week doesn't go far. Expenses had been greater than she had calculated. They always are. Only $1.87 to buy a present for Jim. Her Jim. Many a happy hour she had spent planning for something nice for him. Something fine and rare and sterling—something just a little bit near to being worthy of the honor of being owned by Jim.

There was a pier glass[6] between the windows of the room. Perhaps you have seen a pier glass in an $8 flat. A very thin and very agile person may, by observing his reflection in a rapid sequence of

---

1. **imputation** (im′pyo͞o·tā′shən) **of parsimony** (pär′sə·mō′nē): suggestion of stinginess.
2. **flat:** apartment.
3. **mendicancy** (mɛn′di·kən·sē) **squad:** police who arrested beggars and homeless people.
4. **vestibule:** small entrance hall.
5. **appertaining** (ap′ər·tān′iŋ): belonging.
6. **pier glass:** tall mirror hung between two windows.

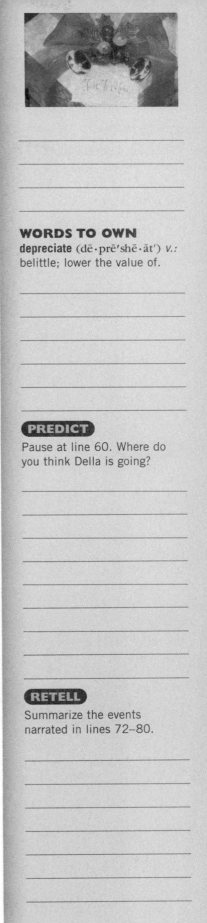

longitudinal strips, obtain a fairly accurate conception of his looks. Della,
40 being slender, had mastered the art.

Suddenly she whirled from the window and stood before the glass.
Her eyes were shining brilliantly, but her face had lost its color within
twenty seconds. Rapidly she pulled down her hair and let it fall to its full
length.

Now, there were two possessions of the James Dillingham Youngs in
which they both took a mighty pride. One was Jim's gold watch that had
been his father's and his grandfather's. The other was Della's hair. Had
the Queen of Sheba lived in the flat across the air shaft,[7] Della would
have let her hair hang out the window some day to dry just to depreciate
50 Her Majesty's jewels and gifts. Had King Solomon been the janitor, with
all his treasures piled up in the basement, Jim would have pulled out his
watch every time he passed, just to see him pluck at his beard from envy.

So now Della's beautiful hair fell about her rippling and shining like
a cascade of brown waters. It reached below her knee and made itself
almost a garment for her. And then she did it up again nervously and
quickly. Once she faltered for a minute and stood still while a tear or two
splashed on the worn red carpet.

On went her old brown jacket; on went her old brown hat. With a
whirl of skirts and with the brilliant sparkle still in her eyes, she fluttered
60 out the door and down the stairs to the street.

Where she stopped, the sign read: "Mme. Sofronie. Hair Goods of All
Kinds." One flight up Della ran, and collected herself, panting. Madame,
large, too white, chilly, hardly looked the "Sofronie."

"Will you buy my hair?" asked Della.

"I buy hair," said Madame. "Take yer hat off and let's have a sight at
the looks of it."

Down rippled the brown cascade.

"Twenty dollars," said Madame, lifting the mass with a practiced hand.

"Give it to me quick," said Della.

70 Oh, and the next two hours tripped by on rosy wings. Forget the
hashed metaphor. She was ransacking the stores for Jim's present.

She found it at last. It surely had been made for Jim and no one else.
There was no other like it in any of the stores, and she had turned all of
them inside out. It was a platinum fob chain,[8] simple and chaste in
design, properly proclaiming its value by substance alone and not by
meretricious[9] ornamentation—as all good things should do. It was even
worthy of The Watch. As soon as she saw it she knew that it must be
Jim's. It was like him. Quietness and value—the description applied to
both. Twenty-one dollars they took from her for it, and she hurried home

---

7. **air shaft:** narrow gap between two buildings.
8. **fob chain:** short chain meant to be attached to a pocket watch.
9. **meretricious** (mer′ə·trish′əs): attractive in a cheap, flashy way.

WORDS TO OWN
depreciate (dē·prē′shē·āt′) *v.*:
belittle; lower the value of.

PREDICT
Pause at line 60. Where do
you think Della is going?

RETELL
Summarize the events
narrated in lines 72–80.

RETELL

Paraphrase lines 84–87 in your own words.

_____

_____

_____

_____

_____

_____

_____

_____

_____

_____

PREDICT

What do you think will happen when Jim sees Della?

_____

_____

_____

_____

INFER

Why do you think Jim is acting so strangely?

_____

_____

_____

_____

_____

_____

_____

_____

_____

80 with the 87 cents. With that chain on his watch, Jim might be properly anxious about the time in any company. Grand as the watch was, he sometimes looked at it on the sly on account of the old leather strap that he used in place of a chain.

When Della reached home, her intoxication gave way a little to prudence and reason. She got out her curling irons and lighted the gas and went to work repairing the ravages made by generosity added to love. Which is always a tremendous task, dear friends—a mammoth task.

Within forty minutes her head was covered with tiny, close-lying curls that made her look wonderfully like a truant schoolboy. She looked
90 at her reflection in the mirror long, carefully, and critically.

"If Jim doesn't kill me," she said to herself, "before he takes a second look at me, he'll say I look like a Coney Island chorus girl. But what could I do—oh! what could I do with a dollar and eighty-seven cents?"

At 7 o'clock the coffee was made and the frying pan was on the back of the stove hot and ready to cook the chops.

Jim was never late. Della doubled the fob chain in her hand and sat on the corner of the table near the door that he always entered. Then she heard his step on the stair away down on the first flight, and she turned white for just a moment. She had a habit of saying little silent prayers
100 about the simplest everyday things, and now she whispered: "Please God, make him think I am still pretty."

The door opened and Jim stepped in and closed it. He looked thin and very serious. Poor fellow, he was only twenty-two—and to be burdened with a family! He needed a new overcoat and he was without gloves.

Jim stepped inside the door, as immovable as a setter at the scent of quail. His eyes were fixed upon Della, and there was an expression in them that she could not read, and it terrified her. It was not anger, nor surprise, nor disapproval, nor horror, nor any of the sentiments that she had been prepared for. He simply stared at her fixedly with that peculiar
110 expression on his face.

Della wriggled off the table and went for him.

"Jim, darling," she cried, "don't look at me that way. I had my hair cut off and sold it because I couldn't have lived through Christmas without giving you a present. It'll grow out again—you won't mind, will you? I just had to do it. My hair grows awfully fast. Say 'Merry Christmas!' Jim, and let's be happy. You don't know what a nice—what a beautiful, nice gift I've got for you."

"You've cut off your hair?" asked Jim, laboriously, as if he had not arrived at that patent[10] fact yet even after the hardest mental labor.
120 "Cut it off and sold it," said Della. "Don't you like me just as well, anyhow? I'm me without my hair, ain't I?"

Jim looked about the room curiously.

---

10. **patent** (pāt′′nt): obvious.

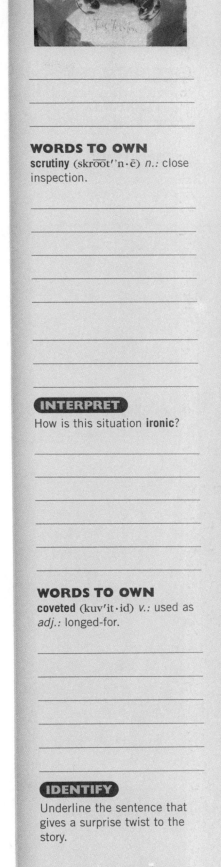

"You say your hair is gone?" he said, with an air almost of idiocy.

"You needn't look for it," said Della. "It's sold, I tell you—sold and gone, too. It's Christmas Eve, boy. Be good to me, for it went for you. Maybe the hairs on my head were numbered," she went on with a sudden serious sweetness, "but nobody could ever count my love for you. Shall I put the chops on, Jim?"

Out of his trance Jim seemed quickly to wake. He enfolded his Della.
130 For ten seconds let us regard with discreet <u>scrutiny</u> some inconsequential object in the other direction. Eight dollars a week or a million a year— what is the difference? A mathematician or a wit would give you the wrong answer. The Magi brought valuable gifts, but that was not among them. This dark assertion will be illuminated later on.

Jim drew a package from his overcoat pocket and threw it upon the table.

"Don't make any mistake, Dell," he said, "about me. I don't think there's anything in the way of a haircut or a shave or a shampoo that could make me like my girl any less. But if you'll unwrap that package,
140 you may see why you had me going awhile at first."

White fingers and nimble tore at the string and paper. And then an ecstatic scream of joy; and then, alas! a quick feminine change to hysterical tears and wails, necessitating the immediate employment of all the comforting powers of the lord of the flat.

For there lay The Combs—the set of combs, side and back, that Della had worshiped for long in a Broadway window. Beautiful combs, pure tortoise shell, with jeweled rims—just the shade to wear in the beautiful vanished hair. They were expensive combs, she knew, and her heart had simply craved and yearned over them without the least hope of
150 possession. And now, they were hers, but the tresses that should have adorned the <u>coveted</u> adornments were gone.

But she hugged them to her bosom, and at length she was able to look up with dim eyes and a smile and say: "My hair grows so fast, Jim!"

And then Della leaped up like a little singed cat and cried, "Oh, oh!"

Jim had not yet seen his beautiful present. She held it out to him eagerly upon her open palm. The dull precious metal seemed to flash with a reflection of her bright and ardent spirit.

"Isn't it a dandy, Jim? I hunted all over town to find it. You'll have to look at the time a hundred times a day now. Give me your watch. I want
160 to see how it looks on it."

Instead of obeying, Jim tumbled down on the couch and put his hands under the back of his head and smiled.

"Dell," said he, "let's put our Christmas presents away and keep 'em a while. They're too nice to use just at present. I sold the watch to get the money to buy your combs. And now suppose you put the chops on."

BUILD FLUENCY

Read the final paragraph aloud. Use an appropriate tone of voice to convey O. Henry's theme or message.

INTERPRET

What is the real "gift" referred to in the title of the story?

170 The Magi, as you know, were wise men—wonderfully wise men—who brought gifts to the Babe in the manger. They invented the art of giving Christmas presents. Being wise, their gifts were no doubt wise ones, possibly bearing the privilege of exchange in case of duplication. And here I have lamely related to you the uneventful chronicle of two foolish children in a flat who most unwisely sacrificed for each other the greatest treasures of their house. But in a last word to the wise of these days, let it be said that of all who give gifts, these two were the wisest. Of all who give and receive gifts, such as they are wisest. Everywhere they are wisest. They are the Magi.

Ironic Situation

An **ironic situation** is one that turns out to be the opposite of what we expected. The mighty Wizard of Oz, for example, turns out to be a little con man. In real life, it is seldom possible to predict the future exactly, and things often turn out differently from the way we had hoped or expected. Irony can move us toward tears or laughter because we sense we are close to the truth of life.

Explore O. Henry's use of irony in "The Gift of the Magi" by filling out the following chart.

Expectation	Reality
1. Della has scrimped and saved in order to buy Jim a Christmas present.	
2. Della expects that the watch chain will be the perfect present for Jim.	
3. Jim hopes that the combs will please Della.	
4. The author calls the story an "uneventful chronicle of two foolish children."	

Vocabulary: How to Own a Word

Synonyms and Context Clues

Word Bank
coveted
instigates
depreciate
scrutiny

In the following sentences, you will find italicized synonyms for the Words to Own. In the blank provided, write the Word to Own that is a synonym for each italicized word. Then, underline any context clues that alert you to the word's meaning.

EXAMPLE: <u>ornamentation</u>   The set of tortoise shell combs would furnish beautiful *decoration* for Della's hair. They would <u>adorn</u> her hair nicely, don't you think?

_____ **1.** Jim and Della's finances, under *examination,* do not give a clear picture of the couple. However, a close inspection of their lives probably would reveal that they are very happy.

_____ **2.** It is not Jim's intention to *disparage* Della's present for him. On the contrary, he values it highly.

_____ **3.** Love *initiates* the sacrifices Della and Jim make for each other in the story.

_____ **4.** Della's *desired* adornments are finally hers. She apparently had wanted them for quite some time.

Selection: _____

Character Analysis

Character _____	Passages
Words	
Actions	
Appearance	
Thoughts	
Effects on Other People	
Direct Characterization	
Analysis of Character	

The Necklace

Make the Connection

The Sharp Tooth of Envy

Have you ever wished to own something that belonged to a friend—a video game, a stereo system, stylish clothes?

What you felt was **envy**. People can be envious of material possessions or of something less material, such as someone's popularity or good looks. When such a feeling is carried to an extreme, the results can be tragic, as in the case of the main character in Guy de Maupassant's story "The Necklace."

Use the chart below to list examples of envious characters in books, fairy tales, or movies with which you are familiar. Then, describe the results of the characters' envious behavior.

Envious Characters	Results

1. Explain whether your examples of envy show more negative results than positive ones, and why.

   _____

   _____

   _____

2. What can these characters do to avoid feelings of envy?

   _____

   _____

   _____

   _____

The Necklace

Guy de Maupassant

INTERPRET

The first paragraph introduces the story's **main character**. From what level of society does she come? Underline two phrases that hint at the answer.

IDENTIFY

According to the narrator, what are the three character traits that make "daughters of the common people" equal to "ladies in high society"? Underline the words giving the answer.

WORDS TO OWN

incessantly (in·ses'ənt·lē) *adv.*: constantly; continually.
disconsolate (dis·kän'sə·lit) *adj.*: very unhappy.

_____

_____

IDENTIFY

Circle three details in this paragraph referring to the style of life that the woman envies.

She was one of those pretty and charming girls, born, as if by an accident of fate, into a family of clerks. With no dowry,[1] no prospects, no way of any kind of being met, understood, loved, and married by a man both prosperous and famous, she was finally married to a minor clerk in the Ministry of Education.

She dressed plainly because she could not afford fine clothes, but she was as unhappy as a woman who has come down in the world; for women have no family rank or social class. With them, beauty, grace, and charm take the place of birth and breeding. Their natural poise, their
10 instinctive good taste, and their mental cleverness are the sole guiding principles which make daughters of the common people the equals of ladies in high society.

She grieved incessantly, feeling that she had been born for all the little niceties and luxuries of living. She grieved over the shabbiness of her apartment, the dinginess of the walls, the worn-out appearance of the chairs, the ugliness of the draperies. All these things, which another woman of her class would not even have noticed, gnawed at her and made her furious. The sight of the little Breton girl[2] who did her humble housework roused in her disconsolate regrets and wild daydreams. She
20 would dream of silent chambers, draped with Oriental tapestries[3] and lighted by tall bronze floor lamps, and of two handsome butlers in knee breeches, who, drowsy from the heavy warmth cast by the central stove, dozed in large overstuffed armchairs.

She would dream of great reception halls hung with old silks, of fine furniture filled with priceless curios,[4] and of small, stylish, scented sitting rooms just right for the four o'clock chat with intimate friends, with distinguished and sought-after men whose attention every woman envies and longs to attract.

When dining at the round table, covered for the third day with the
30 same cloth, opposite her husband, who would raise the cover of the soup tureen, declaring delightedly, "Ah! a good stew! There's nothing I like better . . . ," she would dream of fashionable dinner parties, of gleaming silverware, of tapestries making the walls alive with characters out of history and strange birds in a fairyland forest; she would dream of delicious dishes served on wonderful china, of gallant compliments whispered and listened to with a sphinxlike[5] smile as one eats the rosy flesh of a trout or nibbles at the wings of a grouse.

---

1. **dowry** (dou'rē): property that a woman brings to her husband at marriage.
2. **Breton** (bret''n) **girl:** girl from Brittany, a region in northwestern France.
3. **tapestries** (tap'əs·trēz): heavy cloths woven with decorative designs and pictures, used as wall hangings or furniture coverings.
4. **curios** (kyoor'ē·ōz'): unusual items.
5. **sphinxlike:** mysterious. The sphinx was a creature in Greek mythology who asked riddles.

She had no evening clothes, no jewels, nothing. But those were the things she wanted; she felt that was the kind of life for her. She so much
40 longed to please, be envied, be fascinating and sought after.

She had a well-to-do friend, a classmate of convent-school days whom she would no longer go to see, simply because she would feel so distressed on returning home. And she would weep for days on end from vexation, regret, despair, and anguish.

Then one evening, her husband came home proudly holding out a large envelope.

"Look," he said, "I've got something for you."

She excitedly tore open the envelope and pulled out a printed card bearing these words:

50 "The Minister of Education and Mme. Georges Ramponneau beg M. and Mme. Loisel[6] to do them the honor of attending an evening reception at the Ministerial Mansion on Friday, January 18."

Instead of being delighted, as her husband had hoped, she scornfully tossed the invitation on the table, murmuring, "What good is that to me?"

"But, my dear, I thought you'd be thrilled to death. You never get a chance to go out, and this is a real affair, a wonderful one! I had an awful time getting a card. Everybody wants one; it's much sought after, and not many clerks have a chance at one. You'll see all the most important people there."

60 She gave him an irritated glance and burst out impatiently, "What do you think I have to go in?"

He hadn't given that a thought. He stammered, "Why, the dress you wear when we go to the theater. That looks quite nice, I think."

He stopped talking, dazed and distracted to see his wife burst out weeping. Two large tears slowly rolled from the corners of her eyes to the corners of her mouth; he gasped, "Why, what's the matter? What's the trouble?"

By sheer willpower she overcame her outburst and answered in a calm voice while wiping the tears from her wet cheeks, "Oh, nothing.
70 Only I don't have an evening dress and therefore I can't go to that affair. Give the card to some friend at the office whose wife can dress better than I can."

He was stunned. He resumed, "Let's see, Mathilde. How much would a suitable outfit cost—one you could wear for other affairs too— something very simple?"

She thought it over for several seconds, going over her allowance and thinking also of the amount she could ask for without bringing an immediate refusal and an exclamation of dismay from the thrifty clerk.

---

6. **Mme. Georges Ramponneau** (mȧ·dȧm′ zhôrzh rȧm′pə·nô) . . . **M.** (mə·syͧr′) . . . **Mme. Loisel** (mȧ·dȧm′ lwä·zel′): *M.* and *Mme.* are abbreviations for "Monsieur" and "Madame" and are the French equivalents of *Mr.* and *Mrs.*

INTERPRET

Why would a visit to her friend distress her?

_____

_____

_____

_____

_____

INFER

Why does the invitation upset Mathilde? What does her reaction show about her **character** and her regard for her husband?

_____

_____

_____

_____

_____

_____

_____

EVALUATE

Judging from the dialogue in lines 55–84, what is your opinion of the Loisels' marriage?

_____

_____

_____

_____

_____

_____

_____

_____

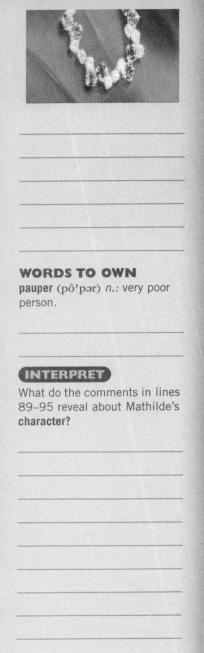

INTERPRET

What do the comments in lines
89–95 reveal about Mathilde's
character?

INTERPRET

What evidence so far hints that
the diamond necklace may
function as a **symbol** in the
story?

Finally, she answered hesitatingly, "I'm not sure exactly, but I think
80 with four hundred francs I could manage it."

He turned a bit pale, for he had set aside just that amount to buy a
rifle so that the following summer, he could join some friends who were
getting up a group to shoot larks on the plain near Nanterre.[7]

However, he said, "All right. I'll give you four hundred francs. But try
to get a nice dress."

As the day of the party approached, Mme. Loisel seemed sad, moody,
ill at ease. Her outfit was ready, however. Her husband said to her one
evening, "What's the matter? You've been all out of sorts for three days."

And she answered, "It's embarrassing not to have a jewel or a gem—
90 nothing to wear on my dress. I'll look like a pauper. I'd almost rather not
go to the party."

He answered, "Why not wear some flowers? They're very fashionable this
season. For ten francs you can get two or three gorgeous roses."

She wasn't at all convinced. "No. . . . There's nothing more
humiliating than to look poor among a lot of rich women."

But her husband exclaimed, "My, but you're silly! Go see your friend
Mme. Forestier,[8] and ask her to lend you some jewelry. You and she know
each other well enough for you to do that."

She gave a cry of joy. "Why, that's so! I hadn't thought of it."
100 The next day she paid her friend a visit and told her of her
predicament.

Mme. Forestier went toward a large closet with mirrored doors, took
out a large jewel box, brought it over, opened it, and said to Mme. Loisel,
"Pick something out, my dear."

At first her eyes noted some bracelets, then a pearl necklace, then
a Venetian cross, gold and gems, of marvelous workmanship. She tried
on these adornments in front of the mirror, but hesitated, unable to
decide which to part with and put back. She kept on asking, "Haven't
you something else?"
110 "Oh, yes, keep on looking. I don't know just what you'd like."

All at once she found, in a black satin box, a superb diamond
necklace; and her pulse beat faster with longing. Her hands trembled
as she took it up. Clasping it around her throat, outside her high-necked
dress, she stood in ecstasy looking at her reflection.

Then she asked, hesitatingly, pleading, "Could I borrow that, just
that and nothing else?"

"Why, of course."

She threw her arms around her friend, kissed her warmly, and fled
with her treasure.

---

7. **Nanterre** (nän·ter′): town near Paris.
8. **Forestier** (fô·rəs·tyā′).

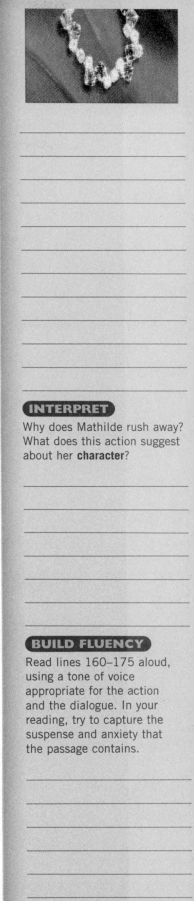

120   The day of the party arrived. Mme. Loisel was a sensation. She was the prettiest one there, fashionable, gracious, smiling, and wild with joy. All the men turned to look at her, asked who she was, begged to be introduced. All the Cabinet officials wanted to waltz with her. The minister took notice of her.

    She danced madly, wildly, drunk with pleasure, giving no thought to anything in the triumph of her beauty, the pride of her success, in a kind of happy cloud composed of all the adulation, of all the admiring glances, of all the awakened longings, of a sense of complete victory that is so sweet to a woman's heart.

130   She left around four o'clock in the morning. Her husband, since midnight, had been dozing in a small, empty sitting room with three other gentlemen whose wives were having too good a time.

    He threw over her shoulders the wraps he had brought for going home, modest garments of everyday life whose shabbiness clashed with the stylishness of her evening clothes. She felt this and longed to escape unseen by the other women, who were draped in expensive furs.

    Loisel held her back.

    "Hold on! You'll catch cold outside. I'll call a cab."

    But she wouldn't listen to him and went rapidly down the stairs.

140 When they were on the street, they didn't find a carriage; and they set out to hunt for one, hailing drivers whom they saw going by at a distance.

    They walked toward the Seine,[9] disconsolate and shivering. Finally, on the docks, they found one of those carriages that one sees in Paris only after nightfall, as if they were ashamed to show their drabness during daylight hours.

    It dropped them at their door in the Rue des Martyrs,[10] and they climbed wearily up to their apartment. For her, it was all over. For him, there was the thought that he would have to be at the Ministry at ten o'clock.

150   Before the mirror, she let the wraps fall from her shoulders to see herself once again in all her glory. Suddenly she gave a cry. The necklace was gone.

    Her husband, already half undressed, said, "What's the trouble?"

    She turned toward him despairingly, "I . . . I . . . I don't have Mme. Forestier's necklace."

    "What! You can't mean it! It's impossible!"

    They hunted everywhere, through the folds of the dress, through the folds of the coat, in the pockets. They found nothing.

    He asked, "Are you sure you had it when leaving the dance?"

160   "Yes, I felt it when I was in the hall of the Ministry."

---

9. **Seine** (sen): river that runs through Paris.
10. **Rue des Martyrs** (rü dā mär·tēr'): street in Paris. The name means "Street of the Martyrs."

INTERPRET

Why does Mathilde rush away? What does this action suggest about her **character**?

BUILD FLUENCY

Read lines 160–175 aloud, using a tone of voice appropriate for the action and the dialogue. In your reading, try to capture the suspense and anxiety that the passage contains.

INFER

Why do you think Madame Loisel's mind is "a blank" here?

EVALUATE

Is this the best way to deal with the loss of a borrowed item? Explain.

WORDS TO OWN
privations (prī·vā′shənz) *n.:* hardships; lack of the things needed for a happy, healthy life.

"But if you had lost it on the street, we'd have heard it drop. It must be in the cab."

"Yes, quite likely. Did you get its number?"

"No. Didn't you notice it either?"

"No."

They looked at each other aghast. Finally Loisel got dressed again.

"I'll retrace our steps on foot," he said, "to see if I can find it."

And he went out. She remained in her evening clothes, without the strength to go to bed, slumped in a chair in the unheated room, her 170 mind a blank.

Her husband came in around seven o'clock. He had had no luck.

He went to the police station, to the newspapers to post a reward, to the cab companies, everywhere the slightest hope drove him.

That evening Loisel returned, pale, his face lined; still he had learned nothing.

"We'll have to write your friend," he said, "to tell her you have broken the catch and are having it repaired. That will give us a little time to turn around."

She wrote to his dictation.

180 At the end of a week, they had given up all hope.

And Loisel, looking five years older, declared, "We must take steps to replace that piece of jewelry."

The next day they took the case to the jeweler whose name they found inside. He consulted his records. "I didn't sell that necklace, madame," he said. "I only supplied the case."

Then they went from one jeweler to another hunting for a similar necklace, going over their recollections, both sick with despair and anxiety.

They found, in a shop in Palais Royal,[11] a string of diamonds which seemed exactly like the one they were seeking. It was priced at forty 190 thousand francs. They could get it for thirty-six.

They asked the jeweler to hold it for them for three days. And they reached an agreement that he would take it back for thirty-four thousand if the lost one was found before the end of February.

Loisel had eighteen thousand francs he had inherited from his father. He would borrow the rest.

He went about raising the money, asking a thousand francs from one, four hundred from another, a hundred here, sixty there. He signed notes, made ruinous deals, did business with loan sharks, ran the whole gamut of money-lenders. He compromised the rest of his life, risked his 200 signature without knowing if he'd be able to honor it, and then, terrified by the outlook of the future, by the blackness of despair about to close around him, by the prospect of all the privations of the body and tortures

---

11. **Palais Royal** (pȧ·lā′ rwä·yȧl′): fashionable shopping district in Paris.

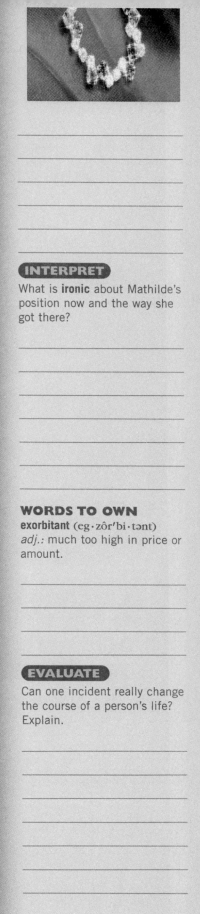

of the spirit, he went to claim the new necklace with the thirty-six thousand francs, which he placed on the counter of the shopkeeper.

When Mme. Loisel took the necklace back, Mme. Forestier said to her frostily, "You should have brought it back sooner; I might have needed it."

She didn't open the case, an action her friend was afraid of. If she had noticed the substitution, what would she have thought? What would she have said? Would she have thought her a thief?

Mme. Loisel experienced the horrible life the needy live. She played her part, however, with sudden heroism. That frightful debt had to be paid. She would pay it. She dismissed her maid; they rented a garret under the eaves.[12]

She learned to do the heavy housework, to perform the hateful duties of cooking. She washed dishes, wearing down her shell-pink nails scouring the grease from pots and pans; she scrubbed dirty linen, shirts, and cleaning rags, which she hung on a line to dry; she took the garbage down to the street each morning and brought up water, stopping on each landing to get her breath. And, clad like a peasant woman, basket on arm, guarding sou[13] by sou her scanty allowance, she bargained with the fruit dealers, the grocer, the butcher, and was insulted by them.

Each month notes had to be paid, and others renewed to give more time.

Her husband labored evenings to balance a tradesman's accounts, and at night, often, he copied documents at five sous a page.

And this went on for ten years.

Finally, all was paid back, everything including the exorbitant rates of the loan sharks and accumulated compound interest.

Mme. Loisel appeared an old woman now. She became heavy, rough, harsh, like one of the poor. Her hair untended, her skirts askew, her hands red, her voice shrill, she even slopped water on her floors and scrubbed them herself. But, sometimes, while her husband was at work, she would sit near the window and think of that long-ago evening when, at the dance, she had been so beautiful and admired.

What would have happened if she had not lost that necklace? Who knows? Who can say? How strange and unpredictable life is! How little there is between happiness and misery!

Then, one Sunday, when she had gone for a walk on the Champs Élysées[14] to relax a bit from the week's labors, she suddenly noticed a woman strolling with a child. It was Mme. Forestier, still young looking, still beautiful, still charming.

---

12. **garret under the eaves:** attic under the overhanging lower edges of a roof.
13. **sou** (sōō): old French coin of little value.
14. **Champs Élysées** (shä*n* zā·lē·zā′): famous avenue in Paris.

INTERPRET

What is **ironic** about Mathilde's position now and the way she got there?

WORDS TO OWN
exorbitant (eg·zôr′bi·tənt) *adj.:* much too high in price or amount.

EVALUATE

Can one incident really change the course of a person's life? Explain.

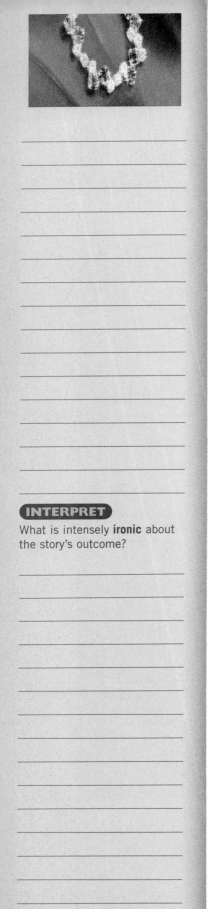

Mme. Loisel felt a rush of emotion. Should she speak to her? Of course. And now that everything was paid off, she would tell her the whole story. Why not?

She went toward her. "Hello, Jeanne."

The other, not recognizing her, showed astonishment at being spoken to so familiarly by this common person. She stammered, "But. . . madame . . . I don't recognize . . . You must be mistaken."

250 "No, I'm Mathilde Loisel."

Her friend gave a cry, "Oh, my poor Mathilde, how you've changed!"

"Yes, I've had a hard time since last seeing you. And plenty of misfortunes—and all on account of you!"

"Of me . . . How do you mean?"

"Do you remember that diamond necklace you loaned me to wear to the dance at the Ministry?"

"Yes, but what about it?"

"Well, I lost it."

"You lost it! But you returned it."

260 "I brought you another just like it. And we've been paying for it for ten years now. You can imagine that wasn't easy for us who had nothing. Well, it's over now, and I am glad of it."

Mme. Forestier stopped short. "You mean to say you bought a diamond necklace to replace mine?"

"Yes. You never noticed, then? They were quite alike."

And she smiled with proud and simple joy.

Mme. Forestier, quite overcome, clasped her by the hands. "Oh, my poor Mathilde. But mine was fake. Why, at most it was worth only five hundred francs!"

INTERPRET

What is intensely **ironic** about the story's outcome?

Limited Point of View

The **point of view** in a story is the vantage point from which the story is told. In **third-person limited point of view,** the storyteller, who is outside the story, zooms in on just one character. In stories with this point of view, we witness the events just as this one character witnesses them. Guy de Maupassant was interested in the psychology of his characters, so it is not surprising that he tells "The Necklace" from the vantage point of Mathilde Loisel.

Review the first seven paragraphs of the story. Then, fill out the following chart to explore what we learn about Mathilde.

Focus on Mathilde Loisel
What do we learn about **a.** her past? _____ _____ _____
b. her dreams? _____ _____ _____
c. what makes her unhappy? _____ _____ _____
d. what she envies in others? _____ _____ _____
e. what she thinks will make her happy? _____ _____ _____

Vocabulary: How to Own a Word

Related Meanings

Word Bank
incessantly
disconsolate
pauper
privations
exorbitant

For each of the following word groups, cross out the word whose meaning or part of speech is different from the meanings or parts of speech of the Word to Own in boldface type and the other two words.

EXAMPLE: **a. gracious**   **b.** kind   **c.** ~~compassion~~   **d.** courteous

1. **a.** cheerless   **b.** deceived   **c.** unhappy   **d. disconsolate**

2. **a. exorbitant**   **b.** excessive   **c.** exceptional   **d.** extravagant

3. **a.** consolations   **b.** hardships   **c.** difficulties   **d. privations**

4. **a.** constantly   **b.** continually   **c. incessantly**   **d.** occasionally

5. **a.** beggar   **b. pauper**   **c.** have-not   **d.** grateful

Selection: _____

Analyzing Point of View

Record the title of the narrative you are analyzing. Then write answers to the following questions about point of view.

1. From what point of view is the selection told?
2. What do we know (or what can we infer) about the narrator?
3. What does this point of view reveal about the characters and the actions of the selection? What does it conceal?
4. Imagine that the narrative were told from a different point of view. How would that alter your understanding of the characters and their motivations?

The Cask of Amontillado

Make the Connection

Grisly Wall of Revenge

In "The Cask of Amontillado," Edgar Allan Poe presents the emotion of revenge, as well as some of its chilling effects. Montresor says that he has received a thousand injuries from Fortunato and that Fortunato has insulted him. He believes he has sufficient cause for revenge.

Using your own knowledge of stories, books, TV shows, or movies, add the names of three other characters to the top row of stones on the "Wall of Revenge" below. Then, in the stone below each name, describe what caused the character to seek revenge and the effects of revenge on each character's personality.

Wall of Revenge

Character:

Cause:

Effects:

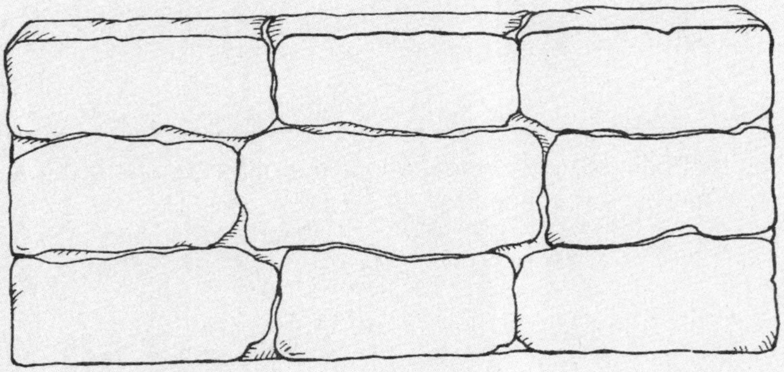

In your opinion, what is a common pattern among the "effects" of revenge? Why?

_____

_____

_____

_____

The Cask of Amontillado

Edgar Allan Poe

The thousand injuries of Fortunato I had borne as best I could; but when he ventured upon insult, I vowed revenge. You, who so well know the nature of my soul, will not suppose, however, that I gave utterance to a threat. At length I would be avenged; this was a point definitively settled—but the very definitiveness with which it was resolved precluded the idea of risk. I must not only punish, but punish with impunity. A wrong is unredressed when retribution overtakes its redresser. It is equally unredressed when the avenger fails to make himself felt as such to him who has done the wrong.

10   It must be understood that neither by word nor deed had I given Fortunato cause to doubt my goodwill. I continued, as was my wont, to smile in his face, and he did not perceive that my smile *now* was at the thought of his immolation.

He had a weak point—this Fortunato—although in other regards he was a man to be respected and even feared. He prided himself on his connoisseurship in wine. Few Italians have the true virtuoso spirit. For the most part their enthusiasm is adopted to suit the time and opportunity—to practice imposture upon the British and Austrian millionaires. In painting and gemmary, Fortunato, like his countrymen,

20   was a quack—but in the matter of old wines he was sincere. In this respect I did not differ from him materially: I was skillful in the Italian vintages myself and bought largely whenever I could.

It was about dusk, one evening during the supreme madness of the carnival season, that I encountered my friend. He accosted me with excessive warmth, for he had been drinking much. The man wore motley.[1] He had on a tight-fitting parti-striped dress, and his head was surmounted by the conical cap and bells. I was so pleased to see him that I thought I should never have done wringing his hand.

I said to him, "My dear Fortunato, you are luckily met. How

30   remarkably well you are looking today! But I have received a pipe[2] of what passes for amontillado, and I have my doubts."

"How?" said he. "Amontillado? A pipe? Impossible! And in the middle of the carnival!"

"I have my doubts," I replied; "and I was silly enough to pay the full amontillado price without consulting you in the matter. You were not to be found, and I was fearful of losing a bargain."

"Amontillado!"

"I have my doubts."

"Amontillado!"

40   "And I must satisfy them."

"Amontillado!"

---

1. **motley** (mät′lē): multicolored costume worn by a clown or jester.
2. **pipe:** barrel.

"As you are engaged, I am on my way to Luchesi. If anyone has a critical turn, it is he. He will tell me—"

"Luchesi cannot tell amontillado from sherry."

"And yet some fools will have it that his taste is a match for your own."

"Come, let us go."

"Whither?"

"To your vaults."[3]

"My friend, no; I will not impose upon your good nature. I perceive
50 you have an engagement. Luchesi—"

"I have no engagement; come."

"My friend, no. It is not the engagement, but the severe cold with which I perceive you are afflicted. The vaults are insufferably damp. They are encrusted with niter."[4]

"Let us go, nevertheless. The cold is merely nothing. Amontillado! You have been imposed upon. And as for Luchesi, he cannot distinguish sherry from amontillado."

Thus speaking, Fortunato possessed himself of my arm. Putting on a mask of black silk and drawing a roquelaure[5] closely about my person, I
60 suffered him to hurry me to my *palazzo.*[6]

There were no attendants at home; they had absconded to make merry in honor of the time. I had told them that I should not return until the morning and had given them explicit orders not to stir from the house. These orders were sufficient, I well knew, to ensure their immediate disappearance, one and all, as soon as my back was turned.

I took from their sconces two flambeaux[7] and, giving one to Fortunato, bowed him through several suites of rooms to the archway that led into the vaults. I passed down a long and winding staircase, requesting him to be cautious as he followed. We came at length to the
70 foot of the descent and stood together on the damp ground of the catacombs of the Montresors.

The gait of my friend was unsteady, and the bells upon his cap jingled as he strode.

"The pipe," said he.

"It is farther on," said I; "but observe the white web-work which gleams from these cavern walls."

He turned toward me, and looked into my eyes with two filmy orbs that distilled the rheum[8] of intoxication.

"Niter?" he asked, at length.

80   "Niter," I replied. "How long have you had that cough?"

WORDS TO OWN
impose (im·pōz′) **upon** v.: take advantage of.

INTERPRET
What does the narrator's attitude toward his servants reveal about his outlook on humanity?

INTERPRET

What strange phrase does the narrator use in line 83 to refer to Fortunato here? Circle the words.

_____

_____

_____

_____

_____

_____

_____

PREDICT

Judging by the **ironic** tone Montresor uses, what do you predict will happen to Fortunato? Will he live a long life?

_____

_____

_____

_____

VISUALIZE

Use the description here to visualize the setting. Why do you think Montresor expresses concern for Fortunato's health?

_____

_____

_____

_____

_____

_____

"Ugh! ugh! ugh!—ugh! ugh! ugh!—ugh! ugh! ugh!—ugh! ugh! ugh!—ugh! ugh! ugh!"

My poor friend found it impossible to reply for many minutes.

"It is nothing," he said, at last.

"Come," I said, with decision, "we will go back; your health is precious. You are rich, respected, admired, beloved; you are happy, as once I was. You are a man to be missed. For me it is no matter. We will go back; you will be ill, and I cannot be responsible. Besides, there is Luchesi—"

90 "Enough," he said; "the cough is a mere nothing; it will not kill me. I shall not die of a cough."

"True—true," I replied; "and, indeed, I had no intention of alarming you unnecessarily—but you should use all proper caution. A draft of this Médoc[9] will defend us from the damps."

Here I knocked off the neck of a bottle which I drew from a long row of its fellows that lay upon the mold.

"Drink," I said, presenting him the wine.

He raised it to his lips with a leer. He paused and nodded to me familiarly, while his bells jingled.

100 "I drink," he said, "to the buried that repose around us."

"And I to your long life."

He again took my arm, and we proceeded.

"These vaults," he said, "are extensive."

"The Montresors," I replied, "were a great and numerous family."

"I forget your arms."[10]

"A huge human foot d'or, in a field azure; the foot crushes a serpent rampant whose fangs are embedded in the heel."[11]

"And the motto?"

"*Nemo me impune lacessit.*"[12]

110 "Good!" he said.

The wine sparkled in his eyes and the bells jingled. My own fancy grew warm with the Médoc. We had passed through walls of piled bones, with casks and puncheons[13] intermingling, into the inmost recesses of the catacombs. I paused again, and this time I made bold to seize Fortunato by an arm above the elbow.

"The niter!" I said. "See, it increases. It hangs like moss upon the vaults. We are below the river's bed. The drops of moisture trickle among the bones. Come, we will go back ere it is too late. Your cough—"

---

9. **Médoc** (mā·dôk'): type of red wine.
10. **arms:** coat of arms, a group of symbols used to represent a family.
11. **foot d'or . . . heel:** The Montresor coat of arms shows a huge golden foot against a blue background, with the foot crushing a snake that is rearing up and biting the heel.
12. *Nemo me impune lacessit* (nā'mō mā im·pōō'nā lä·ke'sit): Latin for "Nobody attacks me without punishment."
13. **puncheons** (pun'chənz): large wine casks.

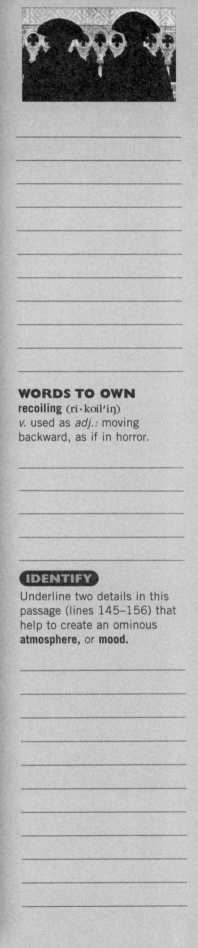

"It is nothing," he said; "let us go on. But first, another draft of the
120 Médoc."

I broke and reached him a flagon of de Grâve.[14] He emptied it at a
breath. His eyes flashed with a fierce light. He laughed and threw the
bottle upward with a gesticulation I did not understand.

I looked at him in surprise. He repeated the movement—a
grotesque one.

"You do not comprehend?" he said.

"Not I," I replied.

"Then you are not of the brotherhood."

"How?"

130   "You are not of the Masons."[15]

"Yes, yes," I said, "yes, yes."

"You? Impossible! A Mason?"

"A mason," I replied.

"A sign," he said.

"It is this," I answered, producing a trowel from beneath the folds of
my roquelaure.

"You jest," he exclaimed, <u>recoiling</u> a few paces. "But let us proceed
to the amontillado."

"Be it so," I said, replacing the tool beneath the cloak and again
140 offering him my arm. He leaned upon it heavily. We continued our route
in search of the amontillado. We passed through a range of low arches,
descended, passed on, and, descending again, arrived at a deep crypt in
which the foulness of the air caused our flambeaux rather to glow than
flame.

At the most remote end of the crypt there appeared another less
spacious. Its walls had been lined with human remains, piled to the
vault overhead, in the fashion of the great catacombs of Paris. Three
sides of this interior crypt were still ornamented in this manner. From the
fourth the bones had been thrown down and lay promiscuously[16] upon
150 the earth, forming at one point a mound of some size. Within the wall
thus exposed by the displacing of the bones, we perceived a still interior
recess, in depth about four feet, in width three, in height six or seven. It
seemed to have been constructed for no especial use within itself, but
formed merely the interval between two of the colossal supports of the
roof of the catacombs and was backed by one of their circumscribing
walls of solid granite.

---

14. **flagon of de Grâve:** narrow-necked bottle with a handle and sometimes a lid, containing
    a wine from the Graves region of France.
15. **Masons** (māˈsənz): Freemasons, a secret society of people who believe in brotherhood,
    giving to the poor, and helping one another. Members use secret signs and gestures to
    recognize one another.
16. **promiscuously** (prō·misˈkyōō·əs·lē): randomly; in a disorganized way.

WORDS TO OWN
recoiling (ri·koilˈiŋ)
v. used as *adj.:* moving
backward, as if in horror.

IDENTIFY

Underline two details in this
passage (lines 145–156) that
help to create an ominous
atmosphere, or **mood.**

It was in vain that Fortunato, uplifting his dull torch, endeavored to pry into the depth of the recess. Its termination the feeble light did not enable us to see.

160 "Proceed," I said; "herein is the amontillado. As for Luchesi—"

"He is an ignoramus," interrupted my friend, as he stepped unsteadily forward, while I followed immediately at his heels. In an instant he had reached the extremity of the niche, and finding his progress arrested by the rock, stood stupidly bewildered. A moment more and I had fettered[17] him to the granite. In its surface were two iron staples, distant from each other about two feet horizontally. From one of these depended a short chain, from the other a padlock. Throwing the links about his waist, it was but the work of a few seconds to secure it. He was too much astounded to resist. Withdrawing the key, I stepped

170 back from the recess.

"Pass your hand," I said, "over the wall; you cannot help feeling the niter. Indeed it is _very_ damp. Once more let me _implore_ you to return. No? Then I must positively leave you. But I must first render you all the little attentions in my power."

"The amontillado!" ejaculated my friend, not yet recovered from his astonishment.

"True," I replied; "the amontillado."

As I said these words, I busied myself among the pile of bones of which I have before spoken. Throwing them aside, I soon uncovered a

180 quantity of building stone and mortar. With these materials and with the aid of my trowel, I began vigorously to wall up the entrance of the niche.

I had scarcely laid the first tier of the masonry when I discovered that the intoxication of Fortunato had in a great measure worn off. The earliest indication I had of this was a low moaning cry from the depth of the recess. It was _not_ the cry of a drunken man. There was then a long and obstinate silence. I laid the second tier, and the third, and the fourth; and then I heard the furious vibrations of the chain. The noise lasted for several minutes, during which, that I might hearken to it with the more satisfaction, I ceased my labors and sat down upon the bones. When at

190 last the clanking subsided, I resumed the trowel and finished without interruption the fifth, the sixth, and the seventh tier. The wall was now nearly upon a level with my breast. I again paused and, holding the flambeaux over the mason-work, threw a few feeble rays upon the figure within.

A succession of loud and shrill screams, bursting suddenly from the throat of the chained form, seemed to thrust me violently back. For a brief moment I hesitated—I trembled. Unsheathing my rapier,[18] I began to grope with it about the recess; but the thought of an instant reassured

---

17. fettered (fet′ərd): chained.
18. rapier (rā′pē·ər): slender two-edged sword.

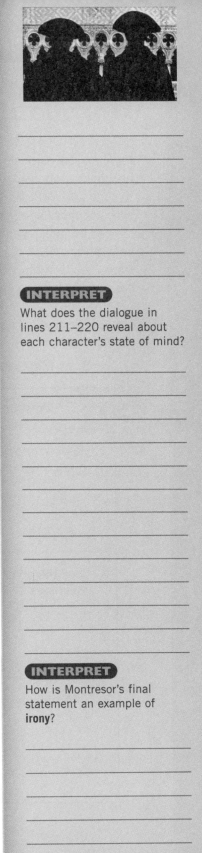

me. I placed my hand upon the solid fabric of the catacombs and felt
200 satisfied. I reapproached the wall; I replied to the yells of him who
clamored. I reechoed—I aided—I surpassed them in volume and in
strength. I did this, and the clamorer grew still.

It was now midnight, and my task was drawing to a close. I had
completed the eighth, the ninth, and the tenth tier. I had finished a
portion of the last and the eleventh; there remained but a single stone to
be fitted and plastered in. I struggled with its weight; I placed it partially
in its destined position. But now there came from out the niche a low
laugh that erected the hairs upon my head. It was succeeded by a sad
voice, which I had difficulty in recognizing as that of the noble
210 Fortunato. The voice said—

"Ha! ha! ha!—he! he! he!—a very good joke indeed—an excellent
jest. We will have many a rich laugh about it at the *palazzo*—he! he!
he!—over our wine—he! he! he!"

"The amontillado!" I said.

"He! he! he!—he! he! he!—yes, the amontillado. But is it not getting
late? Will not they be awaiting us at the *palazzo*—the Lady Fortunato
and the rest? Let us be gone."

"Yes," I said, "let us be gone."

"For the love of God, Montresor!"

220 "Yes," I said, "for the love of God!"

But to these words I hearkened in vain for a reply. I grew impatient. I
called aloud—

"Fortunato!"

No answer. I called again—

"Fortunato!"

No answer still. I thrust a torch through the remaining aperture and
let it fall within. There came forth in return only a jingling of the bells.
My heart grew sick—on account of the dampness of the catacombs. I
hastened to make an end of my labor. I forced the last stone into its
230 position; I plastered it up. Against the new masonry I reerected the old
rampart[19] of bones. For the half of a century no mortal has disturbed
them. *In pace requiescat.*[20]

INTERPRET

What does the dialogue in
lines 211–220 reveal about
each character's state of mind?

INTERPRET

How is Montresor's final
statement an example of
irony?

---

19. **rampart** (ram′pärt′): wall resembling one built for protection or defense.
20. *In pace requiescat* (in pä′chä rä′kwē·es′kät): Latin for "May he rest in peace."

Unreliable Narrator

An **unreliable narrator** is someone who is not always perceptive about what is going on in a story, or someone who is deliberately not telling the whole truth. In several of his best-known stories, including "The Cask of Amontillado," Edgar Allan Poe uses an unreliable narrator to increase our sense of shock and horror.

For example, as the story unfolds, we suspect that Montresor may be deceiving us by concealing part of the truth or by exaggerating or otherwise distorting factual details. In addition, some details in the story may suggest that Montresor—who is outwardly so rational and calculating—may really be insane.

Imagine that you have Montresor on the witness stand and that you are about to cross-examine him. To explore Poe's use of an unreliable narrator further, fill out the following chart.

Does Montresor Tell the Truth, the Whole Truth, and Nothing but the Truth?

Questions	Evidence from the Story
1. Has Fortunato really injured Montresor?	
2. Does the amontillado really exist?	
3. Is Montresor really insane?	

Vocabulary: How to Own a Word

Synonyms and Antonyms

Below are ten word pairs. For each numbered pair, write **S** in the blank if the second word in the pair is a synonym of the Word to Own. Write **A** if the word is an antonym. You may need a dictionary or a thesaurus for this activity.

_____ **1.** impose upon : burden

_____ **2.** retribution : retaliation

_____ **3.** endeavored : avoided

_____ **4.** obstinate : tenacious

_____ **5.** immolation : creation

_____ **6.** impunity : exemption

_____ **7.** succession : precedence

_____ **8.** precluded : included

_____ **9.** recoiling : repulsing

_____ **10.** connoisseurship : apprenticeship

Word Bank
precluded
impunity
retribution
immolation
connoisseurship
impose upon
recoiling
endeavored
obstinate
succession

Marigolds

Make the Connection

Into Adulthood

The setting for this story is the Great Depression of the 1930s, but the story is not just about economic and social conflicts. "Marigolds" also focuses on the internal conflicts of the narrator during adolescence.

Moving from childhood to adulthood can be an emotionally difficult time. Based on your own experience and that of people you know, what are some fears and conflicts that young people have to deal with? What are some practical ways of overcoming these challenges? Explore your thoughts about these questions by filling out the chart below.

FROM CHILDHOOD TO ADULTHOOD

Fears/Conflicts	Ways of Coping

Marigolds

Eugenia W. Collier

When I think of the hometown of my youth, all that I seem to remember is dust—the brown, crumbly dust of late summer—arid, sterile dust that gets into the eyes and makes them water, gets into the throat and between the toes of bare brown feet. I don't know why I should remember only the dust. Surely there must have been lush green lawns and paved streets under leafy shade trees somewhere in town; but memory is an abstract painting—it does not present things as they are, but rather as they *feel*. And so, when I think of that time and that place, I remember only the dry September of the dirt roads and grassless yards

10 of the shantytown where I lived. And one other thing I remember, another incongruency[1] of memory—a brilliant splash of sunny yellow against the dust—Miss Lottie's marigolds.

Whenever the memory of those marigolds flashes across my mind, a strange nostalgia comes with it and remains long after the picture has faded. I feel again the chaotic emotions of adolescence, illusive as smoke, yet as real as the potted geranium before me now. Joy and rage and wild animal gladness and shame become tangled together in the multicolored skein[2] of fourteen-going-on-fifteen as I recall that devastating moment when I was suddenly more woman than child, years ago in Miss Lottie's

20 yard. I think of those marigolds at the strangest times; I remember them vividly now as I desperately pass away the time. . . .

I suppose that futile waiting was the sorrowful background music of our impoverished little community when I was young. The Depression that gripped the nation was no new thing to us, for the black workers of rural Maryland had always been depressed. I don't know what it was that we were waiting for; certainly not for the prosperity that was "just around the corner," for those were white folks' words, which we never believed. Nor did we wait for hard work and thrift to pay off in shining success, as the American Dream promised, for we knew better than

30 that, too. Perhaps we waited for a miracle, amorphous[3] in concept but necessary if one were to have the grit to rise before dawn each day and labor in the white man's vineyard until after dark, or to wander about in the September dust offering one's sweat in return for some meager share of bread. But God was chary[4] with miracles in those days, and so we waited—and waited.

We children, of course, were only vaguely aware of the extent of our poverty. Having no radios, few newspapers, and no magazines, we were somewhat unaware of the world outside our community. Nowadays we would be called culturally deprived and people would write books and

40 hold conferences about us. In those days everybody we knew was just

---

1. **incongruency** (in′kän′grōō·ən·sē): inconsistency; lack of agreement or harmony.
2. **multicolored skein** (skān): The writer is comparing her many feelings to a long coiled piece (a skein) of many- ("multi-") colored yarn.
3. **amorphous** (ə·môr′fəs): vague, shapeless.
4. **chary** (cher′ē): not generous.

as hungry and ill clad as we were. Poverty was the cage in which we all were trapped, and our hatred of it was still the vague, undirected restlessness of the zoo-bred flamingo who knows that nature created him to fly free.

As I think of those days I feel most poignantly the tag end of summer, the bright, dry times when we began to have a sense of shortening days and the imminence of the cold.

By the time I was fourteen, my brother Joey and I were the only children left at our house, the older ones having left home for early
50 marriage or the lure of the city, and the two babies having been sent to relatives who might care for them better than we. Joey was three years younger than I, and a boy, and therefore vastly inferior. Each morning our mother and father trudged wearily down the dirt road and around the bend, she to her domestic job, he to his daily unsuccessful quest for work. After our few chores around the tumbledown shanty, Joey and I were free to run wild in the sun with other children similarly situated.

For the most part, those days are ill-defined in my memory, running together and combining like a fresh watercolor painting left out in the
60 rain. I remember squatting in the road drawing a picture in the dust, a picture which Joey gleefully erased with one sweep of his dirty foot. I remember fishing for minnows in a muddy creek and watching sadly as they eluded my cupped hands, while Joey laughed uproariously. And I remember, that year, a strange restlessness of body and of spirit, a feeling that something old and familiar was ending, and something unknown and therefore terrifying was beginning.

One day returns to me with special clarity for some reason, perhaps because it was the beginning of the experience that in some inexplicable[5] way marked the end of innocence. I was loafing under the great oak tree
70 in our yard, deep in some reverie which I have now forgotten, except that it involved some secret, secret thoughts of one of the Harris boys across the yard. Joey and a bunch of kids were bored now with the old tire suspended from an oak limb, which had kept them entertained for a while.

"Hey, Lizabeth," Joey yelled. He never talked when he could yell. "Hey, Lizabeth, let's go somewhere."

I came reluctantly from my private world. "Where you want to go? What you want to do?"

The truth was that we were becoming tired of the formlessness of
80 our summer days. The idleness whose prospect had seemed so beautiful during the busy days of spring now had degenerated to an almost desperate effort to fill up the empty midday hours.

---

5. **inexplicable** (in·eks′pli·kə·bəl): not explainable or understandable.

INTERPRET

The speaker uses two **metaphors** in lines 41–44. To what does she compare poverty, and to what does she compare the hatred of poverty? Underline the answers. What do the two metaphors have in common?

_____
_____
_____
_____
_____
_____

INTERPRET

What **internal conflict** does the narrator experience?

_____
_____
_____
_____

WORDS TO OWN
clarity (klar′ə·tē) *n.*: clearness.

_____
_____

INTERPRET

List three words to describe the **mood** of the children.

_____
_____
_____
_____
_____

"Let's go see can we find some locusts on the hill," someone suggested.

Joey was scornful. "Ain't no more locusts there. Y'all got 'em all while they was still green."

The argument that followed was brief and not really worth the effort. Hunting locust trees wasn't fun anymore by now.

"Tell you what," said Joey finally, his eyes sparkling. "Let's us go over to Miss Lottie's."

The idea caught on at once, for annoying Miss Lottie was always fun. I was still child enough to scamper along with the group over rickety fences and through bushes that tore our already raggedy clothes, back to where Miss Lottie lived. I think now that we must have made a tragicomic spectacle, five or six kids of different ages, each of us clad in only one garment—the girls in faded dresses that were too long or too short, the boys in patchy pants, their sweaty brown chests gleaming in the hot sun. A little cloud of dust followed our thin legs and bare feet as we tramped over the barren land.

When Miss Lottie's house came into view we stopped, ostensibly[6] to plan our strategy, but actually to reinforce our courage. Miss Lottie's house was the most ramshackle of all our ramshackle homes. The sun and rain had long since faded its rickety frame siding from white to a sullen gray. The boards themselves seemed to remain upright not from being nailed together but rather from leaning together, like a house that a child might have constructed from cards. A brisk wind might have blown it down, and the fact that it was still standing implied a kind of enchantment that was stronger than the elements. There it stood and as far as I know is standing yet—a gray, rotting thing with no porch, no shutters, no steps, set on a cramped lot with no grass, not even any weeds—a monument to decay.

In front of the house in a squeaky rocking chair sat Miss Lottie's son, John Burke, completing the impression of decay. John Burke was what was known as queer-headed. Black and ageless, he sat rocking day in and day out in a mindless stupor, lulled by the monotonous squeak-squawk of the chair. A battered hat atop his shaggy head shaded him from the sun. Usually John Burke was totally unaware of everything outside his quiet dream world. But if you disturbed him, if you intruded upon his fantasies, he would become enraged, strike out at you, and curse at you in some strange enchanted language which only he could understand. We children made a game of thinking of ways to disturb John Burke and then to elude his violent retribution.

But our real fun and our real fear lay in Miss Lottie herself. Miss Lottie seemed to be at least a hundred years old. Her big frame still held traces of the tall, powerful woman she must have been in youth, although it was

---

6. **ostensibly** (ä·sten′sə·blē): seemingly; apparently.

now bent and drawn. Her smooth skin was a dark reddish brown, and her face had Indian-like features and the stern stoicism[7] that one associates with Indian faces. Miss Lottie didn't like intruders either, especially children. She never left her yard, and nobody ever visited her. We never

130 knew how she managed those necessities which depend on human interaction—how she ate, for example, or even whether she ate. When we were tiny children, we thought Miss Lottie was a witch and we made up tales that we half believed ourselves about her exploits. We were far too sophisticated now, of course, to believe the witch nonsense. But old fears have a way of clinging like cobwebs, and so when we sighted the tumbledown shack, we had to stop to reinforce our nerves.

"Look, there she is," I whispered, forgetting that Miss Lottie could not possibly have heard me from that distance. "She's fooling with them crazy flowers."

140 "Yeh, look at 'er."

Miss Lottie's marigolds were perhaps the strangest part of the picture. Certainly they did not fit in with the crumbling decay of the rest of her yard. Beyond the dusty brown yard, in front of the sorry gray house, rose suddenly and shockingly a dazzling strip of bright blossoms, clumped together in enormous mounds, warm and passionate and sun-golden. The old black witch-woman worked on them all summer, every summer, down on her creaky knees, weeding and cultivating and arranging, while the house crumbled and John Burke rocked. For some perverse reason, we children hated those marigolds. They interfered with

150 the perfect ugliness of the place; they were too beautiful; they said too much that we could not understand; they did not make sense. There was something in the vigor with which the old woman destroyed the weeds that <u>intimidated</u> us. It should have been a comical sight—the old woman with the man's hat on her cropped white head, leaning over the bright mounds, her big backside in the air—but it wasn't comical, it was something we could not name. We had to annoy her by whizzing a pebble into her flowers or by yelling a dirty word, then dancing away from her rage, reveling in our youth and mocking her age. Actually, I think it was the flowers we wanted to destroy, but nobody had the nerve

160 to try it, not even Joey, who was usually fool enough to try anything.

"Y'all git some stones," commanded Joey now and was met with instant giggling obedience as everyone except me began to gather pebbles from the dusty ground. "Come on, Lizabeth."

I just stood there peering through the bushes, torn between wanting to join the fun and feeling that it was all a bit silly.

"You scared, Lizabeth?"

I cursed and spat on the ground—my favorite gesture of phony bravado. "Y'all children get the stones, I'll show you how to use 'em."

---

7. **stoicism** (stō′i·siz′əm): calm indifference to pleasure or pain.

INTERPRET

The narrator says that "old fears have a way of clinging like cobwebs," even when a person knows better. What does she mean?

_____

_____

_____

_____

_____

_____

_____

_____

_____

WORDS TO OWN
intimidated (in·tim′ə·dāt′id) v.: frightened.

_____

_____

INFER

Why do you think the children hate the marigolds?

_____

_____

_____

_____

_____

_____

_____

_____

EVALUATE

Reread lines 169–173. Is this a good explanation for what made the children so destructive? Why or why not?

_____

_____

_____

_____

_____

_____

_____

_____

WORDS TO OWN

impotent (im′pə·tənt) *adj.*: powerless; helpless.

BUILD FLUENCY

Read this passage aloud, using an appropriate tone, pace, and volume. Be sure to differentiate between dialogue and narrative and to use an expressive tone of voice for each character.

INTERPRET

What **internal conflict** can you identify in lines 203–204? Which two **external conflicts** seem related to the internal one?

_____

_____

_____

_____

_____

_____

_____

I said before that we children were not consciously aware of how
170 thick were the bars of our cage. I wonder now, though, whether we were not more aware of it than I thought. Perhaps we had some dim notion of what we were, and how little chance we had of being anything else. Otherwise, why would we have been so preoccupied with destruction? Anyway, the pebbles were collected quickly, and everybody looked at me to begin the fun.

"Come on, y'all."

We crept to the edge of the bushes that bordered the narrow road in front of Miss Lottie's place. She was working placidly, kneeling over the flowers, her dark hand plunged into the golden mound. Suddenly *zing*—
180 an expertly aimed stone cut the head off one of the blossoms.

"Who out there?" Miss Lottie's backside came down and her head came up as her sharp eyes searched the bushes. "You better git!"

We had crouched down out of sight in the bushes, where we stifled the giggles that insisted on coming. Miss Lottie gazed warily across the road for a moment, then cautiously returned to her weeding. *Zing*—Joey sent a pebble into the blooms, and another marigold was beheaded.

Miss Lottie was enraged now. She began struggling to her feet, leaning on a rickety cane and shouting. "Y'all git! Go on home!" Then the rest of the kids let loose with their pebbles, storming the flowers and
190 laughing wildly and senselessly at Miss Lottie's impotent rage. She shook her stick at us and started shakily toward the road crying, "Git 'long! John Burke! John Burke, come help!"

Then I lost my head entirely, mad with the power of inciting such rage, and ran out of the bushes in the storm of pebbles, straight toward Miss Lottie, chanting madly, "Old witch, fell in a ditch, picked up a penny and thought she was rich!" The children screamed with delight, dropped their pebbles, and joined the crazy dance, swarming around Miss Lottie like bees and chanting, "Old lady witch!" while she screamed curses at us. The madness lasted only a moment, for John Burke, startled
200 at last, lurched out of his chair, and we dashed for the bushes just as Miss Lottie's cane went whizzing at my head.

I did not join the merriment when the kids gathered again under the oak in our bare yard. Suddenly I was ashamed, and I did not like being ashamed. The child in me sulked and said it was all in fun, but the woman in me flinched at the thought of the malicious attack that I had led. The mood lasted all afternoon. When we ate the beans and rice that was supper that night, I did not notice my father's silence, for he was always silent these days, nor did I notice my mother's absence, for she always worked until well into evening. Joey and I had a particularly bitter argument after
210 supper; his exuberance got on my nerves. Finally I stretched out upon the pallet[8] in the room we shared and fell into a fitful doze.

_____

8. pallet: small bed or cot.

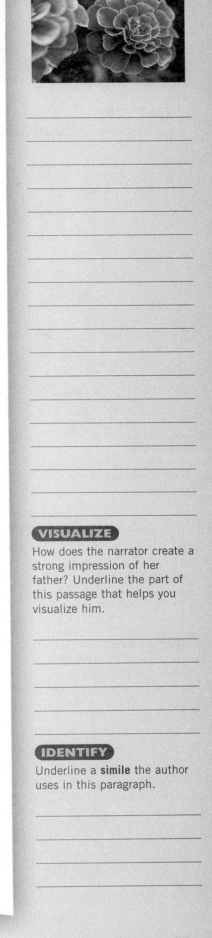

When I awoke, somewhere in the middle of the night, my mother had returned, and I vaguely listened to the conversation that was audible through the thin walls that separated our rooms. At first I heard no words, only voices. My mother's voice was like a cool, dark room in summer—peaceful, soothing, quiet. I loved to listen to it; it made things seem all right somehow. But my father's voice cut through hers, shattering the peace.

"Twenty-two years, Maybelle, twenty-two years," he was saying, 220 "and I got nothing for you, nothing, nothing."

"It's all right, honey, you'll get something. Everybody out of work now, you know that."

"It ain't right. Ain't no man ought to eat his woman's food year in and year out, and see his children running wild. Ain't nothing right about that."

"Honey, you took good care of us when you had it. Ain't nobody got nothing nowadays."

"I ain't talking about nobody else, I'm talking about *me.* God knows I try." My mother said something I could not hear, and my father cried 230 out louder, "What must a man do, tell me that?"

"Look, we ain't starving. I git paid every week, and Mrs. Ellis is real nice about giving me things. She gonna let me have Mr. Ellis's old coat for you this winter—"

"Damn Mr. Ellis's coat! And damn his money! You think I want white folks' leavings? Damn, Maybelle"—and suddenly he sobbed, loudly and painfully, and cried helplessly and hopelessly in the dark night. I had never heard a man cry before. I did not know men ever cried. I covered my ears with my hands but could not cut off the sound of my father's harsh, painful, despairing sobs. My father was a strong 240 man who could whisk a child upon his shoulders and go singing through the house. My father whittled toys for us, and laughed so loud that the great oak seemed to laugh with him, and taught us how to fish and hunt rabbits. How could it be that my father was crying? But the sobs went on, unstifled, finally quieting until I could hear my mother's voice, deep and rich, humming softly as she used to hum to a frightened child.

The world had lost its boundary lines. My mother, who was small and soft, was now the strength of the family; my father, who was the rock on which the family had been built, was sobbing like the tiniest 250 child. Everything was suddenly out of tune, like a broken accordion. Where did I fit into this crazy picture? I do not now remember my thoughts, only a feeling of great bewilderment and fear.

Long after the sobbing and humming had stopped, I lay on the pallet, still as stone with my hands over my ears, wishing that I too could cry and be comforted. The night was silent now except for the sound of the crickets and of Joey's soft breathing. But the room was too crowded with

fear to allow me to sleep, and finally, feeling the terrible aloneness of 4 A.M., I decided to awaken Joey.

260   "Ouch! What's the matter with you? What you want?" he demanded disagreeably when I had pinched and slapped him awake.

"Come on, wake up."

"What for? Go 'way."

I was lost for a reasonable reply. I could not say, "I'm scared and I don't want to be alone," so I merely said, "I'm going out. If you want to come, come on."

The promise of adventure awoke him. "Going out now? Where to, Lizabeth? What you going to do?"

I was pulling my dress over my head. Until now I had not thought of going out. "Just come on," I replied tersely.

270   I was out the window and halfway down the road before Joey caught up with me.

"Wait, Lizabeth, where you going?"

I was running as if the Furies[9] were after me, as perhaps they were—running silently and furiously until I came to where I had half known I was headed: to Miss Lottie's yard.

The half-dawn light was more eerie than complete darkness, and in it the old house was like the ruin that my world had become—foul and crumbling, a grotesque caricature. It looked haunted, but I was not afraid, because I was haunted too.

280   "Lizabeth, you lost your mind?" panted Joey.

I had indeed lost my mind, for all the smoldering emotions of that summer swelled in me and burst—the great need for my mother who was never there, the hopelessness of our poverty and degradation, the bewilderment of being neither child nor woman and yet both at once, the fear unleashed by my father's tears. And these feelings combined in one great impulse toward destruction.

"Lizabeth!"

I leaped furiously into the mounds of marigolds and pulled madly, trampling and pulling and destroying the perfect yellow blooms. The

290 fresh smell of early morning and of dew-soaked marigolds spurred me on as I went tearing and mangling and sobbing while Joey tugged my dress or my waist crying, "Lizabeth, stop, please stop!"

And then I was sitting in the ruined little garden among the uprooted and ruined flowers, crying and crying, and it was too late to undo what I had done. Joey was sitting beside me, silent and frightened, not knowing what to say. Then, "Lizabeth, look."

I opened my swollen eyes and saw in front of me a pair of large, calloused feet; my gaze lifted to the swollen legs, the age-distorted body

---

9. **Furies** (fyoor′ēz): in Greek and Roman mythology, spirits who pursue people who have committed crimes, sometimes driving them mad.

PREDICT

Pause here. What do you predict that Lizabeth may do?

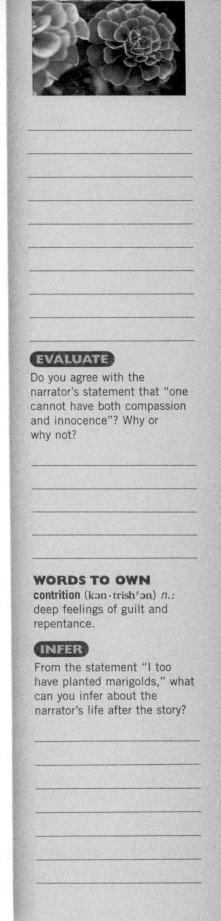

clad in a tight cotton nightdress, and then the shadowed Indian face
300 surrounded by stubby white hair. And there was no rage in the face now,
now that the garden was destroyed and there was nothing any longer to
be protected.

"M-miss Lottie!" I scrambled to my feet and just stood there and
stared at her, and that was the moment when childhood faded and
womanhood began. That violent, crazy act was the last act of childhood.
For as I gazed at the immobile face with the sad, weary eyes, I gazed
upon a kind of reality which is hidden to childhood. The witch was no
longer a witch but only a broken old woman who had dared to create
beauty in the midst of ugliness and sterility. She had been born in
310 squalor and lived in it all her life. Now at the end of that life she had
nothing except a falling-down hut, a wrecked body, and John Burke,
the mindless son of her passion. Whatever verve there was left in her,
whatever was of love and beauty and joy that had not been squeezed out
by life, had been there in the marigolds she had so tenderly cared for.

Of course I could not express the things that I knew about Miss Lottie
as I stood there awkward and ashamed. The years have put words to the
things I knew in that moment, and as I look back upon it, I know that
that moment marked the end of innocence. Innocence involves an
unseeing acceptance of things at face value, an ignorance of the area
320 below the surface. In that humiliating moment I looked beyond myself
and into the depths of another person. This was the beginning of
compassion, and one cannot have both compassion and innocence.

The years have taken me worlds away from that time and that place,
from the dust and squalor of our lives, and from the bright thing that I
destroyed in a blind, childish striking out at God knows what. Miss Lottie
died long ago and many years have passed since I last saw her hut,
completely barren at last, for despite my wild <u>contrition</u> she never
planted marigolds again. Yet, there are times when the image of those
passionate yellow mounds returns with a painful poignancy. For one
330 does not have to be ignorant and poor to find that his life is as barren
as the dusty yards of our town. And I too have planted marigolds.

EVALUATE

Do you agree with the narrator's statement that "one cannot have both compassion and innocence"? Why or why not?

WORDS TO OWN

contrition (kən·trish′ən) *n.*: deep feelings of guilt and repentance.

INFER

From the statement "I too have planted marigolds," what can you infer about the narrator's life after the story?

Internal Conflict

In **internal conflict,** a character struggles to resolve some personal problem, such as fear, shyness, anger, or anxiety. "Marigolds" includes a violent external confrontation between the children and Miss Lottie, as well as arguments between Lizabeth's parents and between Lizabeth and Joey. The main conflicts of the story, however, are internal, inside the mind and heart of fourteen-year-old Lizabeth.

What "personal monsters" are troubling Lizabeth? Fill out the chart to explore how Lizabeth reacts to and copes with the challenges listed.

Challenge	Lizabeth's Feelings
1. family's poverty	
2. relationship with Joey	
3. becoming a woman	
4. beauty of the marigolds	

Vocabulary: How to Own a Word

Word Maps

Create a word map for each Word to Own, using the model shown below. Fill in a synonym, an antonym, and the connotation—positive, negative, or neutral—of each Word to Own. Also provide the dictionary definition, and write a sentence using the word correctly. Be sure that the sentence you write reflects the connotation of the word.

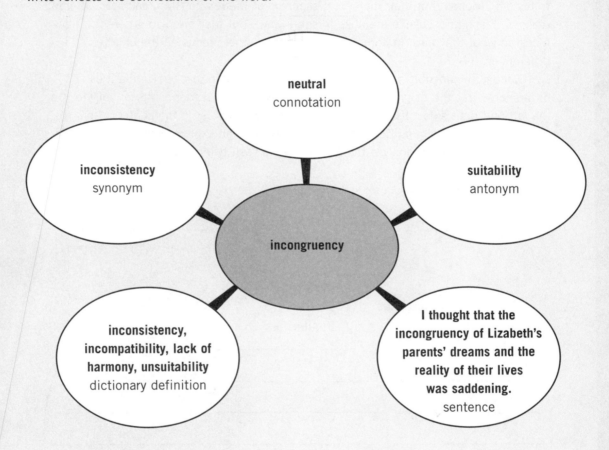

neutral
connotation

inconsistency
synonym

suitability
antonym

incongruency

inconsistency, incompatibility, lack of harmony, unsuitability
dictionary definition

I thought that the incongruency of Lizabeth's parents' dreams and the reality of their lives was saddening.
sentence

American History

Make the Connection

Alike and Different

In "American History," two young people named Elena and Eugene have the chance to become friends, but their mothers disapprove of the relationship, each for different reasons. Elena and Eugene are alike in some ways, but they are also different. They focus on what they have in common, while their mothers focus on the children's differences.

Since no two people are exactly alike, every friendship involves similarities and differences. Use the diagram below to apply this fact about friendship to real life. On the left and right sides, list differences between two friends; in the center, where the circles overlap, list similarities. On your diagram you can explore one of your own friendships, or you can analyze the friendship between two other people you know.

Friend A: Friend B:

(name)_____   (name)_____

Differences   **Differences**

Similarities

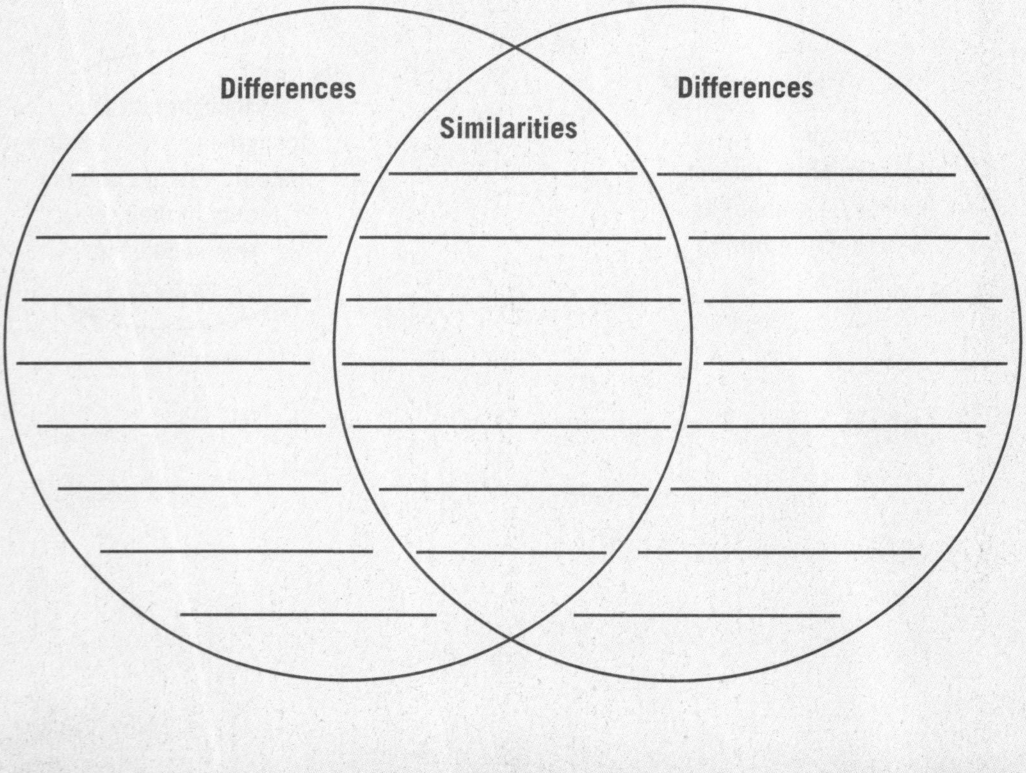

American History

Judith Ortiz Cofer

IDENTIFY

What did El Building sound like at almost any hour of the day? How does the narrator describe most of the residents? What day does the narrator focus on? Underline the answers.

IDENTIFY

Underline three details in lines 29–41 that give you insights into Elena's physical appearance and her **character**.

I once read in a "Ripley's Believe It or Not" column that Paterson, New Jersey, is the place where the Straight and Narrow (streets) intersect. The Puerto Rican tenement known as El Building was one block up on Straight. It was, in fact, the corner of Straight and Market; not "at" the corner, but the corner. At almost any hour of the day, El Building was like a monstrous jukebox, blasting out salsas from open windows as the residents, mostly new immigrants just up from the island, tried to drown out whatever they were currently enduring with loud music. But the day President Kennedy was shot, there was a profound silence in El Building;
10 even the abusive tongues of viragoes,[1] the cursing of the unemployed, and the screeching of small children had been somehow muted. President Kennedy was a saint to these people. In fact, soon his photograph would be hung alongside the Sacred Heart and over the spiritist altars that many women kept in their apartments. He would become part of the hierarchy of martyrs[2] they prayed to for favors that only one who had died for a cause would understand.

On the day that President Kennedy was shot, my ninth-grade class had been out in the fenced playground of Public School Number 13. We had been given "free" exercise time and had been ordered by our
20 PE teacher, Mr. DePalma, to "keep moving." That meant that the girls should jump rope and the boys toss basketballs through a hoop at the far end of the yard. He in the meantime would "keep an eye" on us from just inside the building.

It was a cold gray day in Paterson. The kind that warns of early snow. I was miserable, since I had forgotten my gloves and my knuckles were turning red and raw from the jump rope. I was also taking a lot of abuse from the black girls for not turning the rope hard and fast enough for them.

"Hey, Skinny Bones, pump it, girl. Ain't you got no energy today?"
30 Gail, the biggest of the black girls, had the other end of the rope, yelled, "Didn't you eat your rice and beans and pork chops for breakfast today?"

The other girls picked up the "pork chop" and made it into a refrain: "Pork chop, pork chop, did you eat your pork chop?" They entered the double ropes in pairs and exited without tripping or missing a beat. I felt a burning on my cheeks and then my glasses fogged up so that I could not manage to coordinate the jump rope with Gail. The chill was doing to me what it always did: entering my bones, making me cry, humiliating me. I hated the city, especially in winter. I hated Public School Number 13. I hated my skinny, flat-chested body, and I envied the black girls,
40 who could jump rope so fast that their legs became a blur. They always seemed to be warm, while I froze.

---

1. **viragoes** (vi·rā′gōz): quarrelsome women.
2. **hierarchy** (hī′ər·är′kē) **of martyrs** (märt′ərz): Martyrs are people who have suffered or died rather than give up their faith or principles; here, the author refers to martyrs who are honored and worshiped by Roman Catholics. Hierarchy means "ranking in order of importance."

There was only one source of beauty and light for me that school year—the only thing I had anticipated at the start of the semester. That was seeing Eugene. In August, Eugene and his family had moved into the only house on the block that had a yard and trees. I could see his place from my window in El Building. In fact, if I sat on the fire escape I was <u>literally</u> suspended above Eugene's back yard. It was my favorite spot to read my library books in the summer. Until that August the house had been occupied by an old Jewish couple. Over the years I had

50 become part of their family, without their knowing it, of course. I had a view of their kitchen and their back yard, and though I could not hear what they said, I knew when they were arguing, when one of them was sick, and many other things. I knew all this by watching them at mealtimes. I could see their kitchen table, the sink, and the stove. During good times, he sat at the table and read his newspapers while she fixed the meals. If they argued, he would leave and the old woman would sit and stare at nothing for a long time. When one of them was sick, the other would come and get things from the kitchen and carry them out on a tray. The old man had died in June. The last week of school I had

60 not seen him at the table at all. Then one day I saw that there was a crowd in the kitchen. The old woman had finally emerged from the house on the arm of a stocky middle-aged woman, whom I had seen there a few times before, maybe her daughter. Then a man had carried out suitcases. The house had stood empty for weeks. I had had to resist the temptation to climb down into the yard and water the flowers the old lady had taken such good care of.

By the time Eugene's family moved in, the yard was a tangled mass of weeds. The father had spent several days mowing, and when he finished, from where I sat I didn't see the red, yellow, and purple clusters

70 that meant flowers to me. I didn't see this family sit down at the kitchen table together. It was just the mother, a redheaded, tall woman who wore a white uniform—a nurse's, I guessed it was; the father was gone before I got up in the morning and was never there at dinner time. I only saw him on weekends, when they sometimes sat on lawn chairs under the oak tree, each hidden behind a section of the newspaper; and there was Eugene. He was tall and blond, and he wore glasses. I liked him right away because he sat at the kitchen table and read books for hours. That summer, before we had even spoken one word to each other, I kept him company on my fire escape.

80 Once school started, I looked for him in all my classes, but PS 13 was a huge, overpopulated place and it took me days and many discreet questions to discover that Eugene was in honors classes for all his subjects, classes that were not open to me because English was not my first language, though I was a straight-A student. After much maneuvering I managed to "run into him" in the hallway where his locker was—on

WORDS TO OWN
literally (lit′ər·əl·ē) *adv.:* actually; in fact.

PREDICT

What do the details in lines 42–47 suggest about the role that Eugene may play in the story?

_____

_____

_____

_____

_____

_____

_____

_____

_____

_____

_____

_____

_____

INTERPRET

How do lines 80–84 reinforce the **theme** of prejudice that was suggested earlier in the playground incident?

_____

_____

_____

_____

_____

_____

the other side of the building from mine—and in study hall at the library, where he first seemed to notice me but did not speak, and finally, on the way home after school one day when I decided to approach him directly, though my stomach was doing somersaults.

90   I was ready for rejection, snobbery, the worst. But when I came up to him, practically panting in my nervousness, and blurted out: "You're Eugene. Right?" he smiled, pushed his glasses up on his nose, and nodded. I saw then that he was blushing deeply. Eugene liked me, but he was shy. I did most of the talking that day. He nodded and smiled a lot. In the weeks that followed, we walked home together. He would linger at the corner of El Building for a few minutes, then walk down to his two-story house. It was not until Eugene moved into that house that I noticed that El Building blocked most of the sun and that the only spot that got a little sunlight during the day was the tiny square of earth the old woman had 100 planted with flowers.

I did not tell Eugene that I could see inside his kitchen from my bedroom. I felt dishonest, but I liked my secret sharing of his evenings, especially now that I knew what he was reading since we chose our books together at the school library.

One day my mother came into my room as I was sitting on the windowsill staring out. In her abrupt way she said: "Elena, you are acting 'moony.'" "Enamorada" was what she really said, that is—like a girl stupidly infatuated. Since I had turned fourteen . . . , my mother had been more vigilant than ever. She acted as if I was going to go crazy or explode 110 or something if she didn't watch me and nag me all the time about being a señorita now. She kept talking about virtue, morality, and other subjects that did not interest me in the least. My mother was unhappy in Paterson, but my father had a good job at the bluejeans factory in Passaic and soon, he kept assuring us, we would be moving to our own house there. Every Sunday we drove out to the suburbs of Paterson, Clifton, and Passaic, out to where people mowed grass on Sundays in the summer and where children made snowmen in the winter from pure white snow, not like the gray slush of Paterson, which seemed to fall from the sky in that hue. I had learned to listen to my parents' dreams, which were spoken 120 in Spanish, as fairy tales, like the stories about life in the island paradise of Puerto Rico before I was born. I had been to the island once as a little girl, to Grandmother's funeral, and all I remembered was wailing women in black, my mother becoming hysterical and being given a pill that made her sleep two days, and me feeling lost in a crowd of strangers all claiming to be my aunts, uncles, and cousins. I had actually been glad to return to the city. We had not been back there since then, though my parents talked constantly about buying a house on the beach someday, retiring on the island—that was a common topic among the residents of El Building. As for me, I was going to go to college and become a teacher.

IDENTIFY

What are two **internal conflicts** referred to in this passage? Underline the words giving the answer.

130   But after meeting Eugene I began to think of the present more than
of the future. What I wanted now was to enter that house I had watched
for so many years. I wanted to see the other rooms where the old people
had lived and where the boy spent his time. Most of all I wanted to sit at
the kitchen table with Eugene like two adults, like the old man and his
wife had done, maybe drink some coffee and talk about books. I had
started reading *Gone With the Wind*. I was enthralled by it, with the
daring and the passion of the beautiful girl living in a mansion, and with
her devoted parents and the slaves who did everything for them. I didn't
believe such a world had ever really existed, and I wanted to ask Eugene
140 some questions since he and his parents, he had told me, had come up
from Georgia, the same place where the novel was set. His father worked
for a company that had transferred him to Paterson. His mother was very
unhappy, Eugene said, in his beautiful voice that rose and fell over words
in a strange, lilting way. The kids at school called him "the Hick" and
made fun of the way he talked. I knew I was his only friend so far, and
I liked that, though I felt sad for him sometimes. "Skinny Bones and the
Hick" was what they called us at school when we were seen together.

    The day Mr. DePalma came out into the cold and asked us to line
up in front of him was the day that President Kennedy was shot. Mr.
150 DePalma, a short, muscular man with slicked-down black hair, was the
science teacher, PE coach, and disciplinarian at PS 13. He was the teacher
to whose homeroom you got assigned if you were a troublemaker, and
the man called out to break up playground fights and to escort violently
angry teenagers to the office. And Mr. DePalma was the man who called
your parents in for "a conference."

    That day, he stood in front of two rows of mostly black and Puerto
Rican kids, brittle from their efforts to "keep moving" on a November
day that was turning bitter cold. Mr. DePalma, to our complete shock,
was crying. Not just silent adult tears, but really sobbing. There were
160 a few titters from the back of the line where I stood shivering.

    "Listen," Mr. DePalma raised his arms over his head as if he were
about to conduct an orchestra. His voice broke, and he covered his face
with his hands. His barrel chest was heaving. Someone giggled behind me.

    "Listen," he repeated, "something awful has happened." A strange
gurgling came from his throat, and he turned around and spat on the
cement behind him.

    "Gross," someone said, and there was a lot of laughter.

    "The president is dead, you idiots. I should have known that wouldn't
mean anything to a bunch of losers like you kids. Go home." He was
170 shrieking now. No one moved for a minute or two, but then a big girl let
out a "Yeah!" and ran to get her books piled up with the others against
the brick wall of the school building. The others followed in a mad
scramble to get to their things before somebody caught on. It was still
an hour to the dismissal bell.

WORDS TO OWN
enthralled (en·thrôld') *v.:*
fascinated.

IDENTIFY
Where do Eugene and his
family come from? Circle the
answer.

_____

_____

_____

IDENTIFY
What nicknames are used for
Elena and Eugene at school?
Underline the answer.

INTERPRET
What impression do these
details give you of Mr.
DePalma's **character**?

_____

_____

_____

_____

_____

_____

_____

BUILD FLUENCY
Read the passage, noting how
Mr. DePalma is characterized.
Then, read lines 164–174
aloud, being sure to
distinguish between the
dialogue and the narrative. Use
an appropriate tone of voice
for each speaker in the
passage.

_____

_____

IDENTIFY

Underline four details that demonstrate the shock people felt when they heard that President Kennedy had been shot.

_____

_____

_____

IDENTIFY

What plans had Eugene and Elena made for this day? Underline the words giving the answer.

_____

_____

_____

_____

_____

_____

_____

_____

_____

INTERPRET

This is a key passage for the story's **theme**. What does Elena's mother understand that Elena, as yet, does not? Why does she permit Elena to go to Eugene's house anyway?

_____

_____

_____

_____

_____

_____

_____

A little scared, I headed for El Building. There was an eerie feeling on the streets. I looked into Mario's drugstore, a favorite hangout for the high school crowd, but there were only a couple of old Jewish men at the soda bar talking with the short-order cook in tones that sounded almost angry, but they were keeping their voices low. Even the traffic
180 on one of the busiest intersections in Paterson—Straight Street and Park Avenue—seemed to be moving slower. There were no horns blasting that day. At El Building, the usual little group of unemployed men was not hanging out on the front stoop making it difficult for women to enter the front door. No music spilled out from open doors in the hallway. When I walked into our apartment, I found my mother sitting in front of the grainy picture of the television set.

She looked up at me with a tear-streaked face and just said: "Dios mío," turning back to the set as if it were pulling at her eyes. I went into my room.
190 Though I wanted to feel the right thing about President Kennedy's death, I could not fight the feeling of elation that stirred in my chest. Today was the day I was to visit Eugene in his house. He had asked me to come over after school to study for an American history test with him. We had also planned to walk to the public library together. I looked down into his yard. The oak tree was bare of leaves and the ground looked gray with ice. The light through the large kitchen window of his house told me that El Building blocked the sun to such an extent that they had to turn lights on in the middle of the day. I felt ashamed about it. But the white kitchen table with the lamp hanging just above it looked
200 cozy and inviting. I would soon sit there, across from Eugene, and I would tell him about my perch just above his house. Maybe I should.

In the next thirty minutes I changed clothes, put on a little pink lipstick, and got my books together. Then I went in to tell my mother that I was going to a friend's house to study. I did not expect her reaction.

"You are going out _today_?" The way she said "today" sounded as if a storm warning had been issued. It was said in utter disbelief. Before I could answer, she came toward me and held my elbows as I clutched my books.

"Hija,[3] the president has been killed. We must show respect. He was
210 a great man. Come to church with me tonight."

She tried to embrace me, but my books were in the way. My first impulse was to comfort her, she seemed so distraught, but I had to meet Eugene in fifteen minutes.

"I have a test to study for, Mama. I will be home by eight."

"You are forgetting who you are, Niña.[4] I have seen you staring down at that boy's house. You are heading for humiliation and pain."

---

3. **hija** (ē'hä): Spanish for "daughter."
4. **niña** (nē'nyä): Spanish for "girl."

My mother said this in Spanish and in a resigned tone that surprised me, as if she had no intention of stopping me from "heading for humiliation and pain." I started for the door. She sat in front of the TV holding a
220 white handkerchief to her face.

I walked out to the street and around the chain-link fence that separated El Building from Eugene's house. The yard was neatly edged around the little walk that led to the door. It always amazed me how Paterson, the inner core of the city, had no apparent logic to its architecture. Small, neat single residences like this one could be found right next to huge, dilapidated apartment buildings like El Building. My guess was that the little houses had been there first, then the immigrants had come in droves, and the monstrosities had been raised for them—the Italians, the Irish, the Jews, and now us, the Puerto Ricans and the blacks.
230 The door was painted a deep green: verde, the color of hope. I had heard my mother say it: verde-esperanza.

I knocked softly. A few suspenseful moments later the door opened just a crack. The red, swollen face of a woman appeared. She had a halo of red hair floating over a delicate ivory face—the face of a doll—with freckles on the nose. Her smudged eye makeup made her look unreal to me, like a mannequin[5] seen through a warped store window.

"What do you want?" Her voice was tiny and sweet sounding, like a little girl's, but her tone was not friendly.

"I'm Eugene's friend. He asked me over. To study." I thrust out my
240 books, a silly gesture that embarrassed me almost immediately.

"You live there?" She pointed up to El Building, which looked particularly ugly, like a gray prison, with its many dirty windows and rusty fire escapes. The woman had stepped halfway out and I could see that she wore a white nurse's uniform with "St. Joseph's Hospital" on the name tag.

"Yes. I do."

She looked intently at me for a couple of heartbeats, then said as if to herself, "I don't know how you people do it." Then directly to me: "Listen. Honey. Eugene doesn't want to study with you. He is a smart
250 boy. Doesn't need help. You understand me. I am truly sorry if he told you you could come over. He cannot study with you. It's nothing personal. You understand? We won't be in this place much longer, no need for him to get close to people—it'll just make it harder for him later. Run back home now."

I couldn't move. I just stood there in shock at hearing these things said to me in such a honey-drenched voice. I had never heard an accent like hers, except for Eugene's softer version. It was as if she were singing me a little song.

---

5. **mannequin** (man′i·kin): life-size model of a person.

INFER

A **symbol** is a person, place, object, or event that stands for itself and for something beyond itself as well. Why might the color green be considered a symbol of hope?

EVALUATE

What do you think of Elena's response in lines 255–258? How would you feel if you were Elena, and why?

_____

_____

_____

_____

_____

_____

IDENTIFY

How does this passage (lines
275–279) relate to the **theme**
of the story?

_____

_____

_____

_____

_____

_____

_____

_____

_____

_____

_____

_____

_____

_____

_____

"What's wrong? Didn't you hear what I said?" She seemed very
260 angry, and I finally snapped out of my trance. I turned away from the
green door and heard her close it gently.

Our apartment was empty when I got home. My mother was in
someone else's kitchen, seeking the solace she needed. Father would
come in from his late shift at midnight. I would hear them talking softly
in the kitchen for hours that night. They would not discuss their dreams
for the future, or life in Puerto Rico, as they often did; that night they
would talk sadly about the young widow and her two children, as if
they were family. For the next few days, we would observe luto in our
apartment; that is, we would practice restraint and silence—no loud
270 music or laughter. Some of the women of El Building would wear black
for weeks.

That night, I lay in my bed trying to feel the right thing for our dead
president. But the tears that came up from a deep source inside me were
strictly for me. When my mother came to the door, I pretended to be
sleeping. Sometime during the night, I saw from my bed the streetlight
come on. It had a pink halo around it. I went to my window and pressed
my face to the cool glass. Looking up at the light, I could see the white
snow falling like a lace veil over its face. I did not look down to see it
turning gray as it touched the ground below.

Theme

The **theme** of a literary work is its central idea or underlying message about human life or behavior. In some works, such as fables, the theme is stated explicitly. Most often, however, the theme is implied or unstated. The reader must infer the theme from other elements, such as characterization and plot. Very often, a few key passages in a story help you to identify the theme.

As you go about the process of discovering a story's theme, keep in mind that not everyone sees the same theme in the same story.

Explore the theme of "American History" by re-reading the key passages listed below. On the right-hand side of the chart, comment briefly on how you think each passage relates to the story's central idea.

Key Passage	Relationship to Theme
1. Once school started, I looked for him in all my classes, but . . . it took me days . . . to discover that Eugene was in honors classes for all his subjects, classes that were not open to me because English was not my first language, though I was a straight-A student.	_____ _____ _____ _____ _____ _____ _____
2. "You are forgetting who you are, Niña. I have seen you staring down at that boy's house. You are heading for humiliation and pain."	_____ _____ _____ _____
3. Sometime during the night, I saw from my bed the streetlight come on. It had a pink halo around it. I went to my window and pressed my face to the cool glass. Looking up at the light, I could see the white snow falling like a lace veil over its face. I did not look down to see it turning gray as it touched the ground below.	_____ _____ _____ _____ _____ _____ _____

Vocabulary: How to Own a Word

Word Maps

Create a word map for each Word to Own, providing a synonym, an antonym, and the connotation—positive, negative, or neutral—of each Word to Own. Also provide the dictionary definition, and write a sentence using the word correctly. Be sure that the sentence you write reflects the connotation of the word. Follow the model shown below.

Word Bank
literally
infatuated
vigilant
enthralled
solace

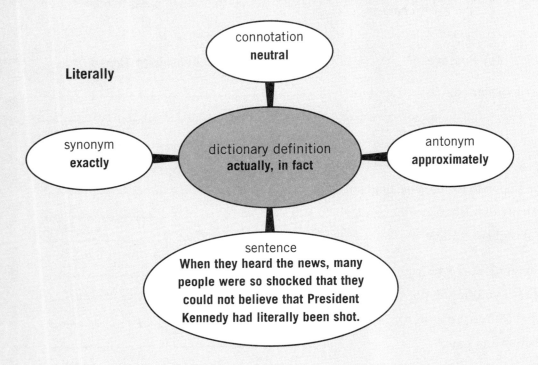

Literally

connotation
neutral

synonym
exactly

dictionary definition
actually, in fact

antonym
approximately

sentence
When they heard the news, many people were so shocked that they could not believe that President Kennedy had literally been shot.

Selection: _____

Understanding Theme

1. What is the *setting* of the story?

2. Who is (are) the main *character(s)?*

3. What central *conflict* does the main *character* face?

4. How does the main character face this conflict?

5. What statement does the selection make about life and/or human relationships?

6. Write one more complete sentence that expresses the *theme* of this literary work.

The Scarlet Ibis

Make the Connection

Moments in Time

The narrator of "The Scarlet Ibis" gives you portraits of his younger brother Doodle at different stages of his life. The story begins with Doodle's birth. Then we follow his growth as a baby, see him as a two-year-old, and finally learn about important events when he is five and six years old.

Have you ever stopped to consider how you yourself, or people you know well, have grown and changed over time? Take "word pictures" of moments in time—either for yourself and your feelings, or for a family member or friend you have known for a considerable period. In each empty box, write words, phrases, or dialogue that tells about or describes the person you have chosen.

Name: _____

Six years ago	Four years ago

Two years ago	Last year

James Hurst

The Scarlet Ibis

IDENTIFY

The first paragraph is full of vivid **images** that appeal to the senses. Circle one word that relates to each of the following: smell, sight, touch, and hearing.

_____

_____

_____

_____

_____

_____

_____

_____

INTERPRET

This paragraph (lines 18–30) reveals a shift in **style** and **tone.** What differences do you notice between this paragraph and the first two paragraphs of the story?

_____

_____

_____

_____

_____

_____

_____

_____

IDENTIFY

Why does Mama sob? Underline the words giving the answer.

_____

_____

_____

_____

It was in the clove of seasons, summer was dead but autumn had not yet been born, that the ibis lit in the bleeding tree. The flower garden was stained with rotting brown magnolia petals, and ironweeds grew rank[1] amid the purple phlox. The five o'clocks by the chimney still marked time, but the oriole nest in the elm was untenanted and rocked back and forth like an empty cradle. The last graveyard flowers were blooming, and their smell drifted across the cotton field and through every room of our house, speaking softly the names of our dead.

It's strange that all this is still so clear to me, now that that summer
10 has long since fled and time has had its way. A grindstone stands where the bleeding tree stood, just outside the kitchen door, and now if an oriole sings in the elm, its song seems to die up in the leaves, a silvery dust. The flower garden is prim, the house a gleaming white, and the pale fence across the yard stands straight and spruce. But sometimes (like right now), as I sit in the cool, green-draped parlor, the grindstone begins to turn, and time with all its changes is ground away—and I remember Doodle.

Doodle was just about the craziest brother a boy ever had. Of course, he wasn't a crazy crazy like old Miss Leedie, who was in love with
20 President Wilson and wrote him a letter every day, but was a nice crazy, like someone you meet in your dreams. He was born when I was six and was, from the outset, a disappointment. He seemed all head, with a tiny body which was red and shriveled like an old man's. Everybody thought he was going to die—everybody except Aunt Nicey, who had delivered him. She said he would live because he was born in a caul[2] and cauls were made from Jesus' nightgown. Daddy had Mr. Heath, the carpenter, build a little mahogany coffin for him. But he didn't die, and when he was three months old, Mama and Daddy decided they might as well name him. They named him William Armstrong, which was like tying a
30 big tail on a small kite. Such a name sounds good only on a tombstone.

I thought myself pretty smart at many things, like holding my breath, running, jumping, or climbing the vines in Old Woman Swamp, and I wanted more than anything else someone to race to Horsehead Landing, someone to box with, and someone to perch with in the top fork of the great pine behind the barn, where across the fields and swamps you could see the sea. I wanted a brother. But Mama, crying, told me that even if William Armstrong lived, he would never do these things with me. He might not, she sobbed, even be "all there." He might, as long as he lived, lie on the rubber sheet in the center of the bed in the front
40 bedroom where the white marquisette[3] curtains billowed out in the afternoon sea breeze, rustling like palmetto fronds.[4]

---

1. **rank:** thick and wild. *Rank* also means "smelly" or "overripe."
2. **caul:** membrane (thin, skinlike material) that sometimes covers a baby's head at birth.
3. **marquisette** (mär′ki·zet′): thin, netlike fabric.
4. **palmetto fronds:** fanlike leaves of a palm tree.

It was bad enough having an invalid brother, but having one who possibly was not all there was unbearable, so I began to make plans to kill him by smothering him with a pillow. However, one afternoon as I watched him, my head poked between the iron posts of the foot of the bed, he looked straight at me and grinned. I skipped through the rooms, down the echoing halls, shouting, "Mama, he smiled. He's all there! He's all there!" and he was.

50 **W**hen he was two, if you laid him on his stomach, he began to try to move himself, straining terribly. The doctor said that with his weak heart this strain would probably kill him, but it didn't. Trembling, he'd push himself up, turning first red, then a soft purple, and finally collapse back onto the bed like an old worn-out doll. I can still see Mama watching him, her hand pressed tight across her mouth, her eyes wide and unblinking. But he learned to crawl (it was his third winter), and we brought him out of the front bedroom, putting him on the rug before the fireplace. For the first time he became one of us.

As long as he lay all the time in bed, we called him William Armstrong, even though it was formal and sounded as if we were
60 referring to one of our ancestors, but with his creeping around on the deerskin rug and beginning to talk, something had to be done about his name. It was I who renamed him. When he crawled, he crawled backward, as if he were in reverse and couldn't change gears. If you called him, he'd turn around as if he were going in the other direction, then he'd back right up to you to be picked up. Crawling backward made him look like a doodlebug[5] so I began to call him Doodle, and in time even Mama and Daddy thought it was a better name than William Armstrong. Only Aunt Nicey disagreed. She said caul babies should be treated with special respect since they might turn out to be saints.
70 Renaming my brother was perhaps the kindest thing I ever did for him, because nobody expects much from someone called Doodle.

Although Doodle learned to crawl, he showed no signs of walking, but he wasn't idle. He talked so much that we all quit listening to what he said. It was about this time that Daddy built him a go-cart, and I had to pull him around. At first I just paraded him up and down the piazza,[6] but then he started crying to be taken out into the yard and it ended up by my having to lug him wherever I went. If I so much as picked up my cap, he'd start crying to go with me, and Mama would call from wherever she was, "Take Doodle with you."
80 He was a burden in many ways. The doctor had said that he mustn't get too excited, too hot, too cold, or too tired and that he must always be

---

5. doodlebug: larva of a type of insect; also, a shuttle train that goes back and forth between stations.
6. piazza: large covered porch.

IDENTIFY

The phrase "all there" is a colloquial expression meaning to be "sane and mentally healthy." How does the narrator know that Doodle is "all there"? Underline the words giving the answer.

INTERPRET

What **character** traits does the baby begin to show at the age of two?

_____

_____

_____

_____

_____

_____

_____

_____

_____

_____

EVALUATE

What do you think of the narrator's opinion that naming his little brother Doodle was a kind act?

_____

_____

_____

_____

_____

_____

_____

_____

treated gently. A long list of don'ts went with him, all of which I ignored once we got out of the house. To discourage his coming with me, I'd run with him across the ends of the cotton rows and careen him around corners on two wheels. Sometimes I accidentally turned him over, but he never told Mama. His skin was very sensitive, and he had to wear a big straw hat whenever he went out. When the going got rough and he had to cling to the sides of the go-cart, the hat slipped all the way down over his ears. He was a sight. Finally, I could see I was licked. Doodle

90　was my brother, and he was going to cling to me forever, no matter what I did, so I dragged him across the burning cotton field to share with him the only beauty I knew, Old Woman Swamp. I pulled the go-cart through the sawtooth fern, down into the green dimness where the palmetto fronds whispered by the stream. I lifted him out and set him down in the soft rubber grass beside a tall pine. His eyes were round with wonder as he gazed about him, and his little hands began to stroke the rubber grass. Then he began to cry.

　　"For heaven's sake, what's the matter?" I asked, annoyed.

　　"It's so pretty," he said. "So pretty, pretty, pretty."

100　　　After that day Doodle and I often went down into Old Woman Swamp. I would gather wildflowers, wild violets, honeysuckle, yellow jasmine, snakeflowers, and waterlilies, and with wire grass we'd weave them into necklaces and crowns. We'd bedeck ourselves with our handiwork and loll about thus beautified, beyond the touch of the everyday world. Then when the slanted rays of the sun burned orange in the tops of the pines, we'd drop our jewels into the stream and watch them float away toward the sea.

　　There is within me (and with sadness I have watched it in others) a knot of cruelty borne by the stream of love, much as our blood

110　sometimes bears the seed of our destruction, and at times I was mean to Doodle. One day I took him up to the barn loft and showed him his casket, telling him how we all had believed he would die. It was covered with a film of Paris green[7] sprinkled to kill the rats, and screech owls had built a nest inside it.

　　Doodle studied the mahogany box for a long time, then said, "It's not mine."

　　"It is," I said. "And before I'll help you down from the loft, you're going to have to touch it."

　　"I won't touch it," he said sullenly.

120　　"Then I'll leave you here by yourself," I threatened, and made as if I were going down.

　　Doodle was frightened of being left. "Don't go leave me, Brother," he cried, and he leaned toward the coffin. His hand, trembling, reached out, and when he touched the casket, he screamed. A screech owl flapped

---

7. Paris green: poisonous green powder used to kill insects

out of the box into our faces, scaring us and covering us with Paris green. Doodle was paralyzed, so I put him on my shoulder and carried him down the ladder, and even when we were outside in the bright sunshine, he clung to me, crying, "Don't leave me. Don't leave me."

When Doodle was five years old, I was embarrassed at having a
130 brother of that age who couldn't walk, so I set out to teach him. We were down in Old Woman Swamp and it was spring and the sick-sweet smell of bay flowers hung everywhere like a mournful song. "I'm going to teach you to walk, Doodle," I said.

He was sitting comfortably on the soft grass, leaning back against the pine. "Why?" he asked.

I hadn't expected such an answer. "So I won't have to haul you around all the time."

"I can't walk, Brother," he said.

"Who says so?" I demanded.

140 "Mama, the doctor—everybody."

"Oh, you can walk," I said, and I took him by the arms and stood him up. He collapsed onto the grass like a half-empty flour sack. It was as if he had no bones in his little legs.

"Don't hurt me, Brother," he warned.

"Shut up. I'm not going to hurt you. I'm going to teach you to walk." I heaved him up again, and again he collapsed.

This time he did not lift his face up out of the rubber grass. "I just can't do it. Let's make honeysuckle wreaths."

"Oh yes you can, Doodle," I said. "All you got to do is try. Now
150 come on," and I hauled him up once more.

It seemed so hopeless from the beginning that it's a miracle I didn't give up. But all of us must have something or someone to be proud of, and Doodle had become mine. I did not know then that pride is a wonderful, terrible thing, a seed that bears two vines, life and death. Every day that summer we went to the pine beside the stream of Old Woman Swamp, and I put him on his feet at least a hundred times each afternoon. Occasionally I too became discouraged because it didn't seem as if he was trying, and I would say, "Doodle, don't you *want* to learn to walk?"

160 He'd nod his head, and I'd say, "Well, if you don't keep trying, you'll never learn." Then I'd paint for him a picture of us as old men, white-haired, him with a long white beard and me still pulling him around in the go-cart. This never failed to make him try again.

Finally, one day, after many weeks of practicing, he stood alone for a few seconds. When he fell, I grabbed him in my arms and hugged him, our laughter pealing through the swamp like a ringing bell. Now we knew it could be done. Hope no longer hid in the dark palmetto thicket but perched like a cardinal in the lacy toothbrush tree, brilliantly visible.

IDENTIFY

In lines 129–137, the narrator gives two different reasons for wishing to teach Doodle to walk. Underline these reasons.

INTERPRET

Identify and explain the **symbol** for hope that the narrator uses in lines 167–168. How do the brothers now feel about Doodle's chances?

WORDS TO OWN
imminent (im′ə·nənt) *adj.:*
near; about to happen.

IDENTIFY

What date do the brothers
choose to reveal their secret?
Circle the words giving the
answer. Why might this date
be **symbolically** significant?

_____

_____

_____

_____

_____

_____

_____

_____

_____

_____

IDENTIFY

What **internal conflict** does
the narrator not reveal to his
family? Underline the answer.

_____

_____

_____

_____

INFER

Why do you think Doodle
tells fantastic lies?

_____

_____

_____

_____

_____

_____

_____

_____

"Yes, yes," I cried, and he cried it too, and the grass beneath us was soft
170 and the smell of the swamp was sweet.

With success so imminent, we decided not to tell anyone until he
could actually walk. Each day, barring rain, we sneaked into Old Woman
Swamp, and by cotton-picking time Doodle was ready to show what he
could do. He still wasn't able to walk far, but we could wait no longer.
Keeping a nice secret is very hard to do, like holding your breath. We
chose to reveal all on October eighth, Doodle's sixth birthday, and for
weeks ahead we mooned around the house, promising everybody a most
spectacular surprise. Aunt Nicey said that, after so much talk, if we
produced anything less tremendous than the Resurrection, she was going
180 to be disappointed.

At breakfast on our chosen day, when Mama, Daddy, and Aunt
Nicey were in the dining room, I brought Doodle to the door in the
go-cart just as usual and had them turn their backs, making them cross
their hearts and hope to die if they peeked. I helped Doodle up, and
when he was standing alone I let them look. There wasn't a sound as
Doodle walked slowly across the room and sat down at his place at the
table. Then Mama began to cry and ran over to him, hugging him and
kissing him. Daddy hugged him too, so I went to Aunt Nicey, who was
thanks-praying in the doorway, and began to waltz her around. We
190 danced together quite well until she came down on my big toe with her
brogans,[8] hurting me so badly I thought I was crippled for life.

Doodle told them it was I who had taught him to walk, so everyone
wanted to hug me, and I began to cry.

"What are you crying for?" asked Daddy, but I couldn't answer. They
did not know that I did it for myself; that pride, whose slave I was, spoke
to me louder than all their voices; and that Doodle walked only because
I was ashamed of having a crippled brother.

Within a few months Doodle had learned to walk well and his
go-cart was put up in the barn loft (it's still there) beside his little
200 mahogany coffin. Now, when we roamed off together, resting often, we
never turned back until our destination had been reached, and to help
pass the time, we took up lying. From the beginning Doodle was a
terrible liar, and he got me in the habit. Had anyone stopped to listen
to us, we would have been sent off to Dix Hill.

My lies were scary, involved, and usually pointless, but Doodle's
were twice as crazy. People in his stories all had wings and flew
wherever they wanted to go. His favorite lie was about a boy named
Peter who had a pet peacock with a ten-foot tail. Peter wore a golden
robe that glittered so brightly that when he walked through the sunflowers
210 they turned away from the sun to face him. When Peter was ready to
go to sleep, the peacock spread his magnificent tail, enfolding the boy

_____

8. brogans (brō′gənz): heavy ankle-high shoes.

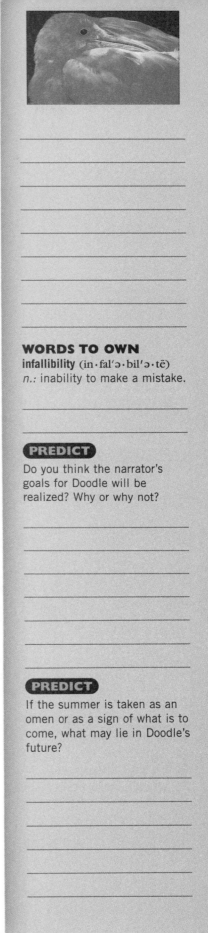

gently like a closing go-to-sleep flower, burying him in the gloriously iridescent,[9] rustling vortex.[10] Yes, I must admit it. Doodle could beat me lying.

Doodle and I spent lots of time thinking about our future. We decided that when we were grown, we'd live in Old Woman Swamp and pick dog's-tongue[11] for a living. Beside the stream, he planned, we'd build us a house of whispering leaves and the swamp birds would be our chickens. All day long (when we weren't gathering dog's-tongue)
220 we'd swing through the cypresses on the rope vines, and if it rained we'd huddle beneath an umbrella tree and play stickfrog. Mama and Daddy could come and live with us if they wanted to. He even came up with the idea that he could marry Mama and I could marry Daddy. Of course, I was old enough to know this wouldn't work out, but the picture he painted was so beautiful and serene that all I could do was whisper yes, yes.

Once I had succeeded in teaching Doodle to walk, I began to believe in my own <u>infallibility</u> and I prepared a terrific development program for him, unknown to Mama and Daddy, of course. I would
230 teach him to run, to swim, to climb trees, and to fight. He, too, now believed in my infallibility, so we set the deadline for these accomplishments less than a year away, when, it had been decided, Doodle could start to school.

That winter we didn't make much progress, for I was in school and Doodle suffered from one bad cold after another. But when spring came, rich and warm, we raised our sights again. Success lay at the end of summer like a pot of gold, and our campaign got off to a good start. On hot days, Doodle and I went down to Horsehead Landing, and I gave him swimming lessons or showed him how to row a boat. Sometimes
240 we descended into the cool greenness of Old Woman Swamp and climbed the rope vines or boxed scientifically beneath the pine where he had learned to walk. Promise hung about us like leaves, and wherever we looked, ferns unfurled and birds broke into song.

That summer, the summer of 1918, was blighted.[12] In May and June there was no rain and the crops withered, curled up, then died under the thirsty sun. One morning in July a hurricane came out of the east, tipping over the oaks in the yard and splitting the limbs of the elm trees. That afternoon it roared back out of the west, blew the fallen oaks around, snapping their roots and tearing them out of the earth like a

---

9. **iridescent** (ir′i·des′ənt): rainbowlike; displaying a shifting range of colors.
10. **vortex:** something resembling a whirlpool.
11. **dog's-tongue:** wild vanilla.
12. **blighted** (blīt′id): suffering from conditions that destroy or prevent growth.

WORDS TO OWN
infallibility (in·fal′ə·bil′ə·tē) *n.:* inability to make a mistake.

PREDICT
Do you think the narrator's goals for Doodle will be realized? Why or why not?

PREDICT
If the summer is taken as an omen or as a sign of what is to come, what may lie in Doodle's future?

THE SCARLET IBIS **121**

250 hawk at the entrails[13] of a chicken. Cotton bolls were wrenched from the stalks and lay like green walnuts in the valleys between the rows, while the cornfield leaned over uniformly so that the tassels touched the ground. Doodle and I followed Daddy out into the cotton field, where he stood, shoulders sagging, surveying the ruin. When his chin sank down onto his chest, we were frightened, and Doodle slipped his hand into mine. Suddenly Daddy straightened his shoulders, raised a giant knuckly fist, and with a voice that seemed to rumble out of the earth itself began cursing heaven, hell, the weather, and the Republican party.[14] Doodle and I, prodding each other and giggling, went back to the house,
260 knowing that everything would be all right.

And during that summer, strange names were heard through the house: Château-Thierry, Amiens, Soissons, and in her blessing at the supper table, Mama once said, "And bless the Pearsons, whose boy Joe was lost in Belleau Wood."[15]

So we came to that clove of seasons. School was only a few weeks away, and Doodle was far behind schedule. He could barely clear the ground when climbing up the rope vines, and his swimming was certainly not passable. We decided to double our efforts, to make that last drive and reach our pot of gold. I made him swim until he turned
270 blue and row until he couldn't lift an oar. Wherever we went, I purposely walked fast, and although he kept up, his face turned red and his eyes became glazed. Once, he could go no further, so he collapsed on the ground and began to cry.

"Aw, come on, Doodle," I urged. "You can do it. Do you want to be different from everybody else when you start school?"

"Does it make any difference?"

"It certainly does," I said. "Now, come on," and I helped him up.

As we slipped through the dog days, Doodle began to look feverish, and Mama felt his forehead, asking him if he felt ill. At night he didn't
280 sleep well, and sometimes he had nightmares, crying out until I touched him and said, "Wake up, Doodle. Wake up."

It was Saturday noon, just a few days before school was to start. I should have already admitted defeat, but my pride wouldn't let me. The excitement of our program had now been gone for weeks, but still we kept on with a tired doggedness. It was too late to turn back, for we had both wandered too far into a net of expectations and had left no crumbs behind.

Daddy, Mama, Doodle, and I were seated at the dining-room table having lunch. It was a hot day, with all the windows and doors open in case a breeze should come. In the kitchen Aunt Nicey was humming

INTERPRET

Where else did the narrator refer to the "clove of seasons"? Why do you think the narrator repeats this **metaphor** here?

WORDS TO OWN
doggedness (dôg′id·nis) *n.:* stubbornness; persistence.

---

13. **entrails** (en′trālz): inner organs; guts.
14. **Republican party:** At this time most Southern farmers were loyal Democrats.
15. **Château-Thierry** (shä′tō tē·er′ē), **Amiens** (á·myan′), **Soissons** (swä·sôn′), **Belleau** (be·lô′) **Wood:** World War I battle sites in France.

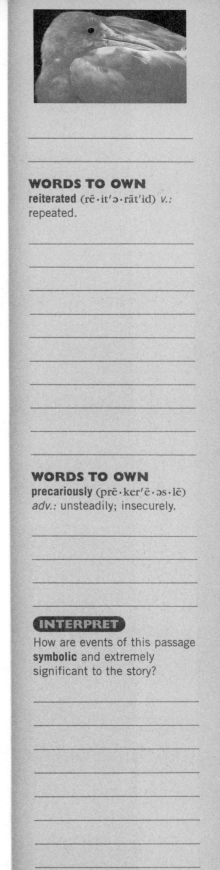

290 softly. After a long silence, Daddy spoke. "It's so calm, I wouldn't be surprised if we had a storm this afternoon."

"I haven't heard a rain frog," said Mama, who believed in signs, as she served the bread around the table.

"I did," declared Doodle. "Down in the swamp."

"He didn't," I said contrarily.

"You did, eh?" said Daddy, ignoring my denial.

"I certainly did," Doodle <u>reiterated</u>, scowling at me over the top of his iced-tea glass, and we were quiet again.

Suddenly, from out in the yard came a strange croaking noise.

300 Doodle stopped eating, with a piece of bread poised ready for his mouth, his eyes popped round like two blue buttons. "What's that?" he whispered.

I jumped up, knocking over my chair, and had reached the door when Mama called, "Pick up the chair, sit down again, and say excuse me."

By the time I had done this, Doodle had excused himself and had slipped out into the yard. He was looking up into the bleeding tree. "It's a great big red bird!" he called.

The bird croaked loudly again, and Mama and Daddy came out into the yard. We shaded our eyes with our hands against the hazy glare of

310 the sun and peered up through the still leaves. On the topmost branch a bird the size of a chicken, with scarlet feathers and long legs, was perched <u>precariously</u>. Its wings hung down loosely, and as we watched, a feather dropped away and floated slowly down through the green leaves.

"It's not even frightened of us," Mama said.

"It looks tired," Daddy added. "Or maybe sick."

Doodle's hands were clasped at his throat, and I had never seen him stand still so long. "What is it?" he asked.

Daddy shook his head. "I don't know, maybe it's—"

320 At that moment the bird began to flutter, but the wings were uncoordinated, and amid much flapping and a spray of flying feathers, it tumbled down, bumping through the limbs of the bleeding tree and landing at our feet with a thud. Its long, graceful neck jerked twice into an S, then straightened out, and the bird was still. A white veil came over the eyes, and the long white beak unhinged. Its legs were crossed and its clawlike feet were delicately curved at rest. Even death did not mar its grace, for it lay on the earth like a broken vase of red flowers, and we stood around it, awed by its exotic beauty.

"It's dead," Mama said.

330 "What is it?" Doodle repeated.

"Go bring me the bird book," said Daddy.

I ran into the house and brought back the bird book. As we watched, Daddy thumbed through its pages. "It's a scarlet ibis," he said, pointing

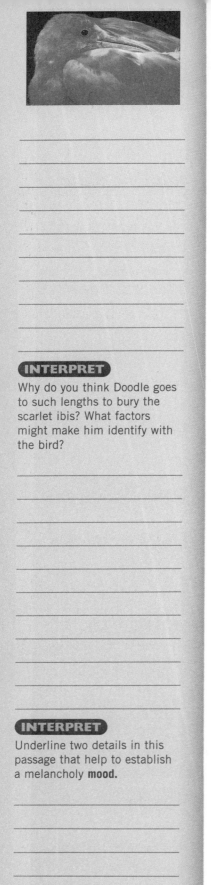

INTERPRET

Why do you think Doodle goes to such lengths to bury the scarlet ibis? What factors might make him identify with the bird?

INTERPRET

Underline two details in this passage that help to establish a melancholy **mood**.

to a picture. "It lives in the tropics—South America to Florida. A storm must have brought it here."

Sadly, we all looked back at the bird. A scarlet ibis! How many miles it had traveled to die like this, in *our* yard, beneath the bleeding tree.

"Let's finish lunch," Mama said, nudging us back toward the dining room.

340 "I'm not hungry," said Doodle, and he knelt down beside the ibis.

"We've got peach cobbler for dessert," Mama tempted from the doorway.

Doodle remained kneeling. "I'm going to bury him."

"Don't you dare touch him," Mama warned. "There's no telling what disease he might have had."

"All right," said Doodle. "I won't."

Daddy, Mama, and I went back to the dining-room table, but we watched Doodle through the open door. He took out a piece of string from his pocket and, without touching the ibis, looped one end around

350 its neck. Slowly, while singing softly "Shall We Gather at the River," he carried the bird around to the front yard and dug a hole in the flower garden, next to the petunia bed. Now we were watching him through the front window, but he didn't know it. His awkwardness at digging the hole with a shovel whose handle was twice as long as he was made us laugh, and we covered our mouths with our hands so he wouldn't hear.

When Doodle came into the dining room, he found us seriously eating our cobbler. He was pale and lingered just inside the screen door. "Did you get the scarlet ibis buried?" asked Daddy.

Doodle didn't speak but nodded his head.

360 "Go wash your hands, and then you can have some peach cobbler," said Mama.

"I'm not hungry," he said.

"Dead birds is bad luck," said Aunt Nicey, poking her head from the kitchen door. "Specially *red* dead birds!"

As soon as I had finished eating, Doodle and I hurried off to Horsehead Landing. Time was short, and Doodle still had a long way to go if he was going to keep up with the other boys when he started school. The sun, gilded with the yellow cast of autumn, still burned fiercely, but the dark green woods through which we passed were shady

370 and cool. When we reached the landing, Doodle said he was too tired to swim, so we got into a skiff and floated down the creek with the tide. Far off in the marsh a rail was scolding, and over on the beach locusts were singing in the myrtle trees. Doodle did not speak and kept his head turned away, letting one hand trail limply in the water.

After we had drifted a long way, I put the oars in place and made Doodle row back against the tide. Black clouds began to gather in the southwest, and he kept watching them, trying to pull the oars a little

faster. When we reached Horsehead Landing, lightning was playing
across half the sky and thunder roared out, hiding even the sound of the
380 sea. The sun disappeared and darkness descended, almost like night.
Flocks of marsh crows flew by, heading inland to their roosting trees,
and two egrets, squawking, arose from the oyster-rock shallows and
careened away.

> Doodle was both tired and frightened, and when he stepped from the
> skiff he collapsed onto the mud, sending an armada[16] of fiddler crabs
> rustling off into the marsh grass. I helped him up, and as he wiped the
> mud off his trousers, he smiled at me ashamedly. He had failed and we
> both knew it, so we started back home, racing the storm. We never
> spoke (what are the words that can solder[17] cracked pride?), but I knew
390 > he was watching me, watching for a sign of mercy. The lightning was
> near now, and from fear he walked so close behind me he kept stepping
> on my heels. The faster I walked, the faster he walked, so I began to run.
> The rain was coming, roaring through the pines, and then, like a bursting
> Roman candle, a gum tree ahead of us was shattered by a bolt of
> lightning. When the deafening peal of thunder had died, and in the
> moment before the rain arrived, I heard Doodle, who had fallen behind,
> cry out, "Brother, Brother, don't leave me! Don't leave me!"

The knowledge that Doodle's and my plans had come to naught was
bitter, and that streak of cruelty within me awakened. I ran as fast as I
400 could, leaving him far behind with a wall of rain dividing us. The drops
stung my face like nettles, and the wind flared the wet, glistening leaves
of the bordering trees. Soon I could hear his voice no more.

I hadn't run too far before I became tired, and the flood of childish
spite evanesced[18] as well. I stopped and waited for Doodle. The sound
of rain was everywhere, but the wind had died and it fell straight down
in parallel paths like ropes hanging from the sky. As I waited, I peered
through the downpour, but no one came. Finally I went back and found
him huddled beneath a red nightshade bush beside the road. He was
sitting on the ground, his face buried in his arms, which were resting on
410 his drawn-up knees. "Let's go, Doodle," I said.

He didn't answer, so I placed my hand on his forehead and lifted his
head. Limply, he fell backward onto the earth. He had been bleeding
from the mouth, and his neck and the front of his shirt were stained a
brilliant red.

"Doodle! Doodle!" I cried, shaking him, but there was no answer but
the ropy rain. He lay very awkwardly, with his head thrown far back,

---

16. **armada** (är·mä′də): group. *Armada* is generally used to mean "fleet, or group, of
   warships."
17. **solder** (säd′ər): patch or repair. Solder is a mixture of metals melted and used to repair
   metal parts.
18. **evanesced** (ev′ə·nest′): faded away; disappeared.

BUILD FLUENCY

Read this passage aloud.
Use a tone that captures
the elements of suspense,
expressive imagery, and
dialogue.

INTERPRET

How is this behavior consistent
with the narrator's earlier
treatment of Doodle?

VISUALIZE

Form a mental picture of the
events narrated in this passage.
What **mood** does the passage
create?

How does the description of Doodle's death resemble the description of the death of the ibis?

_____

_____

_____

_____

_____

_____

_____

_____

_____

_____

_____

_____

_____

_____

_____

_____

_____

_____

_____

_____

_____

_____

_____

making his vermilion[19] neck appear unusually long and slim. His little legs, bent sharply at the knees, had never before seemed so fragile, so thin.

420   I began to weep, and the tear-blurred vision in red before me looked very familiar. "Doodle!" I screamed above the pounding storm, and threw my body to the earth above his. For a long, long time, it seemed forever, I lay there crying, sheltering my fallen scarlet ibis from the heresy[20] of rain.

---

19. **vermilion** (vər·mil′yən): bright red.
20. **heresy** (her′i·sē): here, mockery. *Heresy* generally means "denial of what is commonly believed to be true" or "rejection of a church's teaching."

Symbol

A **symbol** is an object, a person, a place, or an event that functions as itself, but also stands for something more than itself. Symbols in literature may have different shades of meaning for each of us. We generally recognize literary symbols because of the emphasis and context a writer gives them. In James Hurst's story, the title, the elaborate description of the bird, and several other details make clear that the writer intends the scarlet ibis to be interpreted as symbolic.

In the story's final sentence, the narrator calls Doodle his "fallen scarlet ibis." In what ways could the ibis be a symbol for Doodle? Explore the author's use of symbolism by completing the chart below.

Questions	Answers
1. How do Doodle and the ibis resemble each other?	_____ _____ _____ _____
2. How are the deaths of Doodle and the ibis similar?	_____ _____ _____ _____
3. How does Doodle himself identify with the bird?	_____ _____ _____ _____
4. How are both Doodle and the ibis put into worlds where they can't survive?	_____ _____ _____ _____

Vocabulary: How to Own a Word

Making Meanings with Synonyms

Use a dictionary or a thesaurus to find a synonym for each Word to Own below, and write the synonym in the space provided. Next, write a sentence using context clues that make the synonym's meaning clear. An example is provided.

Word to Own	Synonym	Sentence
vermilion	red	The ibis, as red as a cherry, fell from the tree with a thud.
1. imminent	_____	_____ _____
2. infallibility	_____	_____ _____
3. doggedness	_____	_____ _____
4. precariously	_____	_____ _____
5. reiterated	_____	_____ _____

Selection: _____

Understanding Setting

Time

1. In what year, season, or month does the story take place? If you cannot tell, why do you think the author chose not to specify a time?

2. At what time of day does the story take place?

Place

3. Where is the story set? Give some specific details of this location.

Mood

4. What kind of mood does the setting evoke?

Meaning

5. To what extent does the setting contribute to the meaning of the story?

Not Much of Me *and* With a Task Before Me

Make the Connection

History Test

From biographies, history books, films, and television shows, you probably know more about President Abraham Lincoln than you realize. In these selections, you will learn about Lincoln from Lincoln himself—from his own words!

Before you read Lincoln's autobiographical essay and his brief speech, use the lines below to record your **prior knowledge,** or what you already know, about Lincoln. For example, you probably already know that Lincoln was president during the Civil War. What else? Do you know anything about his appearance, his family, or where he grew up? Do you know about the famous speeches he delivered? How did Lincoln die? Record your facts below.

Prior Knowledge Chart
President Abraham Lincoln

Not Much of Me

With a Task Before Me

Abraham Lincoln

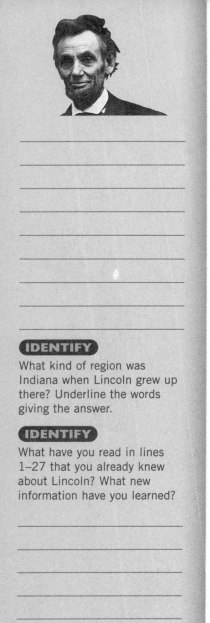

IDENTIFY

What kind of region was Indiana when Lincoln grew up there? Underline the words giving the answer.

IDENTIFY

What have you read in lines 1–27 that you already knew about Lincoln? What new information have you learned?

WORDS TO OWN
elated (ē·lāt'id) v. used as adj.: very happy.

Not Much of Me

I was born Feb. 12, 1809, in Hardin County, Kentucky. My parents were both born in Virginia, of undistinguished families—second families, perhaps I should say. My mother, who died in my tenth year, was of a family of the name of Hanks, some of whom now reside in Adams and others in Macon counties, Illinois. My paternal grandfather, Abraham Lincoln, emigrated from Rockingham County, Virginia, to Kentucky, about 1781 or 2, where, a year or two later, he was killed by indians, not in battle, but by stealth, when he was laboring to open a farm in the forest. His ancestors, who were quakers, went to Virginia from Berks
10 County, Pennsylvania. An effort to identify them with the New-England family of the same name ended in nothing more definite than a similarity of Christian names in both families, such as Enoch, Levi, Mordecai, Solomon, Abraham, and the like.

My father, at the death of his father, was but six years of age; and he grew up, litterally without education. He removed from Kentucky to what is now Spencer county, Indiana, in my eighth year. We reached our new home about the time the State came in the Union. It was a wild region, with many bears and other wild animals still in the woods. There I grew up. There were some schools, so called; but no qualification was
20 ever required of a teacher, beyond *"readin, writin, and cipherin,"* to the Rule of Three. If a straggler supposed to understand latin, happened to sojourn in the neighborhood, he was looked upon as a wizzard. There was absolutely nothing to excite ambition for education. Of course when I came of age I did not know much. Still somehow, I could read, write, and cipher to the Rule of Three; but that was all. I have not been to school since. The little advance I now have upon this store of education, I have picked up from time to time under the pressure of necessity.

I was raised to farm work, which I continued till I was twenty-two. At twenty-one I came to Illinois, and passed the first year in Illinois—
30 Macon county. Then I got to New-Salem, (at that time in Sangamon, now in Menard county), where I remained a year as a sort of Clerk in a store. Then came the Black-Hawk war;[1] and I was elected a Captain of Volunteers—a success which gave me more pleasure than any I have had since. I went the campaign, was <u>elated</u>, ran for the Legislature the same year (1832) and was beaten—the only time I have been beaten by the people. The next, and three succeeding biennial[2] elections, I was elected to the Legislature. I was not a candidate afterwards. During this Legislative period I had studied law, and removed to Springfield to practice

---

1. **Black-Hawk war**: war between the United States and the Sauk and Fox tribes in 1832. Black Hawk (1767–1838) was chief of the Sauk people and a leader in the war.
2. **biennial** (bī·en'ē·əl): happening every two years.

it. In 1846 I was once elected to the lower House of Congress. Was not
a candidate for re-election. From 1849 to 1854, both inclusive, practiced
law more <u>assiduously</u> than ever before. Always a whig[3] in politics, and
generally on the whig electoral tickets, making active canvasses.[4] I was
losing interest in politics, when the repeal of the Missouri Compromise[5]
aroused me again. What I have done since then is pretty well known.

If any personal description of me is thought desirable, it may be said,
I am, in height, six feet, four inches, nearly; lean in flesh, weighing, on
an average, one hundred and eighty pounds; dark complexion, with
coarse black hair, and grey eyes—no other marks or brands recollected.
Yours very truly,

—*Abraham Lincoln*

With a Task Before Me

My friends—No one, not in my situation, can appreciate my feeling of
sadness at this parting. To this place, and the kindness of these people,
I owe every thing. Here I have lived a quarter of a century, and have
passed from a young to an old man. Here my children have been born,
and one is buried. I now leave, not knowing when, or whether ever, I
may return, with a task before me greater than that which rested upon
Washington. Without the assistance of that Divine Being, who ever
attended him, I cannot succeed. With that assistance I cannot fail.
Trusting in Him, who can go with me, and remain with you and be
every where for good, let us confidently hope that all will yet be well.
To His care commending you, as I hope in your prayers you will
commend me, I bid you an affectionate farewell.

---

3. **whig**: Whigs favored a less powerful presidency than Democrats, but both parties split over
the question of slavery.
4. **canvasses**: requests for votes.
5. **Missouri Compromise**: agreement reached in 1820 admitting Maine to the Union as a free
state (one where slavery was illegal) and Missouri as a slave state, but limiting the creation
of other slave states to the area south of Missouri.

WORDS TO OWN
assiduously (ə·sij′o͞o·əs·lē)
adv.: industriously; in a careful
and hard-working manner.

INTERPRET
What words suggest a
comparison to livestock? What
tone does this choice of words
reveal?

IDENTIFY
Underline four details that
contribute to Lincoln's serious
and sad **tone** in this passage.

BUILD FLUENCY
Read the whole speech aloud,
using an appropriate tone of
voice.

Tone

The **tone** of a literary work is the attitude a writer takes toward the audience, a subject, or a character. In speech, tone is expressed through voice, body language, and word choice. In writing, tone is expressed primarily through an author's choice of words. A writer can be modest or boastful, satirical or sincere, comical or serious. When you read any piece of writing, you must be sensitive to the writer's tone. If you misunderstand the tone, you may fail to understand a work's central idea.

Which of the words on the chart below would you use to describe Lincoln's tone as he writes about himself in "Not Much of Me"? Circle the words that you think best describe the tone. Then, in the space provided, write details from the passage to support your answers.

The Writer's Tone		
bitter	critical	serious
playful	humorous	awed
regretful	affectionate	sad
nostalgic	humble	sarcastic

_____

_____

_____

_____

_____

_____

_____

_____

Vocabulary: How to Own a Word

Word Maps

Fill in the ovals below with a synonym, an antonym, and the connotation—positive, negative, or neutral—of the Word to Own. Also provide the dictionary definition, and write a sentence using the word correctly. Be sure that the sentence you write reflects the connotation of the word. If you think an oval does not apply, write "none." Parts of the maps have been done for you.

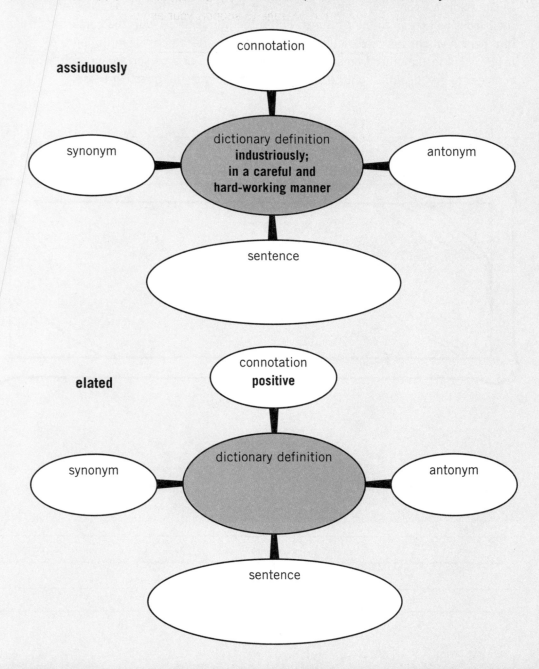

assiduously

- connotation
- synonym
- dictionary definition
  **industriously;
  in a careful and
  hard-working manner**
- antonym
- sentence

elated

- connotation
  positive
- synonym
- dictionary definition
- antonym
- sentence

The Talk

Make the Connection

People with Nice Faces

In Gary Soto's essay, both Gary and Scott are concerned with how they look and what their looks will mean to their futures. Fill in the mirror below with the personality traits of a person whom you or society at large might consider to be "beautiful on the inside." Fill in the outer frame with the physical traits of a person whom society might consider to be "beautiful on the outside." Then, answer the question below.

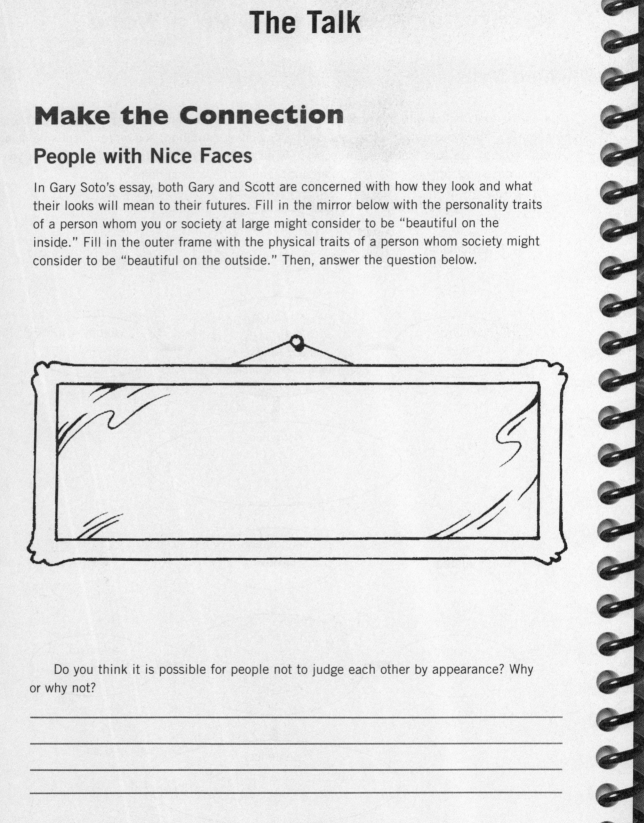

Do you think it is possible for people not to judge each other by appearance? Why or why not?

_____

_____

_____

_____

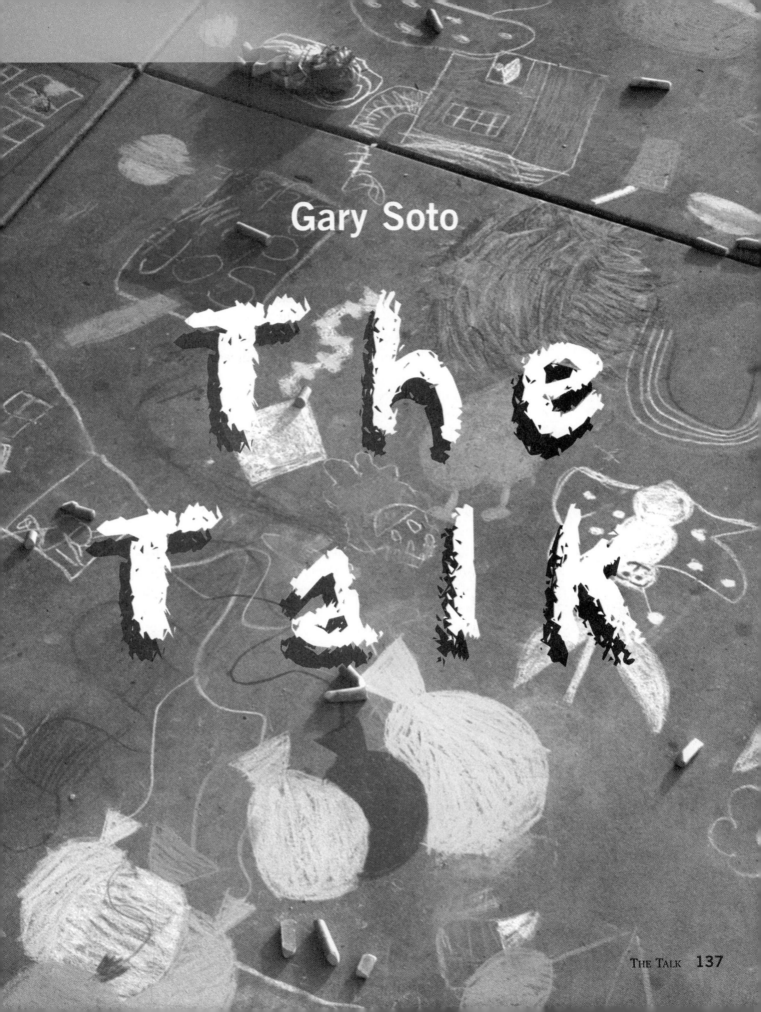

Gary Soto

The Talk

IDENTIFY

What do the boys consider their biggest problem? Underline the answer. Then, circle four details that Soto uses in the first paragraph to develop this **main idea**.

IDENTIFY

Underline the **figures of speech** used to describe the boys' twelve-year-old bodies.

INTERPRET

Do you think the narrator's arms really hang down almost to his kneecaps? Why does he exaggerate?

_____

_____

_____

_____

_____

_____

_____

_____

INFER

What inference can you make about the climate in the town where the boys live?

_____

_____

_____

_____

BUILD FLUENCY

Read this paragraph aloud, using an appropriate tone of voice for the narrator.

_____

_____

_____

_____

My best friend and I knew that we were going to grow up to be ugly. On a backyard lawn—the summer light failing west of the mulberry tree where the house of the most beautiful girl on our street stood—we talked about what we could do: shake the second-base dirt from our hair, wash our hands of frog smells and canal water, and learn to smile without showing our crooked teeth. We had to stop spitting when girls were looking and learn not to pile food onto a fork and into a fat cheek already churning hot grub.

10 We were twelve, with lean bodies that were beginning to grow in weird ways. First, our heads got large, but our necks wavered, frail as crisp tulips. The eyes stayed small as well, receding into pencil dots on each side of an unshapely nose that cast remarkable shadows when we turned sideways. It seemed that Scott's legs sprouted muscle and renegade veins, but his arms, blue with ink markings, stayed short and hung just below his waist. My gangly arms nearly touched my kneecaps. In this way, I was built for picking up grounders and doing cartwheels, my arms swaying just inches from the summery grass.

We sat on the lawn, with the porch light off, waiting for the beautiful girl to turn on her bedroom light and read on her stomach with one leg
20 stirring the air. This stirred us, and our dream was a clean dream of holding hands and airing out our loneliness by walking up and down the block.

When Scott asked whom I was going to marry, I said a brown girl from the valley. He said that he was going to marry a strawberry blonde who would enjoy Millerton Lake, dirty as it was. I said mine would like cats and the sea and would think nothing of getting up at night from a warm, restless bed and sitting in the yard under the icy stars. Scott said his wife would work for the first year or so, because he would go to trade school in refrigeration. Since our town was made with what was
30 left over after God made hell, there was money in air conditioning, he reasoned.

I said that while my wife would clean the house and stir pots of nice grub, I would drive a truck to my job as a carpenter, which would allow me to use my long arms. I would need only a stepladder to hand a fellow worker on the roof a pinch of nails. I could hammer, saw, lift beams into place, and see the work I got done at the end of the day. Of course, she might like to work, and that would be okay, because then we could buy two cars and wave at each other if we should see the other drive by. In the evenings, we would drink Kool-Aid and throw a slipper
40 at our feisty dog at least a hundred times before we went inside for a Pop-Tart and hot chocolate.

Scott said he would work hard too, but now and then he would find money on the street and the two of them could buy extra things like a second TV for the bedroom and a Doughboy swimming pool for his

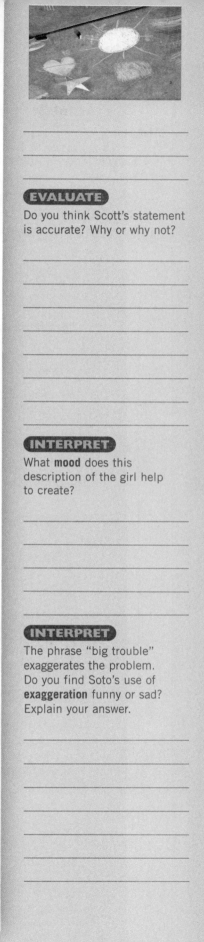

three kids. He planned on having three kids and a ranch house on the river, where he could dip a hand in the water, drink, and say, "Ahh, tastes good."

But that would be years later. Now we had to do something about our looks. We plucked at the grass and flung it into each other's faces.

50 "Rotten luck," Scott said. "My arms are too short. Look at 'em."

"Maybe we can lift weights. This would make up for our looks," I said.

"I don't think so," Scott said, depressed. "People like people with nice faces."

He was probably right. I turned onto my stomach, a stalk of grass in my mouth. "Even if I'm ugly, my wife's going to be good-looking," I said. "She'll have a lot of dresses and I'll have more shirts than I have now. Do you know how much carpenters make?"

Then I saw the bedroom light come on and the beautiful girl walk
60 into the room drying her hair with a towel. I nudged Scott's short arm and he saw what I saw. We flicked the stalks of grass, stood up, and walked over to the fence to look at her scrub her hair dry. She plopped onto the bed and began to comb it, slowly at first because it was tangled. With a rubber band, she tied it back, and picked up a book that was thick as a good-sized sandwich.

Scott and I watched her read a book, now both legs in the air and twined together, her painted toenails like red petals. She turned the pages slowly, very carefully, and now and then lowered her face into the pillow. She looked sad but beautiful, and we didn't know what to do
70 except nudge each other in the heart and creep away to the front yard.

"I can't stand it anymore. We have to talk about this," Scott said.

"If I try, I think I can make myself better looking," I said. "I read an article about a girl whitening her teeth with water and flour."

So we walked up the street, depressed. For every step I took, Scott took two, his short arms pumping to keep up. For every time Scott said, "I think we're ugly," I said two times, "Yeah, yeah, we're in big trouble."

EVALUATE

Do you think Scott's statement is accurate? Why or why not?

INTERPRET

What **mood** does this description of the girl help to create?

INTERPRET

The phrase "big trouble" exaggerates the problem. Do you find Soto's use of **exaggeration** funny or sad? Explain your answer.

Exaggeration

Exaggeration is deliberate overstatement of something to create a specific effect: for example, to express a strong emotion, to be funny, or to emphasize an idea. Writers have been amusing (and sometimes irritating) readers by making the most of exaggeration for thousands—make that billions—of years!

Explore Gary Soto's use of exaggeration by filling out the chart below. On the left are examples of exaggeration from the essay. On the right, comment on the purpose of the exaggeration and give your reaction to each example.

Essay Passage	Author's Purpose/My Reaction
1. The eyes stayed small as well, receding into pencil dots. . . .	
2. My gangly arms nearly touched my kneecaps.	
3. Since our town was made with what was left over after God made hell, there was money in air conditioning, he reasoned.	
4. For every time Scott said, "I think we're ugly," I said two times, "Yeah, yeah, we're in big trouble."	

Vocabulary: How to Own a Word

Analogies

An **analogy** shows the relationship between two pairs of words, stating the relationship in a sentence or expressing the relationship using symbols (: and ::).

There are many ways things can be related. The most common ways include the following:

- Degree
  pink is to red as lavender is to purple
  pink : red :: lavender : purple
- Size
  puddle : lake :: anthill : mountain
- Parts and wholes
  branch : tree :: petal : flower
- Cause and effect
  cold : shiver :: danger : tremble
- Synonyms
  brave : courageous :: friendly : amicable
- Antonyms
  brave : cowardly :: friendly : hostile

Complete the following analogies with the correct word from the group of choices given. Write the letter of the word in the space provided.

_____ **1.** renegade : turncoat :: warrior : ?

      a. lover   **b.** speaker   **c.** fighter   **d.** assistant

_____ **2.** gangly : coordinated :: clumsy : ?

      a. shy   **b.** unintelligent   **c.** eloquent   **d.** graceful

_____ **3.** feisty : frenzied :: comatose : ?

      a. sleepy   **b.** calm   **c.** bored   **d.** intrigued

_____ **4.** hungry : grub :: thirsty : ?

      a. water   **b.** inspiration   **c.** breakfast   **d.** pleasure

The Round Walls of Home

Make the Connection

Earth: Our Common Address

In this essay about the environment, Diane Ackerman comments, ". . . the twentieth century will be remembered as the time when we first began to understand what our address was." Sometimes it's hard to appreciate that everything on Earth is interconnected. Picture yourself on a journey in outer space. What might you think and feel as you look back at your home on Earth?

In the space below, list some global problems or issues that affect everyone on Earth. When you have completed your list, check the items you think pose the most serious danger to Earth's living things.

Global Problems/Issues

_____

_____

_____

_____

_____

_____

The Round Walls of Home

Diane Ackerman

WORDS TO OWN
oasis (ō·ā′sis) *n.:* fertile place. *Oasis* may also mean "place or thing offering welcome relief."

_____
_____
_____

WORDS TO OWN
intricate (in′tri·kit) *adj.:* elaborately detailed.

_____
_____

WORDS TO OWN
anthem (an′thəm) *n.:* song of praise. The writer imagines Earth's vivid greenness as a song of praise.
petitioner (pə·tish′ən·ər) *n.:* person seeking favors.

IDENTIFY
Underline four details the writer identifies with home in lines 18–28.

_____
_____
_____
_____

IDENTIFY
What information does the author give the reader about ecological damage in lines 39–44?

_____
_____
_____
_____
_____
_____

Picture this: everyone you've ever known, everyone you've ever loved, your whole experience of life, floating in one place, on a single planet underneath you. On that dazzling oasis, swirling with blues and whites, the weather systems form and travel. You watch the clouds tingle and swell above the Amazon and know the weather that develops there will affect the crop yield half a planet away in Russia and China. Volcanic eruptions make tiny spangles below. The rain forests are disappearing in Australia, Hawaii, and South America. You see dust bowls developing in Africa and the Near East. Remote sensing devices, judging the humidity
10 in the desert, have already warned you there will be plagues of locusts[1] this year. To your amazement, you identify the lights of Denver and Cairo. And though you were taught about them one by one, as separate parts of a jigsaw puzzle, now you can see that the oceans, the atmosphere, and the land are not separate at all, but part of an intricate recombining web of nature. Like Dorothy in *The Wizard of Oz*, you want to click your magic shoes together and say three times: "There's no place like home."

   You know what home is. For many years, you've tried to be a modest and eager watcher of the skies and of the Earth, whose green
20 anthem you love. Home is a pigeon strutting like a petitioner in the courtyard in front of your house. Home is the law-abiding hickories out back. Home is the sign on a gas station just outside Pittsburgh that reads "If we can't fix it, it ain't broke." Home is springtime on campuses all across America, where students sprawl on the grass like the war-wounded at Gettysburg.[2] Home is the Guatemalan jungle, at times deadly as an arsenal. Home is the pheasant barking hoarse threats at the neighbor's dog. Home is the exquisite torment of love and all the lesser mayhems of the heart. But what you long for is to stand back and see it whole. You want to live out that age-old yearning, portrayed in myths
30 and legends of every culture, to step above the Earth and see the whole world fidgeting and blooming below you.

   I remember my first flying lesson, in the doldrums of summer in upstate New York. Pushing the throttle forward, I zoomed down the runway until the undercarriage began to dance; then the ground fell away below and I was airborne, climbing up an invisible flight of stairs. To my amazement, the horizon came with me (how could it not, on a round planet?). For the first time in my life I understood what a valley was, as I floated above one at 7,000 feet. I could see plainly the devastation of the gypsy moth, whose hunger had leeched[3] the forests
40 to a mottled gray. Later on, when I flew over Ohio, I was saddened to

---

1. **plagues of locusts:** swarms of large grasshoppers that eat all plants in their path.
2. **Gettysburg:** town in Pennsylvania where a bloody Civil War battle was fought in 1863. Some 48,000 men were killed or wounded in the battle.
3. **leeched:** drained. Leeches are worms that suck blood.

discover the stagnant ocher[4] of the air, and to see that the long expanse of the Ohio River, dark and chunky, was the wrong texture for water, even flammable at times, thanks to the fumings of plastics factories, which I could also see, standing like pustules[5] along the river. I began to understand how people settle a landscape, in waves and at crossroads, how they survey a land and irrigate it. Most of all, I discovered that there are things one can learn about the world only from certain perspectives. How can you understand the ocean without becoming part of its intricate fathoms? How can you understand the planet without walking upon it, 50 sampling its marvels one by one, and then floating high above it, to see it all in a single eye-gulp?

Most of all, the twentieth century will be remembered as the time when we first began to understand what our address was. The "big, beautiful blue, wet ball" of recent years is one way to say it. But a more profound way will speak of the orders of magnitude of that bigness, the shades of that blueness, the arbitrary delicacy of beauty itself, the ways in which water has made life possible, and the fragile euphoria of the complex ecosystem[6] that is Earth, an Earth on which, from space, there are no visible fences, or military zones, or national borders. We need 60 to send into space a flurry of artists and naturalists, photographers and painters, who will turn the mirror upon ourselves and show us Earth as a single planet, a single organism that's buoyant, fragile, blooming, buzzing, full of spectacles, full of fascinating human beings, something to cherish. Learning our full address may not end all wars, but it will enrich our sense of wonder and pride. It will remind us that the human context is not tight as a noose, but large as the universe we have the privilege to inhabit. It will change our sense of what a neighborhood is. It will persuade us that we are citizens of something larger and more profound than mere countries, that we are citizens of Earth, her joy 70 riders and her caretakers, who would do well to work on her problems together. The view from space is offering us the first chance we evolutionary toddlers have had to cross the cosmic street and stand facing our own home, amazed to see it clearly for the first time.

---

4. **stagnant ocher** (stag′nənt ō′kər): foul dark yellow.
5. **pustules** (pus′tyo̅o̅lz′): pimples or blisters.
6. **ecosystem** (ek′ō·sis′təm): community of animals and plants and their physical and chemical environment.

WORDS TO OWN
euphoria (yo̅o̅·fôr′ē·ə)
n.: feeling of well-being.

INFER
What is the author's **main idea**?

BUILD FLUENCY
Read the final paragraph aloud. Practice reading the long sentences rhythmically and coherently, and be sure to determine the meanings of any unfamiliar words. In your reading, place additional emphasis on the author's main idea.

Exposition

Exposition is writing that explains a subject, provides information, or clarifies an idea. Exposition is an important ingredient in most kinds of nonfiction. Essayists, biographers, and autobiographers often combine exposition with narration and description.

Referring to lines in the selection, identify some passages from Diane Ackerman's essay that convey **facts** and some passages that express **opinions.** Then, on the lines provided, state whether you think Ackerman's **purpose** is mainly expository—explaining and informing—or whether you think she has a different aim.

Passages Conveying Facts

_____
_____
_____
_____
_____

Passages Expressing Opinions

_____
_____
_____
_____

Comment on Author's Purpose:

_____
_____
_____
_____
_____
_____
_____
_____
_____
_____
_____
_____
_____

Vocabulary: How to Own a Word

Synonyms and Antonyms

Word Bank
oasis
intricate
anthem
petitioner
euphoria

Below are five word pairs. The first word in each pair is a Word to Own. For each numbered pair, write **S** in the blank if the second word in the pair is a synonym of the Word to Own, or **A** if the word is an antonym. You may need a dictionary or a thesaurus for this activity.

_____ **1.** oasis / desert

_____ **2.** intricate / simple

_____ **3.** anthem / hymn

_____ **4.** petitioner / applicant

_____ **5.** euphoria / wretchedness

Now write five sentences using a different Word to Own in each sentence. Use context clues to make each word's meaning clear.

1. _____

_____

_____

2. _____

_____

_____

3. _____

_____

_____

4. _____

_____

_____

5. _____

_____

_____

From An Indian's Views of Indian Affairs

Make the Connection

KWL Chart

In 1877, Chief Joseph was exiled to a reservation in Oklahoma after he had led a three-month-long series of conflicts with federal troops. He spent the rest of his life trying to persuade the government to allow his people to return to their home.

Make a KWL chart like the one shown below. In the **K** column, write what you already *know* about Indian affairs. In the **W** column, write what you *want* to know—some questions you'd like answered. Complete the **L** column—what you have *learned*—after you read Chief Joseph's speech.

K	W	L

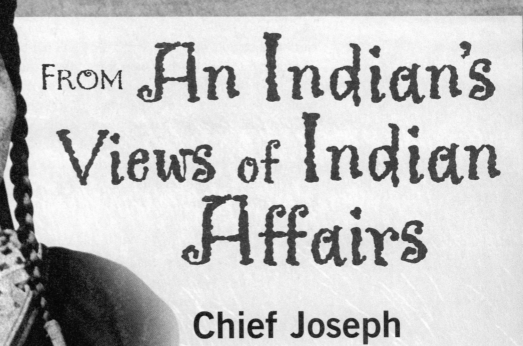

FROM *An Indian's Views of Indian Affairs*

Chief Joseph

INTERPRET

Underline the phrase that Chief Joseph repeats several times in this paragraph. Why do you think he repeats this phrase?

_____

_____

_____

_____

IDENTIFY

Underline three specific things the white man can do in order to live in peace with the Indian, according to Chief Joseph.

IDENTIFY

What logical appeals does Chief Joseph use in lines 20–25 to argue for the tribe's freedom? Underline them.

_____

_____

_____

_____

INTERPRET

What connotations or associations are suggested by the words *outlaws* and *animals*? What point is Chief Joseph making with these words?

_____

_____

_____

_____

_____

_____

_____

. . . **I** have heard talk and talk, but nothing is done. Good words do not last long unless they amount to something. Words do not pay for my dead people. They do not pay for my country, now overrun by white men. They do not protect my father's grave. They do not pay for all my horses and cattle. Good words will not give me back my children. Good words will not make good the promise of your war chief General Miles.[1] Good words will not give my people good health and stop them from dying. Good words will not get my people a home where they can live in peace and take care of themselves.

10   I am tired of talk that comes to nothing. It makes my heart sick when I remember all the good words and all the broken promises. There has been too much talking by men who had no right to talk. Too many misrepresentations have been made, too many misunderstandings have come up between the white men about the Indians.

    If the white man wants to live in peace with the Indian, he can live in peace. There need be no trouble. Treat all men alike. Give them the same law. Give them an even chance to live and grow. All men were made by the same Great Spirit Chief. They are all brothers. The earth is the mother of all people, and all people should have equal rights upon it.

20   You might as well expect the rivers to run backward as that any man who was born a free man should be contented when penned up and denied liberty to go where he pleases. If you tie a horse to a stake, do you expect he will grow fat? If you pen an Indian up on a small spot of earth and compel him to stay there, he will not be contented, nor will he grow and prosper. I have asked some of the great white chiefs where they get their authority to say to the Indian that he shall stay in one place while he sees white men going where they please. They cannot tell me.

    I only ask of the government to be treated as all other men are treated. If I cannot go to my own home, let me have a home in some 30 country where my people will not die so fast. . . .

    When I think of our condition, my heart is heavy. I see men of my race treated as outlaws and driven from country to country or shot down like animals.

I know that my race must change. We cannot hold our own with white men as we are. We ask only an even chance to live as other men live. We ask to be recognized as men. We ask that the same law shall work alike on all men. If the Indian breaks the law, punish him by the law. If the white man breaks the law, punish him also.

    Let me be a free man—free to travel, free to stop, free to work, free 40 to trade where I choose, free to choose my own teachers, free to follow

---

1. **General Miles:** Nelson Appleton Miles (1839–1925), an army officer who led many military campaigns against American Indians. In 1877, he led a campaign against the Nez Percé warriors and captured Chief Joseph.

the religion of my fathers, free to think and talk and act for myself—and I will obey every law or submit to the penalty.

Whenever white men treat Indians as they treat each other, then we will have no more wars. We shall all be alike—brothers of one father and one mother, with one sky above us and one country around us, and one government for all. Then the Great Spirit Chief who rules above will smile upon this land and send rain to wash out the bloody spots made by brothers' hands from the face of the earth.

50 For this time the Indian race is waiting and praying. I hope that no more groans of wounded men and women will ever go to the ear of the Great Spirit Chief above and that all people may be one people.

BUILD FLUENCY

Read the final two paragraphs aloud, using an appropriate tone and pace for the climax of Chief Joseph's speech.

EVALUATE

Are Chief Joseph's appeals for equality persuasive? How do you think his audience reacted to this speech?

_____

_____

_____

_____

_____

_____

_____

_____

_____

_____

_____

_____

_____

_____

_____

_____

_____

_____

_____

_____

Logical and Emotional Appeals

Persuasive writers use both logical and emotional appeals to convince the reader or listener to think or act in a certain way. A **logical appeal** uses reasons, facts, statistics, and examples to support an idea or claim. An **emotional appeal** uses words, phrases, and anecdotes that appeal strongly to the audience's feelings—to their fears, their hopes, and even their prejudices.

Identify each passage below as primarily a logical appeal or as an emotional appeal. Briefly explain each answer in the space provided.

Passage from Speech	Type of Appeal
1. It makes my heart sick when I remember all the good words and all the broken promises.	_____ _____ _____ _____
2. All men were made by the same Great Spirit Chief. They are all brothers. The earth is the mother of all people, and all people should have equal rights upon it.	_____ _____ _____ _____ _____ _____
3. If I cannot go to my own home, let me have a home in some country where my people will not die so fast. . . .	_____ _____ _____ _____
4. I see men of my race treated as outlaws and driven from country to country or shot down like animals.	_____ _____ _____ _____ _____
5. Whenever white men treat Indians as they treat each other, then we will have no more wars.	_____ _____ _____ _____

Vocabulary: How to Own a Word

Synonyms and Antonyms

Synonyms are words that have the same, or nearly the same, meaning. **Antonyms** are words that have opposite meanings. Complete the diagrams below. First, write a sentence correctly using the word given. Then, write one synonym, one antonym, and a sentence for each. You may need a dictionary to help you with this exercise. The first item has been partially completed for you.

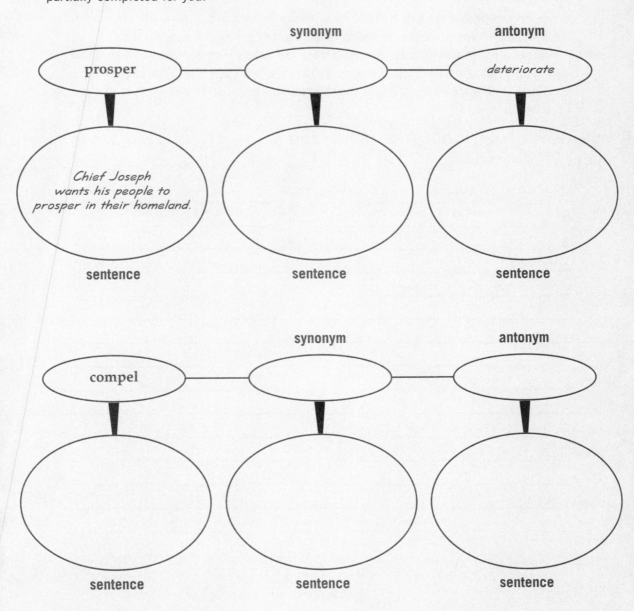

prosper

Chief Joseph wants his people to prosper in their homeland.

sentence

synonym

sentence

antonym

deteriorate

sentence

compel

sentence

synonym

sentence

antonym

sentence

Daily
I Wandered Lonely as a Cloud
Southbound on the Freeway

Make the Connection

Using Your Senses

Since no two people are exactly alike, your sense impressions of daily life are unique. At any given moment, no one is seeing, smelling, or hearing the way you are.

Make a list of five sounds, smells, tastes, and sights from your daily life that make you happy. Call your list "Daily," meaning "they happen every day." Identify the sense that each item appeals to. Then, in the space below your list, briefly explain why you chose each item.

DAILY

Items	Senses
1. _____	_____
2. _____	_____
3. _____	_____
4. _____	_____
5. _____	_____

_____

_____

_____

_____

_____

_____

_____

_____

_____

DAILY
Naomi Shihab Nye

I Wandered Lonely as a Cloud
William Wordsworth

Southbound on the Freeway
May Swenson

IDENTIFY

Underline five specific details connected with daily chores in lines 1–12.

_____

_____

_____

_____

_____

_____

_____

_____

_____

_____

_____

INTERPRET

What is the **metaphor** in line 21, and what might it mean? What is the **metaphor** in line 22, and what might it mean?

_____

_____

_____

_____

_____

_____

_____

_____

_____

_____

_____

_____

_____

_____

Daily

Naomi Shihab Nye

These shriveled seeds we plant,
corn kernel, dried bean,
poke into loosened soil,
cover over with measured fingertips
These T-shirts we fold
into perfect white
squares
These tortillas we slice and fry to crisp strips
This rich egg scrambled in a gray clay bowl
10 This bed whose covers I straighten
smoothing edges till blue quilt fits brown blanket
and nothing hangs out
This envelope I address
so the name balances like a cloud
in the center of the sky
This page I type and retype
This table I dust till the scarred wood shines
This bundle of clothes I wash and hang and wash again
like flags we share, a country so close
20 no one needs to name it
The days are nouns: touch them
The hands are churches that worship the world

I Wandered Lonely as a Cloud

William Wordsworth

I wandered lonely as a cloud
That floats on high o'er vales and hills,
When all at once I saw a crowd,
A host, of golden daffodils,
Beside the lake, beneath the trees,
Fluttering and dancing in the breeze.

Continuous as the stars that shine
And twinkle on the Milky Way,
They stretched in never-ending line
Along the margin of a bay;
Ten thousand saw I at a glance,
Tossing their heads in sprightly dance.

The waves beside them danced, but they
Outdid the sparkling waves in glee;
A poet could not but be gay,
In such a jocund[1] company;
I gazed—and gazed—but little thought
What wealth the show to me had brought:

For oft, when on my couch I lie
In vacant or in pensive mood,
They flash upon that inward eye
Which is the bliss of solitude;
And then my heart with pleasure fills,
And dances with the daffodils.

10

20

---

1. **jocund:** merry.

INTERPRET

What **figure of speech** is used in line 1? What do you think it means to be "lonely as a cloud"?

_____

_____

_____

_____

INTERPRET

What two things are **personified** in lines 11–14? What human qualities are they given?

_____

_____

_____

_____

_____

BUILD FLUENCY

Read the last stanza (lines 19–24) aloud. In your reading, focus on rhythm, rhyme, and units of meaning.

INTERPRET

What do you think is the speaker's message or **theme** in this poem? Use a complete sentence to state the theme.

_____

_____

_____

_____

_____

_____

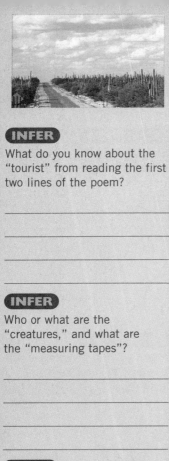

INFER

What do you know about the "tourist" from reading the first two lines of the poem?

_____

_____

_____

_____

INFER

Who or what are the "creatures," and what are the "measuring tapes"?

_____

_____

_____

_____

INFER

What is the 5-eyed creature?

_____

_____

_____

_____

_____

_____

_____

IDENTIFY

What **figure of speech** is used in lines 21–22? Explain the comparison.

_____

_____

_____

_____

_____

_____

_____

A tourist came in from Orbitville,
parked in the air, and said:

The creatures of this star
are made of metal and glass.

Through the transparent parts
you can see their guts.

Their feet are round and roll
on diagrams—or long

measuring tapes—dark
with white lines.   10

They have four eyes.
The two in the back are red.

Sometimes you can see a 5-eyed
one, with a red eye turning

on the top of his head.
He must be special—

the others respect him,
and go slow,

when he passes, winding
among them from behind.   20

They all hiss as they glide,
like inches, down the marked

tapes. Those soft shapes,
shadowy inside

the hard bodies—are they
their guts or their brains?

Imagery

Imagery is language that appeals to one or more of the five senses: sight, hearing, smell, taste, and touch. Imagery is an element in all types of writing, but it is especially important, vivid, and concentrated in poetry. Images are a product of every poet's unique way of perceiving and responding to the world. An image can be so fresh and so powerful that it speaks to our deepest feelings, prompting joy or grief, wonder or horror, love or disgust.

1. What do Nye's particular images in "Daily" tell you about the speaker's life and where she lives?

_____

_____

_____

_____

2. In "I Wandered Lonely as a Cloud," what sense does Wordsworth appeal to in most of the imagery? Give some examples from the text.

_____

_____

_____

3. In "Southbound on the Freeway," where does an image appeal to the sense of hearing?

_____

Vocabulary: How to Own a Word

Prefixes

A **prefix** is a word part added to the beginning of a root or base word. A prefix may change a word's meaning and its function as a part of speech. Use a dictionary to complete the chart below for words from the selections. The first item has been done for you.

Word	Definition	Prefix	Meaning of Prefix	Two Other Words with Same Prefix
retype	type again	re-	again; back	renew; return
continuous				
outdid				
inward				
transparent				

Selection: _____

Understanding Imagery

Sense Organ	Imagery Example

The Seven Ages of Man

Make the Connection

Life in Seven Acts

In the comedy *As You Like It,* Shakespeare's character Jaques compares a person's life to a play in seven acts. In the space provided below, write down what *you* think are the seven stages of a person's life. You might approach this activity by thinking about milestones or turning points: for example, birth, first day of school, graduation, first job, and so forth. On the left-hand side of the chart, list seven landmarks or milestones. Then, on the right-hand side, use two or three appropriate adjectives to describe each stage of life.

Milestones/Turning Points	Stage of Life
1.	
2.	
3.	
4.	
5.	
6.	
7.	

William Shakespeare

THE SEVEN AGES OF MAN

IDENTIFY

What does Shakespeare compare the world and its inhabitants to? Underline the words giving the answer.

INFER

In lines 13–15, what personality trait of the soldier does the speaker emphasize?

_____

_____

_____

IDENTIFY

Underline three physical characteristics that the speaker uses to describe the justice.

INFER

What would you say is the **mood** of the sixth and seventh stages?

_____

_____

_____

_____

_____

BUILD FLUENCY

Read this speech aloud, using appropriate pace, volume, and emphasis. Be sure to use the punctuation (or the lack of punctuation) at the ends of lines to identify units of meaning.

_____

_____

_____

_____

_____

_____

All the world's a stage,
And all the men and women merely players;
They have their exits and their entrances,
And one man in his time plays many parts,
His acts being seven ages. At first the infant,
Mewling and puking in the nurse's arms;
And then the whining schoolboy, with his satchel
And shining morning face, creeping like snail
Unwillingly to school. And then the lover,
10 Sighing like furnace, with a woeful ballad
Made to his mistress' eyebrow. Then a soldier,
Full of strange oaths, and bearded like the pard,[1]
Jealous in honor, sudden and quick in quarrel,
Seeking the bubble reputation
Even in the cannon's mouth. And then the justice,[2]
In fair round belly with good capon[3] lined,
With eyes severe and beard of formal cut,
Full of wise saws[4] and modern instances;
And so he plays his part. The sixth age shifts
20 Into the lean and slippered pantaloon,[5]
With spectacles on nose and pouch on side;
His youthful hose,[6] well saved, a world too wide
For his shrunk shank; and his big manly voice,
Turning again toward childish treble, pipes
And whistles in his sound. Last scene of all,
That ends this strange eventful history,
Is second childishness and mere oblivion,
Sans[7] teeth, sans eyes, sans taste, sans everything.

---

1. **pard:** leopard.
2. **justice:** judge.
3. **capon:** fat chicken.
4. **saws:** sayings.
5. **pantaloon:** silly old man.
6. **hose:** stockings.
7. **sans:** without.

Extended Metaphor

An **extended metaphor** is a comparison developed over several lines of a poem. In "The Seven Ages of Man," Shakespeare compares life to a play in seven acts. Then, he extends that metaphor to include actors for each part of life who play their part and then exit from the stage.

Look back at the notes you made before you read "The Seven Ages of Man." Then, try filling out a new chart such as the one below. Create a program identifying the actors you would choose to play you in each act of your life. In the first two columns, record the age you would be in each act and what role would be played. For example, in Act Four would you be a student or a young lawyer? In the last column, the people you choose to play you can be friends, relatives, television or movie actors, or characters from literature. After you complete the chart, answer the questions below.

My Life in Seven Acts	Cast of Characters	Played by
Act One:		
Act Two:		
Act Three:		
Act Four:		
Act Five:		
Act Six:		
Act Seven:		

1. What would you title this play about your life? Why?

_____

_____

_____

2. How do the seven acts of your play compare with the seven acts referred to in Shakespeare's poem?

_____

_____

_____

Fire and Ice
My Papa's Waltz
Harlem
"Hope" Is the Thing with Feathers

Make the Connection

Exploring Metaphors

In his poem "Fire and Ice," Robert Frost ponders two possible ways the world might end: in fire or in ice. Frost uses **metaphors,** or direct comparisons, to create vivid images of these two endings. He compares desire to fire and hatred to ice.

What do desire and fire have in common, and what do hate and ice have in common? Explore your ideas about these metaphors in the diagrams below. Explore how the elements and emotions evoked in each metaphor could lead to the type of tragedy Frost imagines.

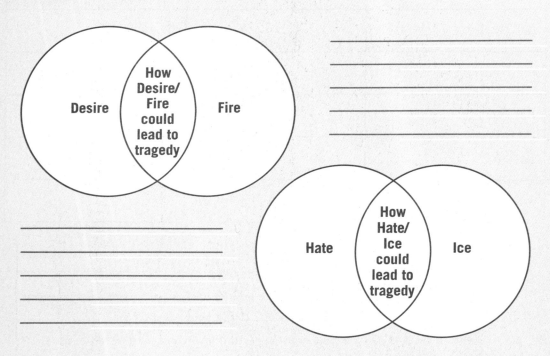

Fire and Ice
Robert Frost

My Papa's Waltz
Theodore Roethke

Harlem
Langston Hughes

"Hope" Is the Thing with Feathers
Emily Dickinson

INFER

With what emotion does the speaker indirectly compare fire? ice? What does the speaker suggest by saying that the world may end in either fire or ice?

_____

_____

_____

_____

_____

_____

INTERPRET

What is the effect of the word *suffice* at the end of the poem? What other word does it suggest?

_____

_____

_____

_____

_____

_____

_____

_____

_____

_____

_____

_____

_____

_____

Fire and Ice

Robert Frost

Some say the world will end in fire,
Some say in ice.
From what I've tasted of desire
I hold with those who favor fire.
But if it had to perish twice,
I think I know enough of hate
To say that for destruction ice
Is also great
And would suffice.

My Papa's Waltz

Theodore Roethke

The whiskey on your breath
Could make a small boy dizzy;
But I hung on like death:
Such waltzing was not easy.

We romped until the pans
Slid from the kitchen shelf;
My mother's countenance
Could not unfrown itself.

10

The hand that held my wrist
Was battered on one knuckle;
At every step you missed
My right ear scraped a buckle.

You beat time on my head
With a palm caked hard by dirt,
Then waltzed me off to bed
Still clinging to your shirt.

INTERPRET

How does the mother react to the antics of the father and son? Circle the words that let you know.

INTERPRET

Find the **similes** in lines 2–5 and tell what words or phrases you associate with each.

_____

_____

_____

_____

_____

_____

_____

INTERPRET

In the last line of the poem, Hughes uses an **implied metaphor** to identify the people who cherish the dream with the dream itself. Tell what the line means.

_____

_____

_____

_____

_____

_____

_____

_____

_____

_____

_____

_____

_____

_____

_____

_____

_____

Harlem

Langston Hughes

What happens to a dream deferred?

Does it dry up
like a raisin in the sun?
Or fester like a sore—
And then run?
Does it stink like rotten meat?
Or crust and sugar over—
like a syrupy sweet?

Maybe it just sags
10   like a heavy load.

Or does it explode?

"Hope" Is the Thing with Feathers

Emily Dickinson

"Hope" is the thing with feathers—
That perches in the soul—
And sings the tune without the words—
And never stops—at all—

And sweetest—in the Gale—is heard—
And sore must be the storm—
That could abash the little Bird
That kept so many warm—

I've heard it in the chillest land—
10   And on the strangest Sea—
Yet, never, in Extremity,
It asked a crumb—of Me.

IDENTIFY

What is the **denotation,** or literal dictionary definition, of the word *hope?*

_____

_____

_____

_____

INTERPRET

In lines 7–8, to what is Dickinson comparing hope? Why are the **connotations** of this comparison appropriate for the concept of hope?

_____

_____

_____

_____

_____

_____

_____

BUILD FLUENCY

Read this poem aloud. Focus especially on Dickinson's rhymes and her use of dashes for emphatic pauses.

_____

_____

_____

_____

_____

_____

_____

_____

Denotation and Connotation

Denotation is the literal dictionary definition of a word. **Connotations** are all the meanings, associations, or emotions suggested by a word. Whenever we use a word, we invoke its connotations—the associations or feelings attached to it. Poets are especially sensitive to the connotations of words.

Think about the words from "'Hope' Is the Thing with Feathers" listed below. Consider the context of each word, and then explore the denotations and connotations of the words by filling out the middle column and the right-hand column of the chart.

Word	Denotation	Connotation(s)
hope (line 1)		
sweetest (line 5)		
gale (line 5)		
storm (line 6)		
chillest (line 9)		
strangest (line 10)		
extremity (line 11)		

Vocabulary: How to Own a Word

Developing Vocabulary

Carefully read each word's definition, explanation, and sample sentence. Then, write a sentence of your own using that word.

1. countenance (koun′tə·nəns) *n.:*
a person's facial expression that shows emotions or thoughts.

- *Countenance* is a near synonym of *appearance*.

Denise's bright smile lit her countenance beautifully.

Original sentence:

_____

_____

2. fester (fes′tər) *v.:*
to putrefy, rot, or deteriorate.

- This word comes from the Latin *fistula*, which means both "pipe" and "ulcer."

The leaves that fell to the bottom of the pond began to fester.

Original sentence:

_____

_____

3. abash (ə·bash′) *v.:*
to disconcert or embarrass.

- The verb *abash* and the noun *abeyance*, which means "temporary inactivity or suspension," both come from the same Old French word for "to gape."

Hyun would try to abash his little sister by teasing her in front of her friends.

Original sentence:

_____

_____

The Road Not Taken
Lucinda Matlock

Make the Connection

Turning Points

There are at least two ways of thinking about turning points. For a missed opportunity that you regret, you might say, "If only I had chosen to . . . " For an important and productive decision, you might say, "I'm very glad I decided to . . ."

Think of a turning point in your life: for example, moving to a new place, meeting a special person, learning a sport, changing your mind about something, having someone help you at the right time. Go back to that moment and pretend it never happened. Then, on the chart below, explore the significance of the turning point. On the left-hand side of the chart, write notes about how your life might have been different if the moment had never occurred. On the right-hand side, write notes about the impact and the consequences of this particular turning point in your life.

Turning point: _____

How things might have been without this turning point	Impact and consequences of this turning point
_____	_____
_____	_____
_____	_____
_____	_____
_____	_____
_____	_____
_____	_____
_____	_____
_____	_____
_____	_____

The Road Not Taken

Robert Frost

Lucinda Matlock

Edgar Lee Masters

RETELL

Use your own words to summarize the first stanza. What is the **speaker's** situation?

_____
_____
_____
_____
_____
_____
_____
_____
_____
_____

INFER

Why do you think Frost titled this poem "The Road Not Taken," rather than "The Road Taken"?

_____
_____
_____
_____
_____
_____
_____
_____
_____
_____
_____
_____
_____
_____
_____
_____
_____

The Road Not Taken
Robert Frost

Two roads diverged in a yellow wood,
And sorry I could not travel both
And be one traveler, long I stood
And looked down one as far as I could
To where it bent in the undergrowth;

Then took the other, as just as fair,
And having perhaps the better claim,
Because it was grassy and wanted wear;
Though as for that the passing there
Had worn them really about the same,

10

And both that morning equally lay
In leaves no step had trodden black.
Oh, I kept the first for another day!
Yet knowing how way leads on to way,
I doubted if I should ever come back.

I shall be telling this with a sigh
Somewhere ages and ages hence:
Two roads diverged in a wood, and I—
I took the one less traveled by,
And that has made all the difference.

20

Lucinda Matlock

Edgar Lee Masters

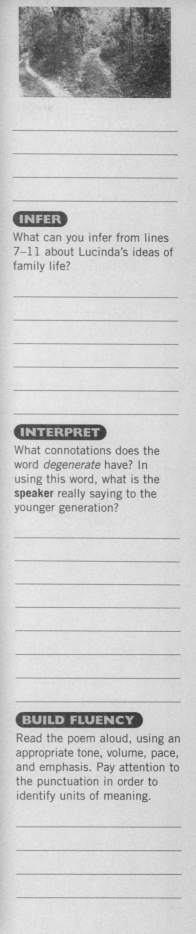

I went to the dances at Chandlerville,
And played snap-out at Winchester.
One time we changed partners,
Driving home in the moonlight of middle June,
And then I found Davis.
We were married and lived together for seventy years,
Enjoying, working, raising the twelve children,
Eight of whom we lost
Ere I had reached the age of sixty.
I spun, I wove, I kept the house, I nursed the sick,
I made the garden, and for holiday
Rambled over the fields where sang the larks,
And by Spoon River gathering many a shell
And many a flower and medicinal weed—
Shouting to the wooded hills, singing to the green valleys.
At ninety-six I had lived enough, that is all,
And passed to a sweet repose.
What is this I hear of sorrow and weariness,
Anger, discontent, and drooping hopes?
Degenerate sons and daughters,
Life is too strong for you—
It takes life to love Life.

10

20

INFER

What can you infer from lines 7–11 about Lucinda's ideas of family life?

INTERPRET

What connotations does the word *degenerate* have? In using this word, what is the **speaker** really saying to the younger generation?

BUILD FLUENCY

Read the poem aloud, using an appropriate tone, volume, pace, and emphasis. Pay attention to the punctuation in order to identify units of meaning.

Speaker

The **speaker** is the voice that is talking to us in a poem. Sometimes the speaker is identical to the poet, but often the speaker and the poet are not the same. The speaker, for example, may be speaking as a child, a woman, a man, a whole people, an animal, or even an object. Poets can imagine almost anyone or anything as the speaker in their poems. The **character** or personality of the speaker emerges from word choice, tone, figurative language, and imagery in the poem itself.

1. How would you describe the speaker in Robert Frost's "The Road Not Taken"? What tone does the speaker set in this poem? Briefly explain your answer.

_____

_____

_____

_____

_____

_____

_____

_____

2. What details in Edgar Lee Masters's "Lucinda Matlock" help you to imagine the speaker? How would you sum up her outlook on life?

_____

_____

_____

_____

_____

_____

_____

Vocabulary: How to Own a Word

Synonyms

Match each word in Column A with the correct synonym in Column B. Write the letter of the correct answer in the blank provided.

Column A

_____ **1.** diverged

_____ **2.** hence

_____ **3.** ere

_____ **4.** rambled

_____ **5.** repose

Column B

a. wandered

b. rest

c. separated

d. from this time forward

e. before

From The Tragedy of Romeo and Juliet

Make the Connection

To Be Young

Some adults criticize kids for being carefree, naive, and irresponsible: "Kids these days! They think that love conquers all and that nothing matters except the way they feel. They have no respect for tradition and no regard for their elders. They don't know that love can't solve all the problems in the world!"

How would you respond to criticisms like these? Take the point of view of a young person, and fill out the chart with ideas and arguments against the criticisms listed on the left-hand side.

Criticism	Response/Rebuttal
1. Kids are too carefree.	_____ _____ _____
2. Kids don't respect tradition.	_____ _____ _____
3. Kids are foolish and naive about the world.	_____ _____ _____
4. Kids disregard their elders.	_____ _____ _____

From The Tragedy of

Romeo and Juliet

William Shakespeare

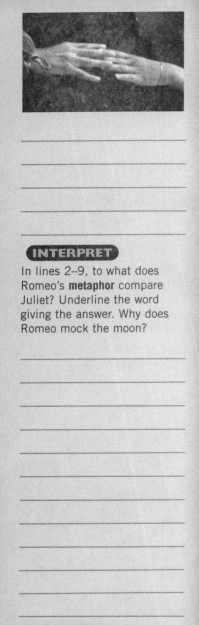

Act II, Scene 2

The balcony scene is one of the most famous scenes in all dramatic literature. In 190 magical lines, the two lovers woo and win each other.

Scene 2. *Capulet's Orchard*

Romeo *(coming forward).*

He jests at scars that never felt a wound.

[*Enter* JULIET *at a window.*]

But soft! What light through yonder window breaks?
It is the East, and Juliet is the sun!
Arise, fair sun, and kill the envious moon,
Who is already sick and pale with grief
That thou her maid[1] art far more fair than she.
Be not her maid, since she is envious.
Her vestal livery[2] is but sick and green,[3]
And none but fools do wear it. Cast it off.

10   It is my lady! O, it is my love!
O, that she knew she were!
She speaks, yet she says nothing. What of that?
Her eye discourses;[4] I will answer it.
I am too bold; 'tis not to me she speaks.
Two of the fairest stars in all the heaven,
Having some business, do entreat her eyes
To twinkle in their spheres till they return.
What if her eyes were there, they in her head?
The brightness of her cheek would shame those stars

20   As daylight doth a lamp; her eyes in heaven
Would through the airy region stream so bright
That birds would sing and think it were not night.
See how she leans her cheek upon her hand!
O, that I were a glove upon that hand,
That I might touch that cheek!

Juliet.   Ay me!

Romeo.   She speaks.

O, speak again, bright angel, for thou art
As glorious to this night, being o'er my head,
As is a wingèd messenger of heaven
Unto the white-upturnèd wond'ring eyes

---

1. **thou her maid:** Juliet, whom Romeo sees as the servant of the virgin goddess of the moon, Diana.
2. **vestal livery:** maidenly clothing.
3. **sick and green:** Unmarried girls supposedly had "greensickness," or anemia.
4. **discourses:** speaks.

Of mortals that fall back to gaze on him
When he bestrides the lazy puffing clouds
And sails upon the bosom of the air.

Juliet.

O Romeo, Romeo! Wherefore art thou Romeo?[5]
Deny thy father and refuse thy name;
Or, if thou wilt not, be but sworn my love,
And I'll no longer be a Capulet.

Romeo *(aside).*

Shall I hear more, or shall I speak at this?

Juliet.

'Tis but thy name that is my enemy.
Thou art thyself, though not[6] a Montague.
What's Montague? It is nor hand, nor foot,
Nor arm, nor face. O, be some other name
Belonging to a man.
What's in a name? That which we call a rose
By any other word would smell as sweet.
So Romeo would, were he not Romeo called,
Retain that dear perfection which he owes[7]
Without that title. Romeo, doff thy name;
And for thy name, which is no part of thee,
Take all myself.

Romeo. I take thee at thy word.
Call me but love, and I'll be new baptized;
Henceforth I never will be Romeo.

Juliet.

What man art thou, that, thus bescreened in night,
So stumblest on my counsel?[8]

Romeo. By a name
I know not how to tell thee who I am.
My name, dear saint, is hateful to myself
Because it is an enemy to thee.
Had I it written, I would tear the word.

Juliet.

My ears have yet not drunk a hundred words
Of thy tongue's uttering, yet I know the sound.
Art thou not Romeo, and a Montague?

Romeo.

Neither, fair maid, if either thee dislike.

---

5. In other words, "Why is your name Romeo?" (It is the name of her enemy.)
6. **though not:** even if you were not.
7. **owes:** owns.
8. **counsel:** private thoughts.

RETELL

Briefly summarize Juliet's speech in lines 38–49. According to Juliet, what is the true significance of a name?

IDENTIFY

What does Romeo call Juliet in line 55? Underline the answer.

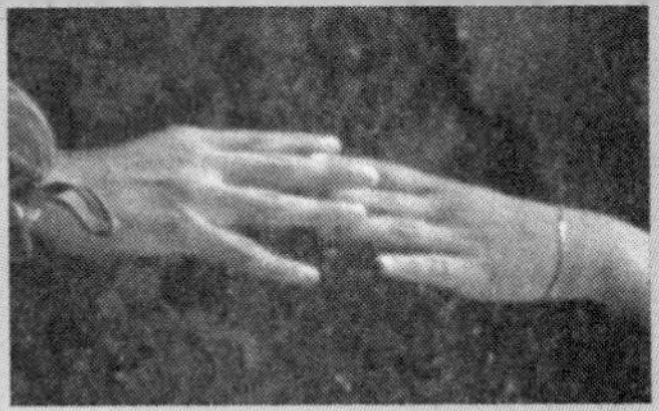

INTERPRET

What new complication threatens the lovers' happiness?

_____
_____
_____
_____
_____
_____
_____
_____
_____
_____
_____
_____
_____
_____
_____
_____

Juliet.

    How camest thou hither, tell me, and wherefore?

    The orchard walls are high and hard to climb,

    And the place death, considering who thou art,

    If any of my kinsmen find thee here.

Romeo.

    With love's light wings did I o'erperch[9] these walls;

    For stony limits cannot hold love out,

    And what love can do, that dares love attempt.

    Therefore thy kinsmen are no stop to me.

Juliet.

70   If they do see thee, they will murder thee.

Romeo.

    Alack, there lies more peril in thine eye

    Than twenty of their swords! Look thou but sweet,

    And I am proof[10] against their enmity.

Juliet.

    I would not for the world they saw thee here.

Romeo.

    I have night's cloak to hide me from their eyes;

    And but[11] thou love me, let them find me here.

    My life were better ended by their hate

    Than death proroguèd,[12] wanting of thy love.

Juliet.

    By whose direction found'st thou out this place?

Romeo.

80   By Love, that first did prompt me to inquire.

    He lent me counsel, and I lent him eyes.

    I am no pilot; yet, wert thou as far

    As that vast shore washed with the farthest sea,

    I should adventure for such merchandise.

INTERPRET

How does Shakespeare use **personification** in line 80? What comparison does the **simile** in lines 82–84 express?

_____
_____
_____
_____
_____
_____
_____
_____

Juliet.

    Thou knowest the mask of night is on my face;

    Else would a maiden blush bepaint my cheek

    For that which thou hast heard me speak tonight.

    Fain would I dwell on form—fain, fain deny

    What I have spoke; but farewell compliment.[13]

90   Dost thou love me? I know thou wilt say "Ay";

    And I will take thy word. Yet, if thou swear'st,

    Thou mayst prove false. At lovers' perjuries,

---

9. **o'erperch:** fly over.
10. **proof:** armored.
11. **but:** if only.
12. **proroguèd:** postponed.
13. **compliment:** good manners.

They say Jove laughs. O gentle Romeo,
If thou dost love, pronounce it faithfully.
Or if thou think'st I am too quickly won,
I'll frown and be perverse and say thee nay,
So thou wilt woo; but else, not for the world.
In truth, fair Montague, I am too fond,[14]
And therefore thou mayst think my havior[15] light;

100   But trust me, gentleman, I'll prove more true
Than those that have more cunning to be strange.[16]
I should have been more strange, I must confess,
But that thou overheard'st, ere I was ware,
My truelove passion. Therefore pardon me,
And not impute this yielding to light love,
Which the dark night hath so discoverèd.[17]

Romeo.

Lady, by yonder blessèd moon I vow,
That tips with silver all these fruit-tree tops—

Juliet.

O, swear not by the moon, the inconstant moon,

110   That monthly changes in her circle orb,
Lest that thy love prove likewise variable.

Romeo.

What shall I swear by?

Juliet.   Do not swear at all;
Or if thou wilt, swear by thy gracious self,
Which is the god of my idolatry,
And I'll believe thee.

Romeo.   If my heart's dear love—

Juliet.

Well, do not swear. Although I joy in thee,
I have no joy of this contract tonight.
It is too rash, too unadvised, too sudden;
Too like the lightning, which doth cease to be

120   Ere one can say it lightens. Sweet, good night!
This bud of love, by summer's ripening breath,
May prove a beauteous flower when next we meet.
Good night, good night! As sweet repose and rest
Come to thy heart as that within my breast!

Romeo.

O, wilt thou leave me so unsatisfied?

---

14. **fond:** affectionate, tender.
15. **havior:** behavior.
16. **strange:** aloof or cold.
17. **discoverèd:** revealed.

BUILD FLUENCY

Read this speech aloud. Where does Juliet shift from embarrassment to frankness, to pleading, to anxiety, to doubt? Why is she worried that Romeo will think poorly of her?

_____
_____
_____
_____
_____
_____

INTERPRET

If you were speaking lines 109–111, would you make them comic, or would you make Juliet sound genuinely frightened?

_____
_____
_____
_____
_____

INTERPRET

How does Shakespeare use **images** of light and darkness in lines 119-120 to **foreshadow** dangers to come?

_____
_____
_____
_____
_____
_____

INTERPRET

What does Juliet's response to Romeo in lines 131–136 reveal about her **character**?

INTERPRET

How does Juliet test Romeo's sincerity in lines 143–146?

Juliet.

What satisfaction canst thou have tonight?

Romeo.

The exchange of thy love's faithful vow for mine.

Juliet.

I gave thee mine before thou didst request it;
And yet I would it were to give again.

Romeo.

130   Wouldst thou withdraw it? For what purpose, love?

Juliet.

But to be frank[18] and give it thee again.
And yet I wish but for the thing I have.
My bounty[19] is as boundless as the sea,
My love as deep; the more I give to thee,
The more I have, for both are infinite.
I hear some noise within. Dear love, adieu!

[NURSE *calls within.*]

Anon, good nurse! Sweet Montague, be true.
Stay but a little, I will come again.   [*Exit.*]

Romeo.

O blessèd, blessèd night! I am afeard,
140   Being in night, all this is but a dream,
Too flattering-sweet to be substantial.

[*Enter* JULIET *again.*]

Juliet.

Three words, dear Romeo, and good night indeed.
If that thy bent[20] of love be honorable,
Thy purpose marriage, send me word tomorrow,
By one that I'll procure to come to thee,
Where and what time thou wilt perform the rite;
And all my fortunes at thy foot I'll lay
And follow thee my lord throughout the world.

Nurse (*within*). Madam!

Juliet.

150   I come anon.—But if thou meanest not well,
I do beseech thee—

18. **frank:** generous.
19. **bounty:** capacity for giving.
20. **bent:** intention.

Nurse (*within*). Madam!

Juliet.   By and by I come.—

>   To cease thy strife[21] and leave me to my grief.
>   Tomorrow will I send.

Romeo.   So thrive my soul—

Juliet.

>   A thousand times good night!   [*Exit.*]

Romeo.

>   A thousand times the worse, to want thy light!
>   Love goes toward love as schoolboys from their books;
>   But love from love, toward school with heavy looks.

[*Enter* JULIET *again.*]

Juliet.

>   Hist! Romeo, hist! O for a falc'ner's voice
> 160   To lure this tassel gentle[22] back again!
>   Bondage is hoarse[23] and may not speak aloud,
>   Else would I tear the cave where Echo[24] lies
>   And make her airy tongue more hoarse than mine
>   With repetition of "My Romeo!"

Romeo.

>   It is my soul that calls upon my name.
>   How silver-sweet sound lovers' tongues by night,
>   Like softest music to attending ears!

Juliet.

>   Romeo!

Romeo.

>   My sweet?

Juliet.   What o'clock tomorrow

>   Shall I send to thee?

Romeo.   By the hour of nine.

Juliet.

> 170   I will not fail. 'Tis twenty years till then.
>   I have forgot why I did call thee back.

Romeo.

>   Let me stand here till thou remember it.

Juliet.

>   I shall forget, to have thee still stand there,
>   Rememb'ring how I love thy company.

---

21. **strife:** efforts to win her.
22. **tassel gentle:** male falcon.
23. **Bondage is hoarse:** Juliet is in "bondage" to her parents and must whisper.
24. **Echo:** mythical girl who could only repeat others' final words.

BUILD FLUENCY

Read lines 159–167 aloud, using an appropriate tone of voice for the characters.

RETELL

Reread lines 177–182. Summarize Juliet's speech in your own words.

_____

_____

_____

_____

_____

_____

_____

IDENTIFY

Where does Romeo say he will go? Underline the words giving the answer.

_____

_____

_____

_____

_____

_____

_____

_____

_____

_____

_____

_____

_____

Romeo.

    And I'll still stay, to have thee still forget,

    Forgetting any other home but this.

Juliet.

    'Tis almost morning. I would have thee gone—

    And yet no farther than a wanton's[25] bird,

    That lets it hop a little from his hand,

180   Like a poor prisoner in his twisted gyves,[26]

    And with a silken thread plucks it back again,

    So loving-jealous of his liberty.

Romeo.

    I would I were thy bird.

Juliet.   Sweet, so would I.

    Yet I should kill thee with much cherishing.

    Good night, good night! Parting is such sweet sorrow

    That I shall say good night till it be morrow.   [*Exit.*]

Romeo.

    Sleep dwell upon thine eyes, peace in thy breast!

    Would I were sleep and peace, so sweet to rest!

    Hence will I to my ghostly friar's[27] close cell,

190   His help to crave and my dear hap[28] to tell.   [*Exit.*]

---

25. wanton's: careless child's.

26. gyves: chains, like the threads that hold the bird captive.

27. ghostly friar's: spiritual father's.

28. hap: luck.

Figurative Language

Figurative language is language that is not intended to be understood literally. Two of the most important figures of speech are simile and metaphor.

> • A **simile** uses words such as *like, as, than,* or *resembles* to compare two unlike things.
> EXAMPLE: "My bounty is as boundless as the sea" (line 133)
>
> • A **metaphor** directly compares two unlike things without using an explicit comparative word such as *like* or *as.*
> EXAMPLE: "Juliet is the sun" (line 3)

The similes and metaphors Shakespeare creates in Act II, Scene 2 of *Romeo and Juliet* (the balcony scene) elevate the young lovers' courtship to the realm of art. Reread the scene and write down, on the left side of the chart, three similes or metaphors the lovers use. On the right side of the chart, describe the comparison in each simile or metaphor. Then, answer the questions below.

Simile/Metaphor	Explanation
a. _____ _____	_____ _____
b. _____ _____	_____ _____
c. _____ _____	_____ _____

1. Of the similes or metaphors you listed above, which do you think is the most romantic— that is, the most unrealistic or idealized? Why?

_____

_____

_____

2. If Shakespeare were to write this scene today, what kinds of similes and metaphors would he use to describe Romeo and Juliet in love?

_____

_____

_____

Vocabulary: How to Own a Word

Developing Vocabulary

Carefully read each word's definition, explanation, and sample sentence. Then, write a sentence of your own using that word.

Word Bank
discourses
counsel
bounty

1. **discourses** (dis′kôrs′iz) *v.:* utters or speaks.

   When the professor discourses on her subject, students pay close attention.

   • This meaning of *discourse* is now archaic, but the word is presently used as a noun to mean "communication of ideas and information" or "a lecture."

   Original sentence:

   _____

   _____

2. **counsel** (koun′səl) *n.:* private thoughts, secret plan.

   Even in the face of threats, the man obstinately kept his counsel.

   • This meaning of *counsel* is rarely used today, except in the expression "to keep one's own counsel," meaning "to keep one's thoughts and plans to oneself."

   Original sentence:

   _____

   _____

3. **bounty** (boun′tē) *n.:* capacity for giving generously.

   The mistress of the castle was much loved for her bounty at holiday time.

   • *Bounty* can also mean "a generous gift," as well as "a reward given by the government for raising certain crops, capturing criminals, etc."

   Original sentence:

   _____

   _____

Act III, Scene 5

After ROMEO *kills* TYBALT *in a duel, he is banished. He and* JULIET
take their final farewell before he leaves for Mantua. JULIET'S
father, LORD CAPULET, *has assured the young suitor,* PARIS, *that*
JULIET *will marry him, and the wedding date is set.*

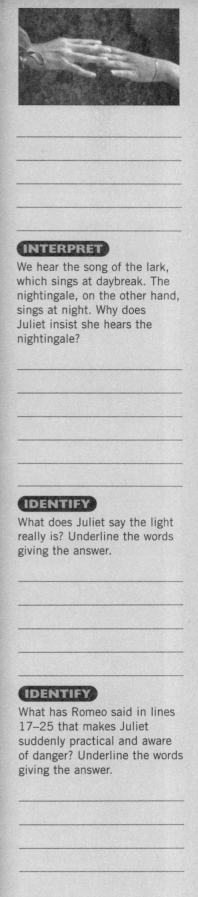

Scene 5. *Capulet's orchard.*

Enter ROMEO *and* JULIET *aloft.*

Juliet.
　　Wilt thou be gone? It is not yet near day.
　　It was the nightingale, and not the lark,
　　That pierced the fearful hollow of thine ear.
　　Nightly she sings on yond pomegranate tree.
　　Believe me, love, it was the nightingale.

Romeo.
　　It was the lark, the herald of the morn;
　　No nightingale. Look, love, what envious streaks
　　Do lace the severing clouds in yonder east.
　　Night's candles are burnt out, and jocund day
10　　Stands tiptoe on the misty mountaintops.
　　I must be gone and live, or stay and die.

Juliet.
　　Yond light is not daylight; I know it, I.
　　It is some meteor that the sun exhales[1]
　　To be to thee this night a torchbearer
　　And light thee on thy way to Mantua.
　　Therefore stay yet; thou need'st not to be gone.

Romeo.
　　Let me be taken, let me be put to death.
　　I am content, so thou wilt have it so.
　　I'll say yon gray is not the morning's eye,
20　　'Tis but the pale reflex[2] of Cynthia's brow;[3]
　　Nor that is not the lark whose notes do beat
　　The vaulty heaven so high above our heads.
　　I have more care to stay than will to go.
　　Come, death, and welcome! Juliet wills it so.
　　How is't, my soul? Let's talk; it is not day.

Juliet.
　　It is, it is! Hie hence, be gone, away!
　　It is the lark that sings so out of tune,

---

1. **exhales:** gives off. (It was believed that the sun drew up vapors and ignited them as meteors.)
2. **reflex:** reflection.
3. **Cynthia's brow:** Cynthia is the moon.

INTERPRET

We hear the song of the lark, which sings at daybreak. The nightingale, on the other hand, sings at night. Why does Juliet insist she hears the nightingale?

_____

_____

_____

_____

IDENTIFY

What does Juliet say the light really is? Underline the words giving the answer.

_____

_____

_____

IDENTIFY

What has Romeo said in lines 17–25 that makes Juliet suddenly practical and aware of danger? Underline the words giving the answer.

_____

_____

_____

INTERPRET

How are references to light and darkness used **ironically** here to suggest the tragedy to come?

BUILD FLUENCY

Read lines 43–47 aloud. In your reading, try to express Juliet's feelings.

Straining harsh discords and unpleasing sharps.
Some say the lark makes sweet division;[4]
30   This doth not so, for she divideth us.
Some say the lark and loathèd toad change eyes;[5]
O, now I would they had changed voices too,
Since arm from arm that voice doth us affray,[6]
Hunting thee hence with hunt's-up[7] to the day.
O, now be gone! More light and light it grows.

Romeo.
More light and light—more dark and dark our woes.

[*Enter* NURSE.]

Nurse. Madam!
Juliet. Nurse?
Nurse.
Your lady mother is coming to your chamber.
40   The day is broke; be wary, look about.   [*Exit.*]
Juliet.
Then, window, let day in, and let life out.
Romeo.
Farewell, farewell! One kiss, and I'll descend.

[*He goes down.*]

Juliet.
Art thou gone so, love-lord, ay husband-friend?
I must hear from thee every day in the hour,
For in a minute there are many days.
O, for this count I shall be much in years
Ere I again behold my Romeo!
Romeo.
Farewell!
I will omit no opportunity
50   That may convey my greetings, love, to thee.
Juliet.
O, think'st thou we shall ever meet again?
Romeo.
I doubt it not; and all these woes shall serve
For sweet discourses in our times to come.

---

4. **division:** literally, a rapid run of notes, but Juliet is punning on the word's other meaning (separation).
5. A fable to explain why the lark, which sings so beautifully, has ugly eyes, and why the toad, which croaks so harshly, has beautiful ones.
6. **affray:** frighten.
7. **hunt's-up:** morning song for hunters.

Juliet.

O God, I have an ill-divining soul!

Methinks I see thee, now thou art so low,

As one dead in the bottom of a tomb.

Either my eyesight fails, or thou look'st pale.

Romeo.

And trust me, love, in my eye so do you.

Dry[8] sorrow drinks our blood. Adieu, adieu!   [*Exit.*]

Juliet.

60   O Fortune, Fortune! All men call thee fickle.

If thou art fickle, what dost thou with him

That is renowned for faith? Be fickle, Fortune,

For then I hope thou wilt not keep him long

But send him back.

[*Enter* JULIET'S *mother,* LADY CAPULET.]

Lady Capulet.

Ho, daughter! Are you up?

Juliet.

Who is't that calls? It is my lady mother.

Is she not down so late,[9] or up so early?

What unaccustomed cause procures her hither?

Lady Capulet.

Why, how now, Juliet?

Juliet.   Madam, I am not well.

Lady Capulet.

70   Evermore weeping for your cousin's death?

What, wilt thou wash him from his grave with tears?

And if thou couldst, thou couldst not make him live.

Therefore have done. Some grief shows much of love;

But much of grief shows still some want of wit.

Juliet.

Yet let me weep for such a feeling loss.[10]

Lady Capulet.

So shall you feel the loss, but not the friend

Which you weep for.

Juliet.   Feeling so the loss,

I cannot choose but ever weep the friend.

Lady Capulet.

Well, girl, thou weep'st not so much for his death

80   As that the villain lives which slaughtered him.

---

8. **Dry:** thirsty (sorrow was thought to drain color from the cheeks).
9. **down so late:** so late getting to bed.
10. **feeling loss:** loss so deeply felt.

PREDICT

What do you think lines 54–56 **foreshadow**?

_____

_____

_____

INTERPRET

According to Juliet, what is the nature of Fortune?

_____

_____

_____

_____

_____

EVALUATE

Actresses playing Lady Capulet have interpreted her character either as loving toward Juliet or as distant and strong-willed. What do you think Lady Capulet's tone is here, and how would you play the part?

_____

_____

_____

_____

_____

_____

_____

_____

INTERPRET

All Juliet's lines in this scene have double meanings. For whom is she really grieving?

_____

_____

_____

_____

_____

_____

_____

_____

_____

BUILD FLUENCY

Read lines 94–103 aloud. Try to express the double meanings that Juliet intends.

_____

_____

_____

_____

_____

INTERPRET

Do you think Juliet has convinced her mother that she wants Romeo dead? Explain.

_____

_____

_____

_____

_____

_____

_____

_____

Juliet.

> What villain, madam?

Lady Capulet.

> That same villain Romeo.

Juliet (*aside*).

> Villain and he be many miles asunder—
> God pardon him! I do, with all my heart;
> And yet no man like he doth grieve my heart.

Lady Capulet.

> That is because the traitor murderer lives.

Juliet.

> Ay, madam, from the reach of these my hands.
> Would none but I might venge my cousin's death!

Lady Capulet.

> We will have vengeance for it, fear thou not.
> Then weep no more. I'll send to one in Mantua,
90   > Where that same banished runagate[11] doth live,
> Shall give him such an unaccustomed dram[12]
> That he shall soon keep Tybalt company;
> And then I hope thou wilt be satisfied.

Juliet.

> Indeed I never shall be satisfied
> With Romeo till I behold him—dead—
> Is my poor heart so for a kinsman vexed.
> Madam, if you could find out but a man
> To bear a poison, I would temper[13] it—
> That Romeo should, upon receipt thereof,
100 > Soon sleep in quiet. O, how my heart abhors
> To hear him named and cannot come to him,
> To wreak[14] the love I bore my cousin
> Upon his body that hath slaughtered him!

Lady Capulet.

> Find thou the means, and I'll find such a man.
> But now I'll tell thee joyful tidings, girl.

Juliet.

> And joy comes well in such a needy time.
> What are they, I beseech your ladyship?

Lady Capulet.

> Well, well, thou hast a careful[15] father, child;
> One who, to put thee from thy heaviness,

---

11. **runagate:** fugitive.
12. **unaccustomed dram:** unexpected drink (of poison).
13. **temper:** mix (she really means "weaken").
14. **wreak:** avenge (she really means "express").
15. **careful:** full of caring (for Juliet).

110   Hath sorted out[16] a sudden day of joy
        That thou expects not nor I looked not for.

Juliet.

        Madam, in happy time![17] What day is that?

Lady Capulet.

        Marry, my child, early next Thursday morn
        The gallant, young, and noble gentleman,
        The County Paris, at Saint Peter's Church,
        Shall happily make thee there a joyful bride.

Juliet.

        Now by Saint Peter's Church, and Peter too,
        He shall not make me there a joyful bride!
        I wonder at this haste, that I must wed
120   Ere he that should be husband comes to woo.
        I pray you tell my lord and father, madam,
        I will not marry yet; and when I do, I swear
        It shall be Romeo, whom you know I hate,
        Rather than Paris. These are news indeed!

Lady Capulet.

        Here comes your father. Tell him so yourself,
        And see how he will take it at your hands.

[*Enter* CAPULET *and* NURSE.]

Capulet.

        When the sun sets the earth doth drizzle dew,
        But for the sunset of my brother's son
        It rains downright.
130   How now? A conduit,[18] girl? What, still in tears?
        Evermore showering? In one little body
        Thou counterfeits a bark,[19] a sea, a wind:
        For still thy eyes, which I may call the sea,
        Do ebb and flow with tears; the bark thy body is,
        Sailing in this salt flood; the winds, thy sighs,
        Who, raging with thy tears and they with them,
        Without a sudden calm will overset
        Thy tempest-tossèd body. How now, wife?
        Have you delivered to her our decree?

Lady Capulet.

140   Ay, sir; but she will none, she gives you thanks.
        I would the fool were married to her grave!

---

16. **sorted out:** selected.
17. **in happy time:** at a lucky time.
18. **conduit:** water pipe (Juliet is weeping).
19. **counterfeits a bark:** imitates a boat.

INTERPRET

How do lines 113–116 illustrate **dramatic irony**? What does the audience know about Juliet's situation that Lady Capulet does not know?

_____
_____
_____
_____
_____
_____
_____
_____
_____
_____
_____
_____

INTERPRET

What **extended metaphor** does Capulet use to describe the weeping Juliet?

_____
_____
_____
_____
_____
_____

EVALUATE

Do you think Capulet is overreacting? Explain.

Capulet.

> Soft! Take me with you,[20] take me with you, wife.
> How? Will she none? Doth she not give us thanks?
> Is she not proud? Doth she not count her blest,
> Unworthy as she is, that we have wrought[21]
> So worthy a gentleman to be her bride?

Juliet.

> Not proud you have, but thankful that you have.
> Proud can I never be of what I hate,
> But thankful even for hate that is meant love.

Capulet.

150
> How, how, how, how, chopped-logic?[22] What is this?
> "Proud"—and "I thank you"—and "I thank you not"—
> And yet "not proud"? Mistress minion[23] you,
> Thank me no thankings, nor proud me no prouds,
> But fettle[24] your fine joints 'gainst Thursday next
> To go with Paris to Saint Peter's Church,
> Or I will drag thee on a hurdle thither.
> Out, you greensickness carrion! Out, you baggage!
> You tallow-face!

Lady Capulet.

>   Fie, fie! What, are you mad?

Juliet.

> Good father, I beseech you on my knees,
160
> Hear me with patience but to speak a word.

Capulet.

> Hang thee, young baggage! Disobedient wretch!
> I tell thee what—get thee to church a' Thursday
> Or never after look me in the face.
> Speak not, reply not, do not answer me!
> My fingers itch. Wife, we scarce thought us blest
> That God had lent us but this only child;
> But now I see this one is one too much,
> And that we have a curse in having her.
> Out on her, hilding!

Nurse.
>   God in heaven bless her!
170
> You are to blame, my lord, to rate[25] her so.

---

20. **Soft! Take me with you:** Wait! Let me understand you.
21. **wrought:** arranged.
22. **chopped-logic:** hair-splitting.
23. **minion:** badly behaved girl.
24. **fettle:** make ready.
25. **rate:** berate, scold.

Capulet.

> And why, my Lady Wisdom? Hold your tongue,
> Good Prudence. Smatter with your gossips,[26] go!

Nurse.

> I speak no treason.

Capulet.   O, God-i-god-en![27]

Nurse.

> May not one speak?

Capulet.   Peace, you mumbling fool!

> Utter your gravity o'er a gossip's bowl,
> For here we need it not.

Lady Capulet.   You are too hot.

Capulet.

> God's bread![28] It makes me mad.
> Day, night; hour, tide, time; work, play;
> Alone, in company; still my care hath been
180   To have her matched; and having now provided
> A gentleman of noble parentage,
> Of fair demesnes, youthful, and nobly trained,
> Stuffed, as they say, with honorable parts,
> Proportioned as one's thought would wish a man—
> And then to have a wretched puling[29] fool,
> A whining mammet,[30] in her fortune's tender,[31]
> To answer "I'll not wed, I cannot love;
> I am too young, I pray you pardon me"!
> But, and you will not wed, I'll pardon you![32]
190   Graze where you will, you shall not house with me.
> Look to't, think on't; I do not use to jest.
> Thursday is near; lay hand on heart, advise.[33]
> And you be mine, I'll give you to my friend;
> And you be not, hang, beg, starve, die in the streets,
> For, by my soul, I'll ne'er acknowledge thee,
> Nor what is mine shall never do thee good.
> Trust to't. Bethink you. I'll not be forsworn.[34]   [*Exit.*]

Juliet.

> Is there no pity sitting in the clouds
> That sees into the bottom of my grief?

---

26. **Smatter with your gossips:** chatter with your gossipy friends.
27. **God-i-god-en!:** Get on with you! ("God give you good evening.")
28. **God's bread!:** oath on the sacrament of Communion.
29. **puling:** whining.
30. **mammet:** puppet.
31. **in her fortune's tender:** with all her good fortunes.
32. **I'll pardon you!:** I'll give you permission to go!
33. **advise:** consider.
34. **forsworn:** guilty of breaking my vow.

PREDICT

Do you think the Nurse's accusation will have any effect on Capulet? Why or why not?

_____
_____
_____
_____
_____
_____
_____
_____
_____
_____
_____
_____
_____
_____
_____
_____
_____
_____
_____
_____
_____
_____
_____
_____

PREDICT

Do you think Capulet's threats will sway Juliet's thinking? Explain.

_____

_____

_____

_____

_____

_____

_____

_____

_____

_____

IDENTIFY

Romeo and Juliet constantly remind us that they take their marriage vows very seriously. According to Juliet, how can these vows be broken? Underline the words giving the answer.

_____

_____

_____

_____

_____

_____

_____

_____

_____

_____

_____

_____

200   O sweet my mother, cast me not away!

      Delay this marriage for a month, a week;

      Or if you do not, make the bridal bed

      In that dim monument where Tybalt lies.

Lady Capulet.

      Talk not to me, for I'll not speak a word.

      Do as thou wilt, for I have done with thee.   [*Exit.*]

Juliet.

      O God!—O nurse, how shall this be prevented?

      My husband is on earth, my faith in heaven.[35]

      How shall that faith return again to earth

      Unless that husband send it me from heaven

210   By leaving earth? Comfort me, counsel me.

      Alack, alack, that heaven should practice stratagems

      Upon so soft a subject as myself!

      What say'st thou? Hast thou not a word of joy?

      Some comfort, nurse.

Nurse.

                Faith, here it is.

      Romeo is banished; and all the world to nothing[36]

      That he dares ne'er come back to challenge you;

      Or if he do, it needs must be by stealth.

      Then, since the case so stands as now it doth,

      I think it best you married with the county.

220   O, he's a lovely gentleman!

      Romeo's a dishclout[37] to him. An eagle, madam,

      Hath not so green, so quick, so fair an eye

      As Paris hath. Beshrew[38] my very heart,

      I think you are happy in this second match,

      For it excels your first; or if it did not,

      Your first is dead—or 'twere as good he were

      As living here and you no use of him.

Juliet.

      Speak'st thou from thy heart?

Nurse.

      And from my soul too; else beshrew them both.

Juliet.

230   Amen!

Nurse.

      What?

---

35. **my faith in heaven:** my wedding vow is recorded in heaven.
36. **all the world to nothing:** it is a safe bet.
37. **dishclout:** literally dishcloth; limp and weak.
38. **Beshrew:** curse.

Juliet.

Well, thou hast comforted me marvelous much.
Go in; and tell my lady I am gone,
Having displeased my father, to Laurence' cell,
To make confession and to be absolved.

Nurse.

Marry, I will; and this is wisely done.   [*Exit.*]

Juliet.

Ancient damnation![39] O most wicked fiend!
Is it more sin to wish me thus forsworn,
Or to dispraise my lord with that same tongue
240   Which she hath praised him with above compare
So many thousand times? Go, counselor!
Thou and my bosom henceforth shall be twain.[40]
I'll to the friar to know his remedy.
If all else fail, myself have power to die.   [*Exit.*]

---

39. Ancient damnation!: Damned old woman!
40. twain: separate.

INFER

What reasons does Juliet have for feeling completely desperate and abandoned at this point in the play?

_____

_____

_____

_____

_____

_____

_____

_____

_____

BUILD FLUENCY

Read lines 237–244 aloud. Note the end-stopped lines and run-on lines. Convey Juliet's emotions as she speaks these lines.

_____

_____

_____

_____

_____

_____

_____

_____

_____

_____

Dramatic Irony

Dramatic irony occurs when the audience or a reader knows something important that a character in a play or story does not know. For example, near the end of *Romeo and Juliet,* Romeo discovers Juliet in the tomb of the Capulets. The audience knows she is merely asleep from the potion Friar Laurence has given her, but Romeo thinks she is dead. When he stabs himself in desperation, we feel a sharp dramatic irony.

You can explore Shakespeare's use of this device in Act III, Scene 5 by filling out the chart below. On the left are some quotations from the scene. In the space provided on the right, briefly explain how each passage is dramatically ironic in context.

Passage from the Play	Dramatic Irony
1. Feeling so the loss, I cannot choose but ever weep the friend. (lines 77–78)	
2. O, how my heart abhors To hear him named and cannot come to him. (lines 100–101)	
3. How now, wife? Have you delivered to her our decree? (lines 138–139)	
4. Delay this marriage for a month, a week; Or, if you do not, make the bridal bed In that dim monument where Tybalt lies. (lines 201–203)	

Vocabulary: How to Own a Word

Synonyms

Match each word in Column A with the correct synonym in Column B.
Write the letter of the correct answer in the blank provided.

Word Bank
exhales
affray
conduit
wrought
forsworn

Column A

_____ 1. exhales

_____ 2. affray

_____ 3. conduit

_____ 4. wrought

_____ 5. forsworn

Column B

a. arranged

b. gives off

c. guilty of breaking a vow

d. water pipe

e. frighten

IDENTIFY

What does Juliet ask the nurse to do? Underline the words giving the answer.

_____

_____

INTERPRET

Lady Capulet is sometimes played here as loving and gentle with Juliet, perhaps suggesting that she is uneasy about her daughter's change of heart. What emotions should her speech in lines 12–13 show?

_____

_____

_____

_____

_____

PREDICT

What may lines 15–17 **foreshadow?**

_____

_____

_____

_____

_____

INFER

Who or what is meant by "thou" in line 23? Underline the answer.

_____

_____

_____

Act IV, Scene 3

JULIET _feigns obedience to her father and says that she will now marry_ PARIS. _Left alone in her chamber, she considers the consequences of taking the potion_ FRIAR LAURENCE _has prepared._

Scene 3. _Juliet's chamber._

Enter JULIET _and_ NURSE.

Juliet.

    Ay, those attires are best; but, gentle nurse,
    I pray thee leave me to myself tonight;
    For I have need of many orisons[1]
    To move the heavens to smile upon my state,
    Which, well thou knowest, is cross and full of sin.

[_Enter_ LADY CAPULET.]

Lady Capulet.

    What, are you busy, ho? Need you my help?

Juliet.

    No, madam; we have culled such necessaries
    As are behoveful[2] for our state[3] tomorrow.
    So please you, let me now be left alone,
10   And let the nurse this night sit up with you;
    For I am sure you have your hands full all
    In this so sudden business.

Lady Capulet.

               Good night.
    Get thee to bed, and rest; for thou hast need.

        [_Exeunt_ LADY CAPULET _and_ NURSE.]

Juliet.

    Farewell! God knows when we shall meet again.
    I have a faint cold fear thrills through my veins
    That almost freezes up the heat of life.
    I'll call them back again to comfort me.
    Nurse!—What should she do here?
    My dismal scene I needs must act alone.
20   Come, vial.
    What if this mixture do not work at all?
    Shall I be married then tomorrow morning?
    No, no! This shall forbid it. Lie thou there.

---

1. **orisons:** prayers.
2. **behoveful:** suitable.
3. **state:** ceremonies.

[Lays down a dagger.]

What if it be a poison which the friar
Subtly hath ministered to have me dead,
Lest in this marriage he should be dishonored
Because he married me before to Romeo?
I fear it is; and yet methinks it should not,
For he hath still been tried⁴ a holy man.

30 How if, when I am laid into the tomb,
I wake before the time that Romeo
Come to redeem me? There's a fearful point!
Shall I not then be stifled in the vault,
To whose foul mouth no healthsome air breathes in,
And there die strangled ere my Romeo comes?
Or, if I live, is it not very like
The horrible conceit of death and night,
Together with the terror of the place—
As in a vault, an ancient receptacle

40 Where for this many hundred years the bones
Of all my buried ancestors are packed;
Where bloody Tybalt, yet but green in earth,⁵
Lies fest'ring in his shroud; where, as they say,
At some hours in the night spirits resort—
Alack, alack, is it not like that I,
So early waking—what with loathsome smells,
And shrieks like mandrakes⁶ torn out of the earth,
That living mortals, hearing them, run mad—
I, if I wake, shall I not be distraught,

50 Environèd with all these hideous fears,
And madly play with my forefathers' joints,
And pluck the mangled Tybalt from his shroud,
And, in this rage, with some great kinsman's bone
As with a club dash out my desp'rate brains?
O, look! Methinks I see my cousin's ghost
Seeking out Romeo, that did spit his body
Upon a rapier's point. Stay, Tybalt, stay!
Romeo, Romeo, Romeo, I drink to thee.

[She falls upon her bed within the curtains.]

---

4. **still been tried:** always been proved.
5. **green in earth:** newly buried.
6. **mandrakes:** plants resembling the human body, which were said to grow beneath the gallows and to scream when torn up.

IDENTIFY

What are Juliet's two worst fears about the potion that Friar Laurence has given her? Underline the words giving the answer.

_____

_____

VISUALIZE

Visualize Juliet awakening in her family tomb. What does she imagine she will find there?

_____

_____

_____

_____

_____

_____

_____

_____

_____

BUILD FLUENCY

Read the whole soliloquy aloud (lines 14–58), using appropriate volume, pacing, and emphasis. Use the punctuation at the end of lines to guide you as you form units of meaning.

_____

_____

_____

_____

Soliloquy

A **soliloquy** is an unusually long speech in which a character who is onstage alone expresses his or her thoughts aloud. The soliloquy is an old dramatic convention in which the audience is supposedly overhearing the thoughts of the character. *Romeo and Juliet* contains several examples of this device. Besides Juliet's speech in this scene, there are soliloquies by Friar Laurence (Act II, Scene 3) and by Romeo (Act V, Scene 3).

Shakespeare structures Juliet's soliloquy as a chain of related questions that produce ever-increasing emotional intensity. Reread the lines listed on the left in the chart below. Write a brief summary of each passage in your own words. Then, comment briefly on Juliet's state of mind, using clues from her language to infer her emotions.

Passage	Summary	Juliet's State of Mind
1. lines 24–29		
2. lines 30–35		
3. lines 36–48		
4. lines 49–54		

Vocabulary: How to Own a Word

Word Maps

Word Bank
dismal
redeem
loathsome
distraught

Fill in the ovals with a synonym, an antonym, and the connotation—positive, negative, or neutral—of each word. Also provide the dictionary definition, and write a sentence using the word correctly. Be sure that the sentence you write reflects the connotation of the word. If you think an oval does not apply, write "none." An example has been partly done for you.

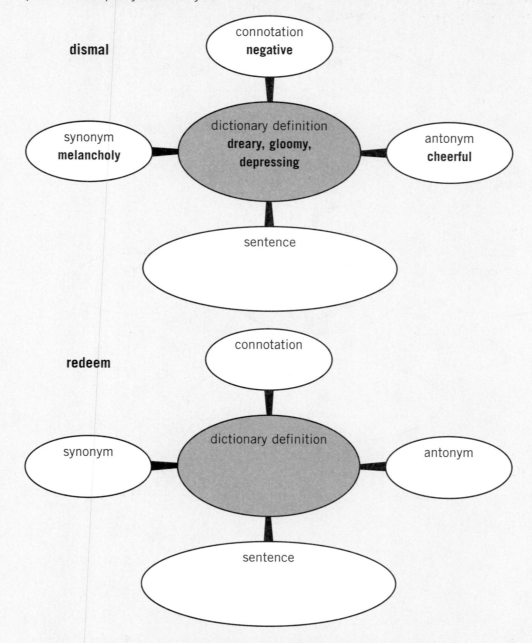

dismal

connotation
negative

synonym
melancholy

dictionary definition
dreary, gloomy, depressing

antonym
cheerful

sentence

redeem

connotation

synonym

dictionary definition

antonym

sentence

loathsome

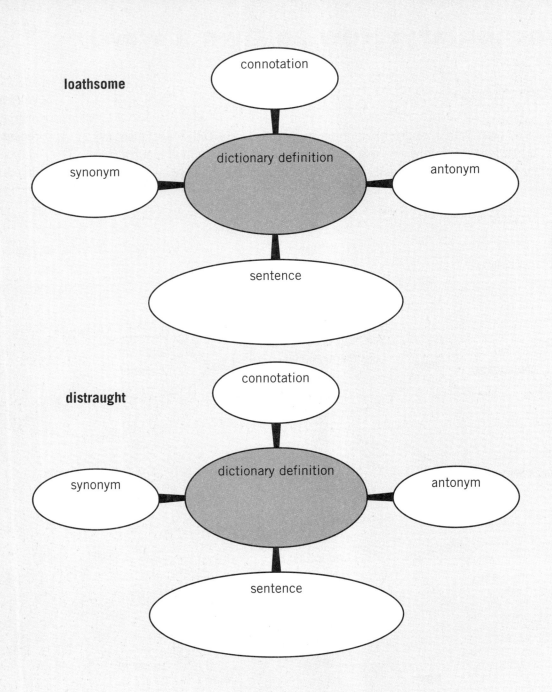

connotation

dictionary definition

synonym

antonym

sentence

distraught

connotation

dictionary definition

synonym

antonym

sentence

Selection: _____

Dramatic Structure

Characters:

_____

_____

_____

_____

Conflict:

_____

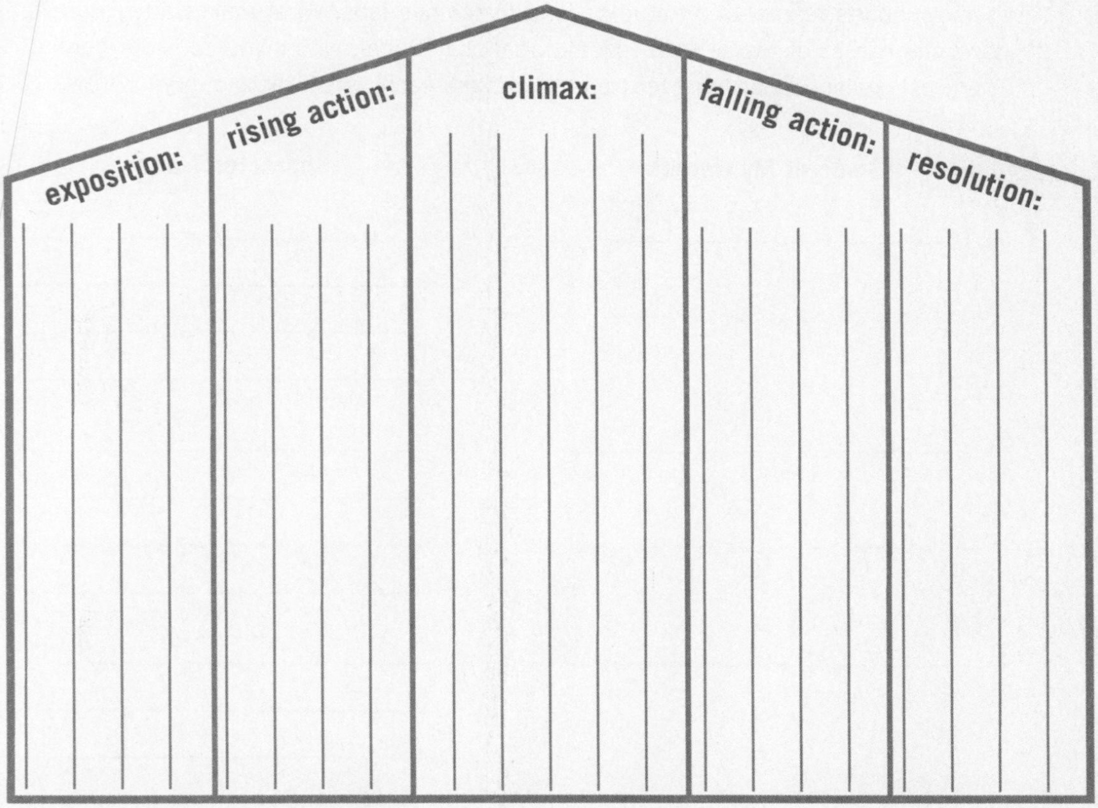

_____

_____

_____

exposition:

rising action:

climax:

falling action:

resolution:

From The Odyssey

Make the Connection

What Makes a Hero?

Homer's epic poems, the *Iliad* and the *Odyssey,* both focus on a hero, a larger-than-life main character whose character traits and deeds sum up the values of society. The hero of the *Iliad* is the great warrior Achilles. The *Odyssey* features a different type of hero: a warrior who is also a wily, diplomatic man, "skilled in all ways of contending." Odysseus is a capable fighter when he has to be, but he is also intelligent and resourceful.

We admire heroes on TV shows, in movies, in books, and in the news; we meet them on sports teams, in art studios, and in science labs. What makes a hero? Write down the names of two or three people, real or fictional, whom you consider heroic. Then, list the specific character traits that make each person heroic in your view.

Some of My Heroes   **Character Traits**

1. _____   _____
                                   _____
                                   _____
                                   _____

2. _____   _____
                                   _____
                                   _____
                                   _____

3. _____   _____
                                   _____
                                   _____
                                   _____

FROM The Odyssey

Homer

The Cyclops

In this adventure Odysseus describes his encounter with the Cyclops named Polyphemus, Poseidon's one-eyed monster son. Polyphemus may well represent the brute forces that any hero must overcome before he can reach home. Now Odysseus must rely on the special intelligence associated with his name.

INFER

Why do you think Odysseus and his men burn an offering for the gods?

_____

_____

_____

VISUALIZE

In lines 3–15, what details does Homer use to emphasize the size and strength of Odysseus' strange opponent? Underline four vivid details in this passage.

_____

_____

INTERPRET

What does the phrase "fair traffic" in line 25 mean? What does the Cyclops mean by these questions?

_____

_____

_____

_____

_____

WORDS TO OWN

ravage (rav′ij) *v.:* destroy violently; ruin.

_____

_____

_____

_____

"We lit a fire, burnt an offering,
and took some cheese to eat; then sat in silence
around the embers, waiting. When he came
he had a load of dry boughs on his shoulder
to stoke his fire at suppertime. He dumped it
with a great crash into that hollow cave,
and we all scattered fast to the far wall.
Then over the broad cavern floor he ushered
the ewes he meant to milk. He left his rams

10   and he-goats in the yard outside, and swung
high overhead a slab of solid rock
to close the cave. Two dozen four-wheeled wagons,
with heaving wagon teams, could not have stirred
the tonnage of that rock from where he wedged it
over the doorsill. Next he took his seat
and milked his bleating ewes. A practiced job
he made of it, giving each ewe her suckling;
thickened his milk, then, into curds and whey,
sieved out the curds to drip in withy baskets,[1]

20   and poured the whey to stand in bowls
cooling until he drank it for his supper.
When all these chores were done, he poked the fire,
heaping on brushwood. In the glare he saw us.

'Strangers,' he said, 'who are you? And where from?
What brings you here by seaways—a fair traffic?
Or are you wandering rogues, who cast your lives
like dice, and <u>ravage</u> other folk by sea?'

We felt a pressure on our hearts, in dread
of that deep rumble and that mighty man.

30   But all the same I spoke up in reply:

'We are from Troy, Achaeans, blown off course
by shifting gales on the Great South Sea;

---

1. **withy baskets:** baskets made from willow twigs.

homeward bound, but taking routes and ways
uncommon; so the will of Zeus would have it.
We served under Agamemnon, son of Atreus[2]—
the whole world knows what city
he laid waste, what armies he destroyed.
It was our luck to come here; here we stand,
beholden for your help, or any gifts
40 you give—as custom is to honor strangers.
We would entreat you, great Sir, have a care
for the gods' courtesy; Zeus will avenge
the unoffending guest.'

　　　　　　　　　　　　　　He answered this
from his brute chest, unmoved:

　　　　　　　　　　　　　　　　'You are a ninny,
or else you come from the other end of nowhere,
telling me, mind the gods! We Cyclopes
care not a whistle for your thundering Zeus
or all the gods in bliss; we have more force by far.
I would not let you go for fear of Zeus—
50 you or your friends—unless I had a whim to.
Tell me, where was it, now, you left your ship—
around the point, or down the shore, I wonder?'

He thought he'd find out, but I saw through this,
and answered with a ready lie:

　　　　　　　　　　　　　　　　　'My ship?
Poseidon Lord, who sets the earth atremble,
broke it up on the rocks at your land's end.
A wind from seaward served him, drove us there.
We are survivors, these good men and I.'

Neither reply nor pity came from him,
60 but in one stride he clutched at my companions
and caught two in his hands like squirming puppies
to beat their brains out, spattering the floor.
Then he dismembered them and made his meal,
gaping and crunching like a mountain lion—
everything: innards, flesh, and marrow bones.
We cried aloud, lifting our hands to Zeus,
powerless, looking on at this, appalled;
but Cyclops went on filling up his belly
with manflesh and great gulps of whey,
70 then lay down like a mast among his sheep.

---

2. **Agamemnon** (ag'ə·mem'nän'). **Atreus** (ā'trē·əs).

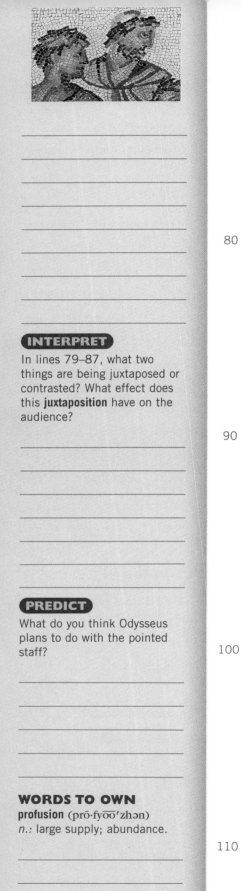

INTERPRET

In lines 79–87, what two things are being juxtaposed or contrasted? What effect does this **juxtaposition** have on the audience?

PREDICT

What do you think Odysseus plans to do with the pointed staff?

WORDS TO OWN
profusion (prō·fyōō′zhən) *n.:* large supply; abundance.

My heart beat high now at the chance of action,
and drawing the sharp sword from my hip I went
along his flank to stab him where the midriff
holds the liver. I had touched the spot
when sudden fear stayed me: if I killed him
we perished there as well, for we could never
move his ponderous doorway slab aside.
So we were left to groan and wait for morning.

When the young Dawn with fingertips of rose
80 lit up the world, the Cyclops built a fire
and milked his handsome ewes, all in due order,
putting the sucklings to the mothers. Then,
his chores being all dispatched, he caught
another brace of men to make his breakfast,
and whisked away his great door slab
to let his sheep go through—but he, behind,
reset the stone as one would cap a quiver.
There was a din of whistling as the Cyclops
rounded his flock to higher ground, then stillness.
90 And now I pondered how to hurt him worst,
if but Athena granted what I prayed for.
Here are the means I thought would serve my turn:

a club, or staff, lay there along the fold—
an olive tree, felled green and left to season
for Cyclops' hand. And it was like a mast
a lugger[3] of twenty oars, broad in the beam—
a deep-seagoing craft—might carry:
so long, so big around, it seemed. Now I
chopped out a six-foot section of this pole
100 and set it down before my men, who scraped it;
and when they had it smooth, I hewed again
to make a stake with pointed end. I held this
in the fire's heart and turned it, toughening it,
then hid it, well back in the cavern, under
one of the dung piles in <u>profusion</u> there.
Now came the time to toss for it: who ventured
along with me? Whose hand could bear to thrust
and grind that spike in Cyclops's eye, when mild
sleep had mastered him? As luck would have it,
110 the men I would have chosen won the toss—
four strong men, and I made five as captain.

---

3. lugger: type of sailboat.

At evening came the shepherd with his flock,
his woolly flock. The rams as well, this time,
entered the cave: by some sheepherding whim—
or a god's bidding—none were left outside.
He hefted his great boulder into place
and sat him down to milk the bleating ewes
in proper order, put the lambs to suck,
and swiftly ran through all his evening chores.
120 Then he caught two more men and feasted on them.
My moment was at hand, and I went forward
holding an ivy bowl of my dark drink,
looking up, saying:

                                    'Cyclops, try some wine.
Here's liquor to wash down your scraps of men.
Taste it, and see the kind of drink we carried
under our planks. I meant it for an offering
if you would help us home. But you are mad,
unbearable, a bloody monster! After this,
will any other traveler come to see you?'

130 He seized and drained the bowl, and it went down
so fiery and smooth he called for more:

'Give me another, thank you kindly. Tell me,
how are you called? I'll make a gift will please you.
Even Cyclopes know the wine grapes grow
out of grassland and loam in heaven's rain,
but here's a bit of nectar and ambrosia!'

Three bowls I brought him, and he poured them down.
I saw the fuddle and flush come over him,
then I sang out in cordial tones:

                                    'Cyclops,
140 you ask my honorable name? Remember
the gift you promised me, and I shall tell you.
My name is Nohbdy: mother, father, and friends,
everyone calls me Nohbdy.'

                                    And he said:
'Nohbdy's my meat, then, after I eat his friends.
Others come first. There's a noble gift, now.'
Even as he spoke, he reeled and tumbled backward,

PREDICT

Odysseus says that the rams may have entered the cave at "a god's bidding" (line 115). What does this mean, and what might it **foreshadow** about the role the rams will play in this conflict?

_____
_____
_____
_____
_____
_____
_____
_____
_____
_____
_____
_____
_____
_____
_____
_____
_____
_____
_____
_____
_____
_____

RETELL

Briefly summarize the action
in lines 150–167.

_____

_____

_____

_____

_____

_____

_____

_____

_____

_____

_____

IDENTIFY

In the **Homeric simile** in lines
167–171, to what is the
blinding of the Cyclops
compared?

_____

_____

_____

_____

_____

_____

_____

_____

_____

_____

_____

his great head lolling to one side; and sleep
took him like any creature. Drunk, hiccuping,
he dribbled streams of liquor and bits of men.

150   Now, by the gods, I drove my big hand spike
deep in the embers, charring it again,
and cheered my men along with battle talk
to keep their courage up: no quitting now.
The pike of olive, green though it had been,
reddened and glowed as if about to catch.
I drew it from the coals and my four fellows
gave me a hand, lugging it near the Cyclops
as more than natural force nerved them; straight
forward they sprinted, lifted it, and rammed it
160   deep in his crater eye, and I leaned on it
turning it as a shipwright turns a drill
in planking, having men below to swing
the two-handled strap that spins it in the groove.
So with our brand we bored that great eye socket
while blood ran out around the red-hot bar.
Eyelid and lash were seared; the pierced ball
hissed broiling, and the roots popped.

                                In a smithy[4]
one sees a white-hot axhead or an adze[5]
plunged and wrung in a cold tub, screeching steam—
170   the way they make soft iron hale and hard—
just so that eyeball hissed around the spike.
The Cyclops bellowed and the rock roared round him,
and we fell back in fear. Clawing his face
he tugged the bloody spike out of his eye,
threw it away, and his wild hands went groping;
then he set up a howl for Cyclopes
who lived in caves on windy peaks nearby.
Some heard him; and they came by divers[6] ways
to clump around outside and call:

                               'What ails you,
180   Polyphemus? Why do you cry so sore
in the starry night? You will not let us sleep.
Sure no man's driving off your flock? No man
has tricked you, ruined you?'

---

4. **smithy:** blacksmith's shop, where iron tools are made.
5. **adze:** tool like an ax but with a longer, curved blade.
6. **divers:** diverse; various.

Out of the cave
the mammoth Polyphemus roared in answer:

'Nohbdy, Nohbdy's tricked me. Nohbdy's ruined me!'

To this rough shout they made a <u>sage</u> reply:

'Ah well, if nobody has played you foul
there in your lonely bed, we are no use in pain
given by great Zeus. Let it be your father,
Poseidon Lord, to whom you pray.'

So saying
190   they trailed away. And I was filled with laughter
to see how like a charm the name deceived them.
Now Cyclops, wheezing as the pain came on him,
fumbled to wrench away the great doorstone
and squatted in the breach with arms thrown wide
for any silly beast or man who bolted—
hoping somehow I might be such a fool.
But I kept thinking how to win the game:
death sat there huge; how could we slip away?
200   I drew on all my wits, and ran through tactics,
reasoning as a man will for dear life,
until a trick came—and it pleased me well.
The Cyclops's rams were handsome, fat, with heavy
fleeces, a dark violet.

Three abreast
I tied them silently together, twining
cords of willow from the ogre's bed;
then slung a man under each middle one
to ride there safely, shielded left and right.
So three sheep could convey each man. I took
210   the woolliest ram, the choicest of the flock,
and hung myself under his kinky belly,
pulled up tight, with fingers twisted deep
in sheepskin ringlets for an iron grip.
So, breathing hard, we waited until morning.

When Dawn spread out her fingertips of rose
the rams began to stir, moving for pasture,
and peals of bleating echoed round the pens
where dams with udders full called for a milking.

WORDS TO OWN
sage (sāj) *adj.:* wise.

INFER
What is **ironic** about lines 187–190?

_____

_____

_____

_____

_____

_____

INTERPRET
How would you characterize Odysseus here?

_____

_____

_____

_____

IDENTIFY
Underline the three steps or stages of Odysseus' trick.

_____

_____

INTERPRET
What **figure of speech** is used in line 215?

_____

_____

_____

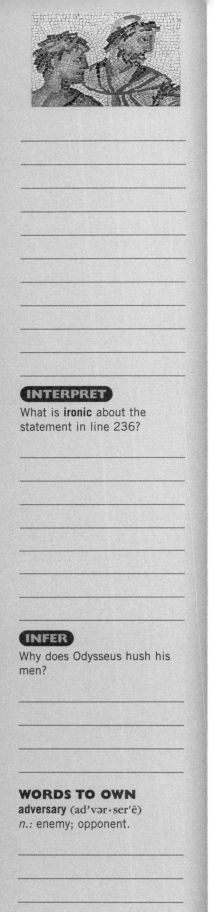

INTERPRET

What is **ironic** about the statement in line 236?

INFER

Why does Odysseus hush his men?

WORDS TO OWN
adversary (ad′vər·ser′ē)
n.: enemy; opponent.

220 Blinded, and sick with pain from his head wound,
the master stroked each ram, then let it pass,
but my men riding on the pectoral fleece[7]
the giant's blind hands blundering never found.
Last of them all my ram, the leader, came,
weighted by wool and me with my meditations.
The Cyclops patted him, and then he said:

'Sweet cousin ram, why lag behind the rest
in the night cave? You never linger so,
but graze before them all, and go afar
230 to crop sweet grass, and take your stately way
leading along the streams, until at evening
you run to be the first one in the fold.
Why, now, so far behind? Can you be grieving
over your Master's eye? That carrion rogue[8]
and his accurst companions burnt it out
when he had conquered all my wits with wine.
Nohbdy will not get out alive, I swear.
Oh, had you brain and voice to tell
where he may be now, dodging all my fury!
Bashed by this hand and bashed on this rock wall
240 his brains would strew the floor, and I should have
rest from the outrage Nohbdy worked upon me.'

He sent us into the open, then. Close by,
I dropped and rolled clear of the ram's belly,
going this way and that to untie the men.
With many glances back, we rounded up
his fat, stiff-legged sheep to take aboard,
and drove them down to where the good ship lay.
We saw, as we came near, our fellows' faces
shining; then we saw them turn to grief
250 tallying those who had not fled from death.
I hushed them, jerking head and eyebrows up,
and in a low voice told them: 'Load this herd;
move fast, and put the ship's head toward the breakers.'
They all pitched in at loading, then embarked
and struck their oars into the sea. Far out,
as far offshore as shouted words would carry,
I sent a few back to the adversary:

---

7. **pectoral fleece:** wool on an animal's chest.
8. **carrion rogue:** rotten scoundrel. Carrion is decaying flesh.

'O Cyclops! Would you feast on my companions?
Puny, am I, in a Caveman's hands?
260 How do you like the beating that we gave you,
you damned cannibal? Eater of guests
under your roof! Zeus and the gods have paid you!'

The blind thing in his doubled fury broke
a hilltop in his hands and heaved it after us.
Ahead of our black prow it struck and sank
whelmed in a spuming geyser, a giant wave
that washed the ship stern foremost back to shore.
I got the longest boathook out and stood
fending us off, with furious nods to all
270 to put their backs into a racing stroke—
row, row or perish. So the long oars bent
kicking the foam sternward, making head
until we drew away, and twice as far.
Now when I cupped my hands I heard the crew
in low voices protesting:

                              'Godsake, Captain!
Why bait the beast again? Let him alone!'

'That tidal wave he made on the first throw
all but beached us.'

                              'All but stove us in!'

'Give him our bearing with your trumpeting,
he'll get the range and lob[9] a boulder.'

                                        'Aye
280 He'll smash our timbers and our heads together!'

I would not heed them in my glorying spirit,
but let my anger flare and yelled:

                              'Cyclops,
if ever mortal man inquire
how you were put to shame and blinded, tell him
Odysseus, raider of cities, took your eye:
Laertes' son, whose home's on Ithaca!'

---

9. lob: toss.

EVALUATE

Is it wise for Odysseus to taunt Polyphemus? Explain.

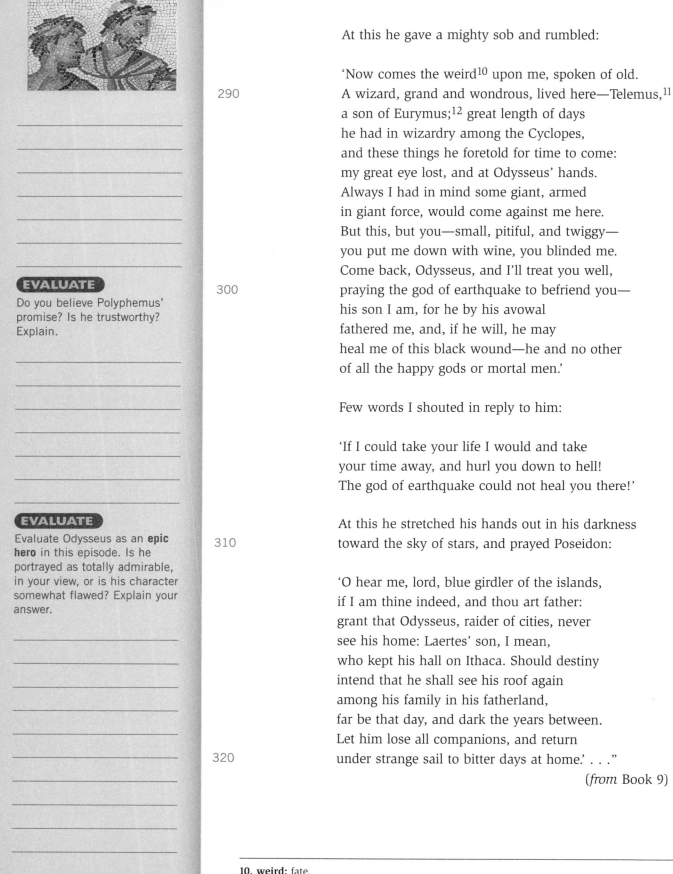

At this he gave a mighty sob and rumbled:

'Now comes the weird[10] upon me, spoken of old.
290   A wizard, grand and wondrous, lived here—Telemus,[11]
a son of Eurymus;[12] great length of days
he had in wizardry among the Cyclopes,
and these things he foretold for time to come:
my great eye lost, and at Odysseus' hands.
Always I had in mind some giant, armed
in giant force, would come against me here.
But this, but you—small, pitiful, and twiggy—
you put me down with wine, you blinded me.
Come back, Odysseus, and I'll treat you well,
300   praying the god of earthquake to befriend you—
his son I am, for he by his avowal
fathered me, and, if he will, he may
heal me of this black wound—he and no other
of all the happy gods or mortal men.'

Few words I shouted in reply to him:

'If I could take your life I would and take
your time away, and hurl you down to hell!
The god of earthquake could not heal you there!'

At this he stretched his hands out in his darkness
310   toward the sky of stars, and prayed Poseidon:

'O hear me, lord, blue girdler of the islands,
if I am thine indeed, and thou art father:
grant that Odysseus, raider of cities, never
see his home: Laertes' son, I mean,
who kept his hall on Ithaca. Should destiny
intend that he shall see his roof again
among his family in his fatherland,
far be that day, and dark the years between.
Let him lose all companions, and return
320   under strange sail to bitter days at home.' . . ."

(from Book 9)

EVALUATE

Do you believe Polyphemus' promise? Is he trustworthy? Explain.

EVALUATE

Evaluate Odysseus as an **epic hero** in this episode. Is he portrayed as totally admirable, in your view, or is his character somewhat flawed? Explain your answer.

---

10. **weird:** fate.
11. **Telemus** (tel'ə·məs).
12. **Eurymus** (yōō'rē·məs).

The Epic Hero

So far, from what you've observed of Odysseus, how would you describe what the Greeks valued in a hero? Do we value these same characteristics today? In the space below, write a paragraph answering these questions. (Be sure to refer to the notes you made about heroism before you read the selection.)

_____

_____

_____

_____

_____

_____

_____

_____

_____

_____

_____

_____

_____

Vocabulary: How to Own a Word

Word Maps

Fill in the ovals with a synonym, an antonym, and the connotation–positive, negative, or neutral–of each Word to Own. Also, provide the dictionary definition and write a sentence using the word correctly. Be sure that the sentence you write reflects the connotation of the word. If you think an oval does not apply, write "none." An example has been done for you.

Word Bank
ravage
profusion
sage
adversary

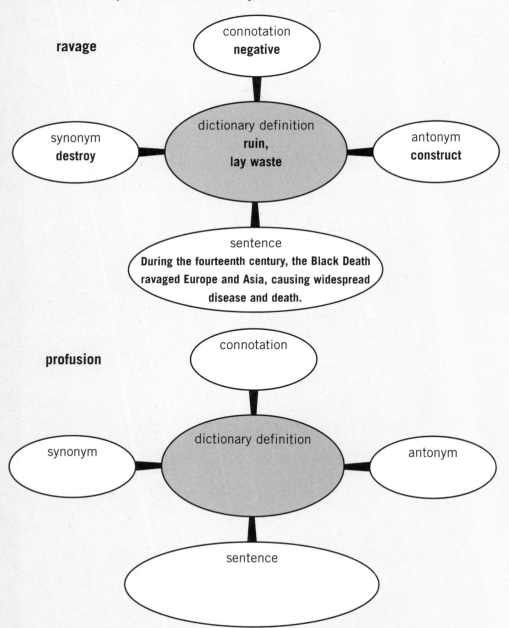

ravage

connotation
negative

synonym
destroy

dictionary definition
**ruin,
lay waste**

antonym
construct

sentence
During the fourteenth century, the Black Death ravaged Europe and Asia, causing widespread disease and death.

profusion

connotation

synonym

dictionary definition

antonym

sentence

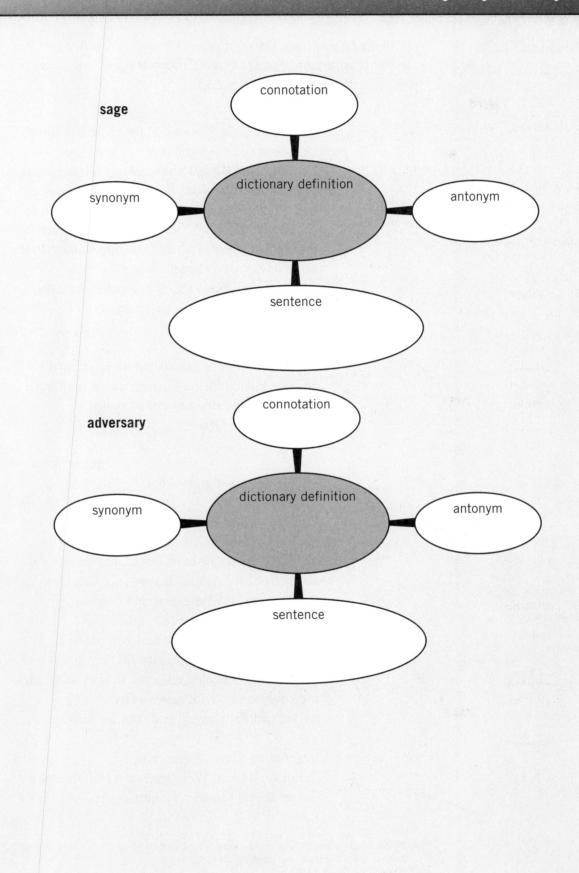

sage

connotation

dictionary definition

synonym

antonym

sentence

adversary

connotation

dictionary definition

synonym

antonym

sentence

IDENTIFY

Which characters are in the mountain hut? Underline the words giving the answer.

_____

_____

_____

INFER

What inference does Odysseus draw when he sees the watchdogs fawning on the new arrival?

_____

_____

_____

_____

_____

_____

_____

_____

INTERPRET

To whom does the **Homeric simile** in lines 19–25 compare Telemachus? To whom does it compare the swineherd? Given the presence of Odysseus in disguise, what added meaning does the simile take on?

_____

_____

_____

_____

_____

_____

_____

_____

_____

The Meeting of Father and Son

With the help of the goddess Athena, Odysseus is reunited with his son, Telemachus, whom he has not seen for twenty years. They meet in the hut of a swineherd on the island of Ithaca.

But there were two men in the mountain hut—
Odysseus and the swineherd. At first light
blowing their fire up, they cooked their breakfast
and sent their lads out, driving herds to root
in the tall timber.

         When Telemachus came,
the wolfish troop of watchdogs only fawned on him
as he advanced. Odysseus heard them go
and heard the light crunch of a man's footfall—
at which he turned quickly to say:

                      "Eumaeus,

10   here is one of your crew come back, or maybe
another friend: the dogs are out there snuffling
belly down; not one has even growled.
I can hear footsteps—"

                But before he finished
his tall son stood at the door.

                   The swineherd
rose in surprise, letting a bowl and jug
tumble from his fingers. Going forward,
he kissed the young man's head, his shining eyes
and both hands, while his own tears brimmed and fell.
Think of a man whose dear and only son,

20   born to him in exile, reared with labor,
has lived ten years abroad and now returns:
how would that man embrace his son! Just so
the herdsman clapped his arms around Telemachus
and covered him with kisses—for he knew
the lad had got away from death. He said:

"Light of my days, Telemachus,
you made it back! When you took ship for Pylos[1]
I never thought to see you here again.

---

1. **Pylos:** home of Nestor, one of Odysseus' fellow soldiers in the Trojan War. Telemachus had gone to see if Nestor knew anything about Odysseus.

Come in, dear child, and let me feast my eyes;
here you are, home from the distant places!
How rarely, anyway, you visit us,
your own men, and your own woods and pastures!
Always in the town, a man would think
you loved the suitors' company, those dogs!"

Telemachus with his clear candor said:

"I am with you, Uncle.[2] See now, I have come
because I wanted to see you first, to hear from you
if Mother stayed at home—or is she married
off to someone, and Odysseus' bed
left empty for some gloomy spider's weaving?"
Gently the forester replied to this:

"At home indeed your mother is, poor lady
still in the women's hall. Her nights and days
are wearied out with grieving."

                                                    Stepping back
he took the bronze-shod lance, and the young prince
entered the cabin over the worn door stone.
Odysseus moved aside, yielding his couch,
but from across the room Telemachus checked him:

"Friend, sit down; we'll find another chair
in our own hut. Here is the man to make one!"

The swineherd, when the quiet man sank down,
built a new pile of evergreens and fleeces—
a couch for the dear son of great Odysseus—
then gave them trenchers[3] of good meat, left over
from the roast pork of yesterday, and heaped up
willow baskets full of bread, and mixed
an ivy bowl of honey-hearted wine.
Then he in turn sat down, facing Odysseus,
their hands went out upon the meat and drink
as they fell to, ridding themselves of hunger. . . .

30
40
50
60

---

2. **Uncle:** here, a term of affection.
3. **trenchers:** wooden platters.

INTERPRET

Why did Telemachus want to see the swineherd first? Underline the words giving the answer.

INTERPRET

What important Greek value is illustrated in this treatment of the beggar?

Not realizing that the stranger is his father, Telemachus agrees to protect him as best he can. But he says that the beggar cannot stay in the palace hall because he will be abused by the drunken suitors.

The swineherd is sent to Penelope with news of her son's return. Now even Athena cannot stand the suspense any longer. She turns to Odysseus, who is still in beggar's rags:

> . . . She tipped her golden wand upon the man,
> making his cloak pure white, and the knit tunic
> fresh around him. Lithe[4] and young she made him,
> ruddy with sun, his jawline clean, the beard
> no longer gray upon his chin. And she
> withdrew when she had done.
>
>   Then Lord Odysseus
> reappeared—and his son was thunderstruck.
> Fear in his eyes, he looked down and away
> as though it were a god, and whispered:
>
>   "Stranger,

70
> you are no longer what you were just now!
> Your cloak is new; even your skin! You are
> one of the gods who rule the sweep of heaven!
> Be kind to us, we'll make you fair oblation[5]
> and gifts of hammered gold. Have mercy on us!"
>
> The noble and enduring man replied:
>
> "No god. Why take me for a god? No, no.
> I am that father whom your boyhood lacked
> and suffered pain for lack of. I am he."

> Held back too long, the tears ran down his cheeks
> as he embraced his son.
>
80
>   Only Telemachus,
> uncomprehending, wild
> with incredulity,[6] cried out:
>
>   "You cannot
> be my father Odysseus! Meddling spirits
> conceived this trick to twist the knife in me!
> No man of woman born could work these wonders
> by his own craft, unless a god came into it
> with ease to turn him young or old at will.

---

4. **lithe:** limber.
5. **oblation:** offering of a sacrifice. Telemachus thinks the stranger is a god.
6. **incredulity:** disbelief.

IDENTIFY

An **epithet** is an adjective or descriptive phrase that is regularly used to describe a person, place, or thing. Homer created many epithets in the *Iliad* and the *Odyssey*. What epithet is used to characterize Odysseus here? Underline the answer.

BUILD FLUENCY

Read lines 79–89 aloud as expressively as you can, observing the distinction between narrative and dialogue. Also, pay attention to the end-stopped lines and run-on lines.

I swear you were in rags and old,
and here you stand like one of the immortals!"

90 Odysseus brought his ranging mind to bear
and said:

"This is not princely, to be swept
away by wonder at your father's presence.
No other Odysseus will ever come,
for he and I are one, the same; his bitter
fortune and his wanderings are mine.
Twenty years gone, and I am back again
on my own island. . . ."

Then, throwing
his arms around this marvel of a father,
Telemachus began to weep. Salt tears
100 rose from the wells of longing in both men,
and cries burst from both as keen and fluttering
as those of the great taloned hawk,
whose nestlings[7] farmers take before they fly.
So helplessly they cried, pouring out tears,
and might have gone on weeping so till sundown. . . .

(*from* Book 16)

INTERPRET

To what are the cries of Odysseus and Telemachus compared in the **Homeric simile** in lines 101–105? What strikes you as odd or inconsistent about the comparison?

EVALUATE

Which part of this recognition scene between father and son do you think is most moving or most dramatic?

Homeric Simile

A **Homeric simile** is an extended, explicit comparison of two unlike things, using words such as *like, as, than,* or *resembles.* Occasionally Homer includes surprising details that make his comparisons evocative and thought-provoking.

Explore Homeric similes by filling out the chart below. Re-read each passage carefully. Then, explain what is compared to what, and briefly comment on the fit, or match, between the simile and the narrative context.

Passage	Comparison	Comment
1. Lines 19–25: "Think of a man whose dear and only son . . . "		
2. Lines 101–105: "and cries burst from both as keen and fluttering . . . "		

Vocabulary: How to Own a Word

Synonyms

Match each word in Column A with the correct synonym in Column B. Write the letter of the correct answer in the blank provided.

Column A

Column B

_____ **1.** troop

a. agile; limber

_____ **2.** snuffling

b. group; pack

_____ **3.** gloomy

c. sullen; depressing

_____ **4.** lithe

d. disbelief

_____ **5.** incredulity

e. breathing audibly

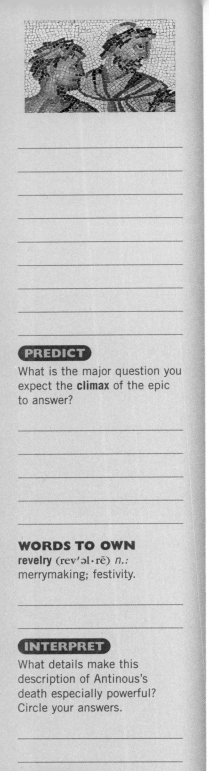

Death at the Palace

After all the suitors fail to string Odysseus' huge bow, Odysseus, still in beggar's clothes, successfully wins the contest. He now turns to face the suitors.

Now shrugging off his rags the wiliest fighter of the
    islands
leapt and stood on the broad doorsill, his own bow in his
    hand.
He poured out at his feet a rain of arrows from the quiver
and spoke to the crowd:

                "So much for that. Your clean-cut game is over.
Now watch me hit a target that no man has hit before,
if I can make this shot. Help me, Apollo."[1]

He drew to his fist the cruel head of an arrow for
    Antinous
just as the young man leaned to lift his beautiful
    drinking cup,
embossed, two-handled, golden: the cup was in his
    fingers,
the wine was even at his lips, and did he dream of
    death?

10How could he? In that <u>revelry</u> amid his throng of friends
who would imagine a single foe—though a strong foe
    indeed—
could dare to bring death's pain on him and darkness on
    his eyes?
Odysseus' arrow hit him under the chin
and punched up to the feathers through his throat.

Backward and down he went, letting the wine cup fall
from his shocked hand. Like pipes his nostrils jetted
crimson runnels,[2] a river of mortal red,
and one last kick upset his table
20knocking the bread and meat to soak in dusty blood.
Now as they craned to see their champion where he lay
the suitors jostled in uproar down the hall,

---

1. Odysseus prays to Apollo because this particular day is one of the god's feast days. Apollo is also the god of archery.
2. **runnels:** streams.

Sidebar

PREDICT

What is the major question you expect the **climax** of the epic to answer?

WORDS TO OWN
revelry (rev′əl·rē) *n.:* merrymaking; festivity.

INTERPRET

What details make this description of Antinous's death especially powerful? Circle your answers.

PREDICT

What do you think will happen next?

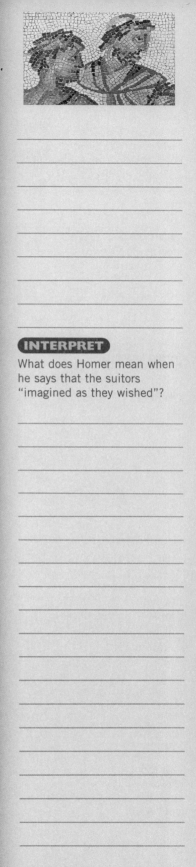

everyone on his feet. Wildly they turned and scanned
the walls in the long room for arms; but not a shield,
not a good ashen spear was there for a man to take and
    throw.
All they could do was yell in outrage at Odysseus:

"Foul! to shoot at a man! That was your last shot!"

"Your own throat will be slit for this!"

                              "Our finest lad is down!
You killed the best on Ithaca."

                    "Buzzards will tear your eyes out!"

For they imagined as they wished—that it was a wild
    shot,
an unintended killing—fools, not to comprehend
they were already in the grip of death.
But glaring under his brows Odysseus answered:

"You yellow dogs, you thought I'd never make it
home from the land of Troy. You took my house to
    plunder,
twisted my maids to serve your beds. You dared
bid for my wife while I was still alive.
Contempt was all you had for the gods who rule wide
    heaven,
contempt for what men say of you hereafter.
Your last hour has come. You die in blood."

As they all took this in, sickly green fear
pulled at their entrails,³ and their eyes flickered
looking for some hatch or hideaway from death.
Eurymachus alone could speak. He said:

"If you are Odysseus of Ithaca come back,
all that you say these men have done is true.
Rash actions, many here, more in the countryside.
But here he lies, the man who caused them all.
Antinous was the ringleader, he whipped us on
to do these things. He cared less for a marriage

30

40

50

---

3. **entrails:** guts.

EVALUATE

Is Odysseus right to insist on
revenge? Why or why not?

INTERPRET

To what are the suitors
compared in this **Homeric
simile** (lines 70–73)?

INTERPRET

In the **Homeric simile** in
lines 74–83, to what
are Odysseus and his men
compared?

than for the power Cronion[4] has denied him
as king of Ithaca. For that
he tried to trap your son and would have killed him.
He is dead now and has his portion. Spare
your own people. As for ourselves, we'll make
restitution of wine and meat consumed,
and add, each one, a tithe of twenty oxen
with gifts of bronze and gold to warm your heart.
Meanwhile we cannot blame you for your anger."

60   Odysseus glowered under his black brows
and said:

              "Not for the whole treasure of your fathers,
all you enjoy, lands, flocks, or any gold
put up by others, would I hold my hand.
There will be killing till the score is paid.
You forced yourselves upon this house. Fight your
    way out,
or run for it, if you think you'll escape death.
I doubt one man of you skins by." . . .

*Telemachus joins his father in the fight. They are helped by the swineherd
and cowherd. Now the suitors, trapped in the hall without weapons, are
struck right and left by arrows, and many of them lie dying on the floor.*

        At this moment that unmanning thundercloud,
the aegis, Athena's shield,
took form aloft in the great hall.
70   And the suitors mad with fear
at her great sign stampeded like stung cattle by a river
when the dread shimmering gadfly strikes in summer,
in the flowering season, in the long-drawn days.
After them the attackers wheeled, as terrible as falcons
from eyries[5] in the mountains veering over and diving
    down
with talons wide unsheathed on flights of birds,
who cower down the sky in chutes and bursts along the
    valley—

---

4. **Cronion:** another name for Zeus, meaning "son of Cronus."
5. **eyries** (er′ēz): nests built in high places.

but the pouncing falcons grip their prey, no frantic wing
        avails,
and farmers love to watch those beakèd hunters.
So these now fell upon the suitors in that hall,
turning, turning to strike and strike again,
while torn men moaned at death, and blood ran smoking
over the whole floor. . . .

(*from* Book 22)

80

INFER

What does this scene add to the epic's **theme** about the value of hospitality and the punishment of those who mock divine laws?

_____

_____

_____

_____

_____

_____

_____

_____

_____

_____

_____

_____

_____

_____

_____

_____

_____

_____

_____

_____

_____

_____

Conflict and Climax

In the *Odyssey,* the hero Odysseus faces many **conflicts,** both external and internal. The clash with the Cyclops, for example, is an external struggle for survival. Odysseus' character trait of curiosity sometimes involves him in internal conflicts, which pit his desire for adventure against his yearning to return to his homeland of Ithaca.

Perhaps the most daunting conflict in the epic, however, sets Odysseus and his family against the suitors of Penelope. The suitors' ringleader is the arrogant Antinous. He hit Odysseus with a stool when the hero appeared in the hall as a beggar, and he ridiculed the disguised king by calling him a bleary vagabond, a pest, and a tramp.

The **climax** of a literary work is the moment of greatest suspense or emotional intensity, when the conflict is resolved one way or another. Re-read the description of the death of Antinous in lines 7–20. Then, in the space provided below, briefly comment on the vivid details that make this scene appropriate for the climax of the *Odyssey.*

_____

_____

_____

_____

_____

_____

_____

_____

_____

_____

_____

_____

Vocabulary: How to Own a Word

Word Maps

Following the model on this page, create word maps for each Word to Own. Fill in the ovals with a synonym, an antonym, and the connotation—positive, negative, or neutral—of each Word to Own. Also, provide the dictionary definition, and write a sentence using the word correctly. Be sure that the sentence you write reflects the connotation of the word. If you think an oval does not apply, write "none."

Revelry

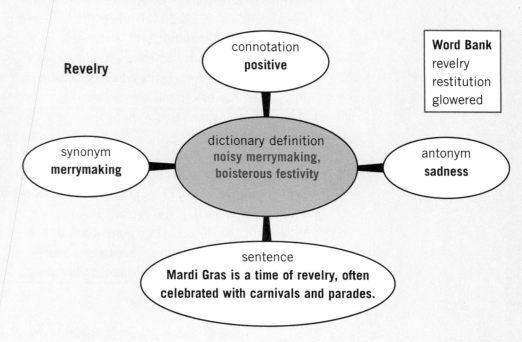

connotation
positive

synonym
merrymaking

dictionary definition
noisy merrymaking, boisterous festivity

antonym
sadness

sentence
Mardi Gras is a time of revelry, often celebrated with carnivals and parades.

Word Bank
revelry
restitution
glowered

Odysseus and Penelope

The nurse Eurycleia runs to Penelope to announce the return of Odysseus and the defeat of the suitors. The faithful wife—the perfect mate for the wily Odysseus—suspects a trick from the gods and decides to test this stranger who claims to be her husband.

INFER

Why does Penelope have so much trouble recognizing Odysseus?

_____

_____

_____

_____

_____

_____

_____

BUILD FLUENCY

Read Telemachus's speech in lines 11–18 aloud as expressively as you can.

_____

_____

_____

_____

_____

_____

_____

_____

_____

_____

INFER

Why do you think a smile comes to Odysseus' lips here?

_____

_____

_____

_____

_____

_____

Crossing the doorsill she sat down at once
in firelight, against the nearest wall,
across the room from the lord Odysseus.

There

leaning against a pillar, sat the man
and never lifted up his eyes, but only waited
for what his wife would say when she had seen him.
And she, for a long time, sat deathly still
in wonderment—for sometimes as she gazed
she found him—yes, clearly—like her husband,
10   but sometimes blood and rags were all she saw.

Telemachus's voice came to her ears:

"Mother,
cruel mother, do you feel nothing,
drawing yourself apart this way from Father?
Will you not sit with him and talk and question him?
What other woman could remain so cold?
Who shuns her lord, and he come back to her
from wars and wandering, after twenty years?
Your heart is hard as flint and never changes!"

Penelope answered:

"I am stunned, child.
20   I cannot speak to him. I cannot question him.
I cannot keep my eyes upon his face.
If really he is Odysseus, truly home,
beyond all doubt we two shall know each other
better than you or anyone. There are
secret signs we know, we two."

A smile
came now to the lips of the patient hero, Odysseus,
who turned to Telemachus and said:

"Peace: let your mother test me at her leisure.
Before long she will see and know me best.

30   These tatters, dirt—all that I'm caked with now—
      make her look hard at me and doubt me still. . . ."

*Odysseus orders Telemachus, the swineherd, and the cowherd to bathe
and put on fresh clothing.*

      Greathearted Odysseus, home at last,
      was being bathed now by Eurynome
      and rubbed with golden oil, and clothed again
      in a fresh tunic and a cloak. Athena
      lent him beauty, head to foot. She made him
      taller, and massive, too, with crisping hair
      in curls like petals of wild hyacinth
      but all red-golden. Think of gold infused
40   on silver by a craftsman, whose fine art
      Hephaestus taught him, or Athena: one
      whose work moves to delight: just so she <u>lavished</u>
      beauty over Odysseus' head and shoulders.
      He sat then in the same chair by the pillar,
      facing his silent wife, and said:
                                    "Strange woman,
      the immortals of Olympus made you hard,
      harder than any. Who else in the world
      would keep <u>aloof</u> as you do from her husband
      if he returned to her from years of trouble,
50   cast on his own land in the twentieth year?

      Nurse, make up a bed for me to sleep on.
      Her heart is iron in her breast."
                                          Penelope
      spoke to Odysseus now. She said:
                                    "Strange man,
      if man you are . . . This is no pride on my part
      nor scorn for you—not even wonder, merely.
      I know so well how you—how he—appeared
      boarding the ship for Troy. But all the same . . .

      Make up his bed for him, Eurycleia.
      Place it outside the bedchamber my lord
60   built with his own hands. Pile the big bed
      with fleeces, rugs, and sheets of purest linen."

      With this she tried him to the breaking point,
      and he turned on her in a flash, raging:

IDENTIFY

Who intervenes to change Odysseus' physical appearance? Circle the answer.

_____
_____
_____
_____

WORDS TO OWN
lavished (lav′isht) *v.*: gave generously.
aloof (ə·lo͞of′) *adj.*: at a distance; unfriendly.

_____
_____
_____
_____
_____
_____
_____
_____

IDENTIFY/INFER

How does Penelope's greeting to Odysseus in line 53 echo his earlier greeting to her? What is Penelope implying in line 54?

_____
_____
_____
_____
_____

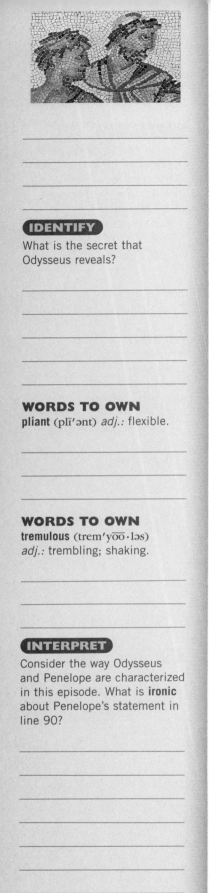

IDENTIFY

What is the secret that Odysseus reveals?

WORDS TO OWN
pliant (plī'ənt) *adj.:* flexible.

WORDS TO OWN
tremulous (trem'yōō·ləs) *adj.:* trembling; shaking.

INTERPRET

Consider the way Odysseus and Penelope are characterized in this episode. What is **ironic** about Penelope's statement in line 90?

"Woman, by heaven you've stung me now!
Who dared to move my bed?
No builder had the skill for that—unless
a god came down to turn the trick. No mortal
in his best days could budge it with a crowbar.
There is our pact and pledge, our secret sign,
70 built into that bed—my handiwork
and no one else's!

                      An old trunk of olive
grew like a pillar on the building plot,
and I laid out our bedroom round that tree,
lined up the stone walls, built the walls and roof,
gave it a doorway and smooth-fitting doors.
Then I lopped off the silvery leaves and branches,
hewed and shaped the stump from the roots up
into a bedpost, drilled it, let it serve
80 as model for the rest, I planed them all,
inlaid them all with silver, gold, and ivory,
and stretched a bed between—a pliant web
of oxhide thongs dyed crimson.

                         There's our sign!
I know no more. Could someone else's hand
have sawn that trunk and dragged the frame away?"

Their secret! as she heard it told, her knees
grew tremulous and weak, her heart failed her.
With eyes brimming tears she ran to him,
throwing her arms around his neck, and kissed him,
murmuring:

                      "Do not rage at me, Odysseus!
90 No one ever matched your caution! Think
what difficulty the gods gave: they denied us
life together in our prime and flowering years,
kept us from crossing into age together.
Forgive me, don't be angry. I could not
welcome you with love on sight! I armed myself
long ago against the frauds of men,
impostors who might come—and all those many
whose underhanded ways bring evil on! . . .
But here and now, what sign could be so clear
100 as this of our own bed?
No other man has ever laid eyes on it—

only my own slave, Actoris, that my father
sent with me as a gift—she kept our door.
You make my stiff heart know that I am yours."

Now from his breast into his eyes the ache
of longing mounted, and he wept at last,
his dear wife, clear and faithful, in his arms,
longed for
    as the sun-warmed earth is longed for by a swimmer
spent in rough water where his ship went down
under Poseidon's blows, gale winds and tons of sea.
Few men can keep alive through a big surf
to crawl, clotted with brine, on kindly beaches
in joy, in joy, knowing the abyss behind:
and so she too rejoiced, her gaze upon her husband,
her white arms round him pressed, as though forever. . . .

110

(*from* Book 23)

INTERPRET

To whom is Odysseus compared in the **Homeric simile** in this passage? Given what you know about Odysseus' adventures and his struggle to get home, why is this comparison especially appropriate?

_____

_____

_____

_____

_____

_____

_____

_____

_____

_____

_____

_____

_____

_____

_____

_____

_____

Characterization

Characterization is the process of revealing the personality of a character in a literary work. In the *Odyssey,* the hero Odysseus is given a perfect mate in Penelope, who shares many of his qualities. Given what you know about Odysseus and Penelope in the epic, fill out the diagram below listing their similarities and differences.

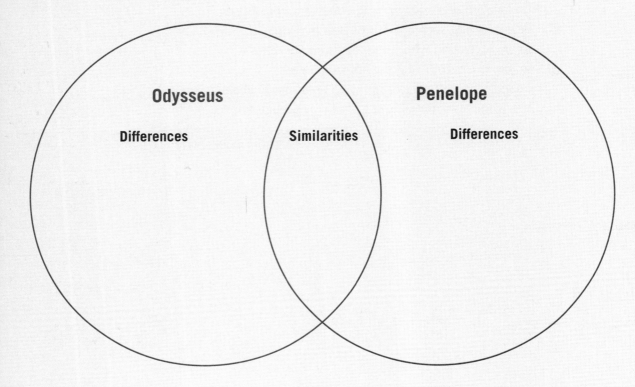

Odysseus

Differences

Similarities

Penelope

Differences

Vocabulary: How to Own a Word

Related Meanings

For each of the following word groups, cross out the word whose meaning or part of speech is different from that of any of the other words, including the Word to Own in boldface type. On the line following each word group, write an original sentence correctly using the Word to Own.

EXAMPLE: **adversities**   misfortunes   ~~successes~~   hardships
Through patience and determination, Odysseus triumphed over many adversities.

1. confident   **tremulous**   shaky   trembling

_____

_____

_____

2. involved   reserved   **aloof**   unfriendly

_____

_____

_____

3. showered   withheld   **lavished**   bestowed

_____

_____

_____

4. bendable   flexible   rigid   **pliant**

_____

_____

_____

PART 2 READING INFORMATIONAL MATERIALS

From One Belfast Boy
From Introduction to Children of "The Troubles"

Make the Connection

Synthesizing Several Sources: Balancing Act

When you do research, you need to get a balanced view of your subject by using several types of sources and examining different points of view. Here are some guidelines:

- **Determine the author's purpose and audience.** Was the piece written, for example, to tell a personal story, to change an unsympathetic reader's mind, or to provide background information?
- **Compare and contrast your sources.** On what do your sources agree and disagree? Do your sources offer a range of opinions? What type of information do you find in your source? For example, does a source provide only objective facts and explain the historical background of an event? Does a source present the author's feelings and thoughts and tell what is was like to experience an event? Are objective facts and personal feeling combined in a source?
- **Connect to other sources or related topics.** Try to connect your resources to other works you've read, both nonfiction and fiction. Look for similarities between your subject and a similar topic, perhaps one related to another time or place.

The pieces you are about to read are about the Irish Civil War. What do you know about the American Civil War? In the left column, write any information you can think of about this topic. In the right column, tell where you read or heard it and whether it is fact or someone's opinion.

Information	Source
1. Northern states fought southern states	1. textbook—fact
2.	2.
3.	3.

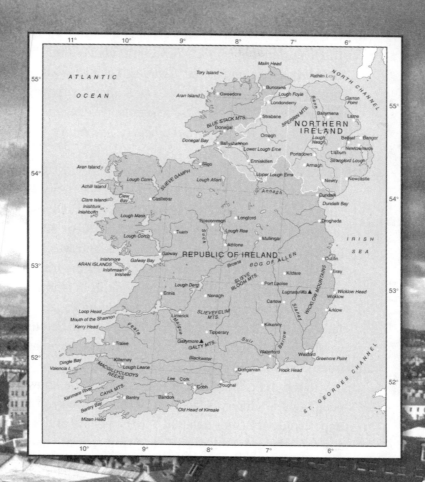

From

One Belfast Boy

Patricia McMahon

From

Children of "The Troubles"

Laurel Holliday

Our Lives in the Crossfire of Northern Ireland

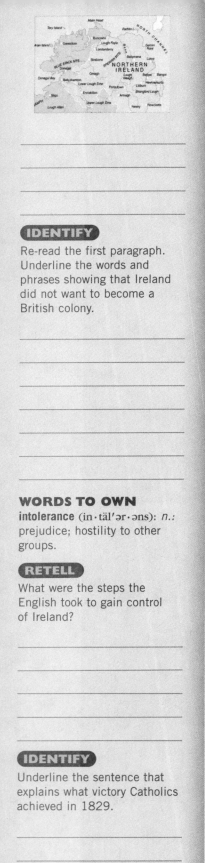

From One Belfast Boy

Patricia McMahon

From One Belfast Boy

Patricia McMahon

The long-standing conflicts between Catholics and Protestants in Ireland have become known as the Troubles. They have pitted brother against brother (like the characters in "The Sniper," on page 3) and torn the country apart. The following selections tell how the conflict began, what might be done to end it, and what it's like to live in a place where your home is a battleground.

Around the year 1170 the king of England, Henry II, declared himself king of Ireland as well. Gradually, with great bloodshed, Ireland was brought under the control of England, or Great Britain, as England came to be known. Through the centuries, Ireland was held as a colony of the British Empire—held against the wishes of the Irish people.

There were also other people living in Ireland, however. English settlers had been going to Ireland for centuries, and beginning in 1609, James I, then king of England, offered land to Scottish settlers if they would move to Ireland and farm the land—land that was being taken
10   from the native Irish.

To the Irish, these new arrivals came to be known as the strangers: people with a different language, a different way of life, and, most important, a different religion. For the people of Ireland were Catholic and the strangers taking over their land were Protestant. At that time in England and in much of Europe, a terrible intolerance existed between different religions.

The English gradually put laws into place that said Catholics could not own land, could not vote, could not be elected to public office or work for the government. Catholics were not allowed to be lawyers.
20   They were not allowed to speak the Irish language or study Irish history or literature. They were forbidden to hold Mass. Bishops, priests, and monks[1] were forced to leave the country. By 1780 the Irish people owned only 5 percent of their own land, and in 1800 the British government passed the Act of Union, declaring Ireland part of the United Kingdom of Great Britain and Ireland.

Through the long years of British rule, the Irish fought for their freedom. They fought with what weapons they had, in rebellions great and small—rebellions that the vast British army always put down. The Irish fought with words as well as weapons. They organized and signed

---

1. hold Mass . . . monks: Mass is the Roman Catholic service consisting of prayers, scripture readings, and the celebration of the Eucharist. Bishops and priests are members of the Catholic clergy. Monks live in religious communities governed by strict rules.

IDENTIFY

Re-read the first paragraph. Underline the words and phrases showing that Ireland did not want to become a British colony.

WORDS TO OWN

intolerance (in·täl′ər·əns): *n.:* prejudice; hostility to other groups.

RETELL

What were the steps the English took to gain control of Ireland?

IDENTIFY

Underline the sentence that explains what victory Catholics achieved in 1829.

30 petitions, held massive nonviolent protests, and after Catholics regained
the vote in 1829, they lobbied[2] in the English Parliament[3] for their freedom.

In 1916, during World War I, a small rebellion broke out in Dublin[4]
on Easter Monday. The Irish rebels were quickly defeated. Sixteen of the
leaders were shot, and many men and women were jailed, including
some who had not been involved. Anger grew in Ireland. People began
to join Sinn Fein, a political group working for Irish freedom. In the Irish
language, Sinn Fein means "ourselves alone." Those who felt it was
necessary to fight with weapons joined the IRA—the Irish Republican
Army—and fought the British army where and when they could. The
40 outnumbered IRA, led by a man named Michael Collins, managed to
inflict losses on the superior British forces. The Irish people began to
believe that this time would be different, this time freedom would
finally come.

But the Protestants of Ireland did not approve of the rebellion. They
had lived in Ireland for generations. They owned land and businesses.
And they knew who they were: They were British subjects, and they
believed Ireland should remain part of the United Kingdom. They were
willing to fight to keep it so. "No surrender" became their motto. Great
numbers of Protestants were living in the North; their cry was "Ulster[5]
50 will fight, and Ulster will be right."

The damages inflicted by the Irish rebels grew, and the British
government agreed in 1920 to meet with the Irish for peace talks. After
difficult negotiations, the British agreed to the Irish demands for self-
government and freedom. But they did not agree to freedom for all of
Ireland. Ulster, where so many British Protestants lived, would become
Northern Ireland and would become part of the United Kingdom of
Great Britain and Northern Ireland. But not all of Ulster would become
Northern Ireland. A new border would be drawn to create a place
where there would be more Protestants than Catholics. Three counties—
60 Donegal, Cavan, and Monaghan—of the original nine making up Ulster
were not included in Northern Ireland. This was the deal the British
offered. If it was not accepted, the talks would be ended, and the fighting
would begin again.

In Ireland, the arguments over the proposal were fierce. Some
believed there should be no division of the country—no deal. Others
thought it was the best deal possible at that time. They believed that
creating Northern Ireland was a temporary measure and Ireland would
soon be reunited. In the end, Ireland took the offer. But anger over the
division of the country was so strong that civil war broke out. Friends
70 who had fought together against the British now turned on one another.

---

2. **lobbied** (lăb′ēd) *v.:* attempted to influence public officials to do something.
3. **English Parliament:** branch of government with the power to make laws for the country.
4. **Dublin:** Ireland's capital.
5. **Ulster:** name often given to the northern, predominantly Protestant, portion of Ireland.

EVALUATE

Do you think the name "Sinn Fein" is appropriate for this group? Why or why not?

_____

_____

_____

_____

_____

_____

_____

_____

_____

WORDS TO OWN
negotiations
(ni·gō′shē·a′shənz) *n.:* discussions aimed at reaching an agreement.

IDENTIFY

Re-read lines 52–63. Underline the sentences that describe the deal the British offered.

_____

_____

IDENTIFY

Underline the reason why some Irish were in favor of creating Northern Ireland.

IDENTIFY

Pause at line 69. What was the cause of the civil war?

_____

_____

_____

INFER

Why do you think the Catholics in Northern Ireland would be inspired by Martin Luther King's teachings?

_____

_____

_____

_____

INFER

Re-read lines 90–97. What do you think life was like during this period? List as many adjectives as you can.

_____

_____

_____

_____

IDENTIFY

Re-read lines 98–101. Underline the sentence in which the writer suggests that the deaths caused by "the Troubles" have been in vain.

INTERPRET

What is the writer suggesting in lines 107–109 about the future of the conflict in Northern Ireland?

_____

_____

_____

_____

_____

_____

And so in 1921, while most of the Irish gained their freedom, the Catholics of Northern Ireland remained under British rule. In the new Ulster, Catholics could not vote unless they owned land, and few did. Businesses, government, public housing, and jobs were all controlled by Protestants.

In 1968, Catholics began to form civil rights organizations, inspired by the work of people like Dr. Martin Luther King, Jr., in the United States. Catholics wanted to have the same rights as Protestants. They began a series of protest marches across Northern Ireland. The government 80 forbade the marches. Catholic demonstrators were attacked and gassed.[6] Catholic homes, neighborhoods, and churches were attacked by mobs who believed that the Catholics were not entitled to equal rights.

The Catholics began to fight back, arming themselves. The Irish Republican Army, whose numbers had dwindled since the country was divided, gained new recruits and became active again. The British army moved in to try to stop the fighting, but the battles grew worse. After fourteen unarmed protesters were killed by a British army regiment in 1972, on a day that became known as Bloody Sunday, the IRA's membership swelled. Soon the cities and towns of Northern Ireland were battlegrounds.

90 Both the Protestants and the Catholics made bombs, blew up buildings, and created armies. The IRA began to argue within its ranks about tactics, splitting into different groups. One group, called the Provisional IRA, or the Provos, became the present-day IRA. Both Catholics and Protestants were guilty of murder and mayhem. At one point there were as many as seven armed groups on the streets of Belfast.[7] Even the question of civil rights seemed to have been lost amidst the violence and the constant calls for revenge.

More than 3,200 people have died in the Troubles[8]—men, women, and children—Protestant and Catholic alike. They died over the question "Are 100 we British or are we Irish?" And after all this time, there are still two very different answers to that question. The deaths have not changed this.

The habit of hating is a hard one to break. But many people believe it is worth a try. People on both sides of the walls[9] who want peace keep working to stop the fighting. In 1997, a new cease-fire went into effect. Peace talks began, which led to the signing of a peace accord in 1998. A new government for Northern Ireland was formed, intending to guarantee the rights of Catholics. Some say there will be no peace until the entire island of Ireland is united. Some say there will be no peace if that ever happens.

---

6. **gassed** _v._: exposed to tear gas or some other airborne substance released in order to cause great discomfort.
7. **Belfast:** capital of Northern Ireland.
8. **More than . . . Troubles:** This figure refers to the number of deaths at the time of the book's publication in 1999.
9. **both sides of the walls:** walls in some parts of Belfast that separate Catholics and Protestants.

From Children of "The Troubles": Our Lives in the Crossfire of Northern Ireland

Laurel Holliday

DECEMBER 20, 1976

I would love to risk sleeping some Christmas night with curtains flung back from the windows, nothing but shiny black glass between me and the stars and sky, the drizzle and the horses, but [IRA] bombs ruthlessly silence my wishes, for a while at least.

—*from the diary of Sharon Ingram*
eighteen years old, Ballygawley

28th APRIL, 1994

I am frightened living on this street across from the Protestants. I am frightened they will come and kill us because this is the eleventh time they have shot people in our street. I don't know why they want to kill us.

—*from the diary of Bridie Murphy*
eleven years old, Belfast

From the moment children are born in Northern Ireland, they begin to live in a majority Protestant or a majority Catholic neighborhood. They go to either a Catholic or a Protestant school, and their friends are likely to be exclusively one or the other. They are taught to shop only in their "own" shops in some towns and, eventually, to socialize only in their "own" pubs. And, of course, when they die they will go to a segregated graveyard.

Amazingly, I think, to those who haven't been raised there, in Belfast even the taxis divide along religious lines, with one fleet heading
10 to Catholic and another to Protestant neighborhoods. In some parts of the country even the sidewalks are painted to <u>designate</u> political/religious loyalties.

In addition to these very obvious distinctions that children need to learn in order to survive in Northern Ireland, they also <u>absorb</u> differences in language and perspective[1] that set them apart from one another for the rest of their lives. If you are Catholic, for example, you call Northern Ireland's second largest city Derry; if you are Protestant, it is Londonderry to you. If you are Catholic, you call the nearly three decades of the Troubles a war; if you are Protestant, you are careful to point out that
20 there has been a terrorist uprising, not a war, in Northern Ireland.

---

1. **perspective** (pər·spek′tiv) *n.*: point of view.

WORDS TO OWN
reunification
(rē·yōo′nə·fi·kā′shən) *n.:*
the joining together of things
that had been divided.

_____

_____

WORDS TO OWN
divergent (dī·vur′jənt) *adj.:*
separate; going in different
directions.
coerced (kō·ursd′) *v.:* forced.
abhor (ab·hôr′) *v.:* hate.

INTERPRET

Re-read lines 35–38. According
to the author, how is this war
different from other wars?

_____

_____

_____

_____

_____

_____

_____

_____

_____

_____

_____

_____

_____

_____

_____

_____

In fact, even the name you call your country will be in question. If you are raised in a Catholic family wanting the reunification of Ireland, you will refer to the North of Ireland as your homeland or call it the Six Counties, rather than making it sound as if it were a separate country called Northern Ireland. And if you were raised in a Protestant environment, you will be more likely to call your country Northern Ireland or Ulster.

Not only are most children in Northern Ireland set on divergent sectarian[2] courses from birth, but from the age of seven some Protestant
30 and Catholic children are coerced into running secret errands for terrorists and assembling and hiding their weapons.

Although the majority of people in Northern Ireland abhor the violence and take no part in it themselves, virtually every family in Northern Ireland has had members beaten, tortured, or murdered, and the country's children have been witness to it all. For this is not a private war, conducted behind closed doors, nor a war where the men go away to fight the enemy. This is an everyday, in-your-face war, where the enemy lives on the next block and speaks (almost) the same language.

---

2. sectarian (sek·ter′ē·ən) *adj.:* pertaining to a particular religious group.

Resource Source Chart

Comparison and Contrast

The two selections you just read are about the Irish Civil War. However, they contain different types of information and different perspectives. Use the chart below to compare and contrast *One Belfast Boy* and *Children of "The Troubles."*

Comparison-Contrast Chart

Features	One Belfast Boy	Children of "The Troubles"
Author's purpose and audience:	**Audience:** Anyone interested in learning about history of Ireland. **Purpose:** To give an overview of the Irish-British conflict.	
Type of Information: • Objective facts? • Historical background? • Author's thoughts and feelings? • A combination?	Mostly facts and historical background. Very little of author's thoughts.	
Connections to other sources/related topics:	Other sources: "The Sniper," *Braveheart.* Related topics: History of Irish immigration, civil wars, freedom fighters.	

Analyzing Informational Materials

Reading Check

1. What caused civil war to break out in Ireland in the 1920s, according to *One Belfast Boy*?

_____

_____

2. Give two examples of how the division between Catholics and Protestants affects daily life, according to "Introduction to *Children of 'The Troubles.'*" _____

_____

_____

Test Practice

Circle the letter of the correct answer.

1. What is the main point of "Introduction to *Children of 'The Troubles'*"?

A Violence is not productive.

B The Troubles affect the daily life of children, as well as that of adults, in Northern Ireland.

C Most people in Northern Ireland oppose violence.

D It is impossible to judge which side is right in the conflict.

2. Which of the following statements comparing *One Belfast Boy* to "Introduction to *Children of 'The Troubles'*" is *not* true?

F Neither author expresses a bias in the selection.

G Both include facts.

H Both are secondary sources.

J Both explain the causes of the conflict.

3. What **conclusion** can you draw from **synthesizing** the content of the selections?

A Peace has not been established because no one is trying to achieve it.

B The long-standing conflict has been deadly, and it has divided the Irish people.

C The conflict is between political leaders, and it does not affect the lives of citizens.

D If the conflict doesn't end soon, many Irish will leave the country.

Vocabulary: How to Own a Word

Word Families: Meet the Relatives

Most words are members of **word families,** groups of related words that have slightly different forms and that function as different parts of speech. Learning one new word opens the door for you to meet the rest of its family. Take a look at the word *know*, for example. This one verb will introduce you to the noun *knowledge*, the adjectives *knowable, knowing*, and *knowledgeable*, and the adverbs *knowingly* and *knowledgeably*, among others. Study the word-family chart below for *intolerance*. Then, try completing one for *negotiations*.

Word Bank

intolerance

negotiations

designate

absorb

reunification

divergent

coerced

abhor

Part I

Word Bank Word **intolerance** *n.:* prejudice; hostility to other groups	**Sentence** Intolerance is a great evil.
Related Words intolerant *adj.:* unwilling to tolerate others' opinions or beliefs, or people of other backgrounds or races. intolerable *adj.:* unbearable.	**Sentence(s)** The school administration is intolerant to new ideas. I find loud noises intolerable.
Word Bank Word **negotiations** *n.:*	**Sentence**
Related Words negotiate *v.:* negotiable *adj.:*	**Sentence(s)**

Part II

On a separate piece of paper, make a word-family chart like the ones above for each remaining Word Bank word. Define the Word Bank word, and give its part of speech. Then, use a dictionary to help you list related words, their definitions, and their parts of speech. Write a sentence for each word in the family.

Can Animals Think?

Make the Connection

Generating Research Questions

Posing good questions is the key to doing research that will lead to an interesting, informative report. To develop good research questions based on informational materials, keep the following in mind:

- Stay focused on your subject. Don't stray into topics that are unrelated to the specific topic you're investigating.
- Focus on subsections of an informational article, which may be indicated by subheads. In this way you will narrow the scope of your subject so that you can explore it in more depth.
- Ask the *5W-How?* questions: *Who* was involved? *What* happened? *When* and *where* did it happen? *Why* and *how* did it happen? Such questions will help you get more information about your subject.
- Ask questions that can be answered within the scope of your research. Don't ask questions so broad that you cannot present a complete answer.

In the space provided below, list five questions that most intrigue you about the ways animals communicate or solve problems. Use the *5W-How?* questions to get yourself started.

1.
2.
3.
4.
5.

Can Animals Think?

Eugene Linden

INFER

Why might the keepers at
Omaha Zoo have assumed that
Fu Manchu's first escape was
the result of human error?

_____

_____

_____

_____

_____

_____

_____

IDENTIFY

Underline the detail in
the second paragraph that
suggests Fu Manchu possesses
high-level problem-solving
skills.

_____

_____

_____

_____

_____

_____

EVALUATE

Based on your prior knowledge
and what you've read so far,
write your own answer to the
question in lines 37–38.

_____

_____

_____

_____

_____

_____

The first time Fu Manchu broke out, zookeepers chalked it up to human error. On a balmy day, the orangutans at the Omaha Zoo had been playing in their big outdoor enclosure. Not long thereafter, shocked keepers looked up and saw Fu and his family hanging out in some trees near the elephant barn. Later investigation revealed that the door that connects the furnace room to the orangutan enclosure was open. Head keeper Jerry Stones chewed out his staff, and the incident was forgotten. But the next time the weather was nice, Fu Manchu escaped again. Fuming, Stones recalls, "I was getting ready to fire someone."

10 The next nice day, alerted by keepers desperate to keep their jobs, Stones finally managed to catch Fu Manchu in the act. First, the young ape climbed down some air-vent louvers into a dry moat. Then, taking hold of the bottom of the furnace door, he used brute force to pull it back just far enough to slide a wire into the gap, slip a latch, and pop the door open. The next day, Stones noticed something shiny sticking out of Fu's mouth. It was the wire lock pick, bent to fit between his lip and gum and stowed there between escapes.

Fu Manchu's jailbreaks made headlines in 1968, but his clever tricks didn't make a big impression on the scientists who specialize in looking
20 for signs of higher mental processes in animals. At the time, much of the action in animal intelligence was focused on efforts to teach apes to use human languages. No researcher cared much about ape escape artists.

And neither did I. In 1970, I began following studies of animal intelligence, particularly the early reports of chimpanzees who learned how to use human words. The big breakthrough in these experiments came when two psychologists,[1] R. Allen and Beatrice Gardner, realized their chimps were having trouble forming wordlike sounds and decided to teach a young female named Washoe sign language instead. Washoe eventually learned more than 130 words from the language of the deaf
30 called American Sign Language.

Washoe's success spurred more language studies and created such ape celebrities as Koko the gorilla and Chantek the orangutan. The work also set off a fierce debate in scientific circles about the nature of animal intelligence—one that continues to this day. Indeed, it has been easier to defeat communism than to get scientists to agree on what Washoe meant three decades ago when she saw a swan on a pond and made the signs for "water bird." Was she inventing a phrase to describe waterfowl, or merely generating signs vaguely associated with the scene in front of her?

I began to wonder whether there might be better windows on animal
40 minds than experiments designed to teach them human signs and symbols. When I heard about Fu Manchu, I realized what to me now seems obvious: If animals can think, they will probably do their best thinking when it serves their purposes, not when some scientist asks them to.

---

1. **psychologists** (sī·käl′ə·jists) n.: specialists who study the mind and emotions.

Lending a Helping Tail

Why would an animal want to cooperate with a human? The behaviorist[2] would say that animals cooperate when, through reinforcement, they learn it is in their interest to cooperate. This is true as far as it goes, but I don't think it goes far enough. Certainly with humans, the <u>intangible</u> reinforcement that comes with respect, dignity, and accomplishment can be far more motivating than material rewards.

50   Gail Laule, a consultant on animal behavior with Active Environments Inc., uses rewards to encourage an animal to do something, but also recognizes that animals are more than windup toys that blindly respond to tempting treats. "It's much easier to work with a dolphin if you assume that it is intelligent. . . . That was certainly the case with Orky," says Laule, referring to her work with one of the giant dolphins called orcas or killer whales. "Of all the animals I've worked with, Orky was the most intelligent. . . . He would assess a situation and then do something based on the judgments he made."

    Like the time he helped save a member of the family. Orky's mate
60 Corky gave birth in the late 1970s, but the baby did not thrive at first, and the keepers took the little killer whale out of the tank by stretcher for emergency care and feeding. Things began to go <u>awry</u> when they returned the orca to the tank. The boom operator halted the stretcher when it was still a few feet above the water. Suddenly the baby began throwing up, through both its mouth and its blowhole. The keepers feared it would aspirate[3] some vomit, which could bring on a fatal case of pneumonia, but they could not reach the baby dangling above.

    Orky had been watching the procedure, and, apparently sizing up the problem, he swam under the stretcher and allowed one of the men
70 to stand on his head. This was remarkable since Orky had never been trained to carry people on his head like Sea World's Shamu. Then, using the amazing power of his tail flukes to keep steady, Orky provided a platform that allowed the keeper to reach up and release the bridle so that the 420-pound baby could slide into the water within reach of help.

The Keeper Always Falls for That One

A sad fact of life is that it is easier to spot evidence of intelligence in <u>devious</u> behavior than in acts of cooperation or love.

    While psychologists have studied various forms of animal deception, zookeepers are its targets every day. Helen Shewman, of the Woodland Park Zoo in Seattle, Washington, recalls that one day she dropped an
80 orange through a feeding porthole for Meladi, one of the female orangutans. Instead of moving away, Meladi looked Helen in the eye and held out her hand. Thinking that the orange must have rolled off

---

2. **behaviorist** (bē·hāv′yər·ist) *n.*: psychologist who studies behavior.
3. **aspirate** (as′pə·rāt) *v.*: breathe in.

IDENTIFY
Underline the research question that focuses the topic of this subsection.

WORDS TO OWN
intangible (in·tan′jə·bəl) *adj.*: cannot be touched or held.

_____
_____
_____
_____
_____
_____

WORDS TO OWN
awry (ə·rī′) *adv.*: in the wrong manner.

_____
_____
_____
_____
_____
_____
_____
_____

WORDS TO OWN
devious (dē′vē·əs) *adj.*: sneaky; deceptive.

EVALUATE
Do you think the statement in lines 75–76 is true?

_____
_____
_____
_____
_____
_____

WORDS TO OWN
beguile (bē·gīl′) v.: charm;
deceive.

INTERPRET

Scientists often study animals
with the hope of learning more
about humans. Use a piece of
information from this article to
write a research question
about human intelligence.

somewhere inaccessible, Helen gave her another one. When Meladi
shuffled off, Helen noticed that she had hidden the original orange in
her other hand.

Tawan, the colony's dominant male, watched this whole charade,
and the next day he too looked Helen in the eye and pretended that he
had not yet received an orange. "Are you sure you don't have one?"
Helen asked. He continued to hold her gaze and held out his hand.
90 Relenting, she gave him another, then noticed that he had been hiding
his orange under his foot.

Countless creatures draw on their abilities not only to secure food and
compete with their peers, but also to deal with, deceive, and <u>beguile</u> the
humans they encounter. Every so often, they do something extraordinary,
and we gain insight into our own abilities and what it's like to be an
orangutan or an orca.

—From *Time*, September 6, 1999

Generating Research Questions Chart

Try using a *KWL* chart to begin researching a specific aspect of animal intelligence. After you read "Can Animals Think?" list what you already know about the topic in the *K* column. In the *W* column, list the questions you have—what you want to learn. You can use the five questions about animal intelligence you posed before you read the article or change them based on what you learned from the article. When you've finished your research, complete column *L* by telling what you've learned. Which question yielded the best research results and why?

K	W	L

Analyzing Informational Materials

Reading Check

1. How did Fu Manchu get out of his enclosure? _____
   _____

2. What did Orky do that was so remarkable? _____
   _____

3. How did Meladi and Tawan deceive their zookeeper? _____
   _____

Test Practice

Circle the letter of the correct answer.

1. What is the **main idea** of "Can Animals Think?"

   A Animals are often smarter than humans.

   B Animals are most likely to show intelligence not to please us but to serve their own needs.

   C Apes have a difficult time mastering the sounds of human speech.

   D Human beings cannot or will not recognize animal intelligence.

2. If you want to do further research on the topic of animal intelligence, which question would help limit your investigation?

   F Do we value intelligence more than it deserves to be valued?

   G Will humans ever be able to communicate extensively with animals?

   H What are other instances in which orcas have made judgments?

   J What does *intelligence* mean?

3. Why is *How did the Gardners teach Washoe sign language?* a more useful first research question than *Did Washoe like learning sign language?*

   A It is a broad question about Washoe.

   B It will lead you to detailed information rather than a yes-or-no answer.

   C It covers a lengthy period of time.

   D It includes the psychologists who worked with Washoe.

4. Which research question would yield the *most* useful information about the intelligence of apes?

   F Who was smarter, Chantek or Koko?

   G What intelligent actions have observers seen orangutans perform in the wild?

   H How many times did Fu Manchu try to escape his enclosure?

   J What did Helen Shewman do the next time an orangutan tried to trick her into giving him an extra orange?

Vocabulary: How to Own a Word

Synonyms

Synonyms are words that mean the same thing or almost the same thing. When you choose a word or when you examine why a writer uses a particular word, you should think about its precise meaning as well as its context.

Look, for example, at what Gail Laule says about Orky in "Can Animals Think?":

"He would <u>assess</u> a situation and then do something based on the judgments he made."

If you were using your own words to express that idea, you might have said that Orky would "think about" the situation. Why might *assess* be a better word to describe Orky's behavior? *Think* is a vague word; it can be used in many different contexts. For instance, *think* can mean "reflect." You might think about a piece of advice that applies to your life. *Assess,* however, is more precise. It implies evaluation or calculation. *Assess* conveys that Orky thinks logically. The word suits the scientific context of the sentence because the statement is an observation made by a specialist in animal behavior.

Practice

Use a dictionary and a thesaurus to make a synonym chart like the one below for each word from the Word Bank. Write a sentence for each synonym. Try to make your sentences show any slight (or not so slight) differences in meaning among the synonyms.

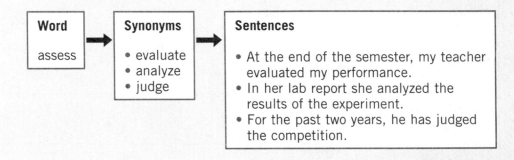

Word

assess

Synonyms
- evaluate
- analyze
- judge

Sentences
- At the end of the semester, my teacher evaluated my performance.
- In her lab report she analyzed the results of the experiment.
- For the past two years, he has judged the competition.

Teaching Chess, and Life; Feeding Frenzy

Make the Connection

Identifying and Using Primary and Secondary Sources

Research sources generally fall into one of two basic categories: primary or secondary sources.

- A **primary source** is a firsthand account. The writers present experiences, opinions, and ideas. Primary sources include autobiographies, interviews, oral histories, essays, eyewitness news reports, and speeches.
- A **secondary source** is a secondhand account. The writers summarize, interpret, or analyze events in which they did not participate. Secondary sources include encyclopedias, textbooks, biographies, and many magazine and journal articles. Most newspaper articles are secondary sources, unless, for example, they are firsthand accounts written at the time of an event.

The authors of the following articles convey useful information on volunteering. However, one author writes from personal experience and the other from research. Thus, "Teaching Chess, and Life" is considered a primary source and "Feeding Frenzy" is considered a secondary source.

Below is a list of sources you might encounter while researching a report on volunteering. Indicate which are primary and which are secondary sources.

A television interview with volunteers	
Chapter of a biography on someone known for his or her community service	
Newspaper editorial about a new volunteering program	
Transcript of a speech by the founder of a new volunteering program	
A pamphlet from the Chamber of Commerce on volunteering	
A chapter in a civics textbook on volunteering	
An encyclopedia article on volunteering	

Teaching Chess, and Life

The Game, and a Mentor, Showed the Way Out of 160th Street

FROM *The New York Times,*
September 3, 2000

Carlos Capellan

FEEDING FRENZY

FROM *People,* June 2, 1997

Peter Ames Carlin and Don Sider

Teaching Chess, and Life

The Game, and a Mentor, Showed the Way Out of 160th Street
from *The New York Times*, September 3, 2000

Carlos Capellan

If you were to walk down West 160th Street in Washington Heights, you would see drug dealers whistling to people in cars and handing off small packages to passers-by. As you walk further down the block, you would see residents who are too scared to sit and talk to their neighbors on the front steps. These families stay inside most of the time. You would see parents pick up their children from P.S. 4 and hurry off the block before trouble can start. This is my block and this is my neighborhood.

Many kids my age in Washington Heights wind up in gangs, as drug dealers, in jail or dead. I decided long ago that I would not end up in
10 one of those situations because of the consequences I saw others suffer. I have stuck by this decision with help from several important people. One of the most influential people in my life is my former chess coach and current boss, Jeremy Chiappetta, who has taught me a lot about chess and more about life.

As an eighth-grader at a gang-infested junior high school, I joined the chess team as a way to stay out of trouble. I already knew the coach, Mr. Chiappetta, because he was my social studies teacher.

As a ninth- and tenth-grader, I volunteered to help Chia with his chess team at Intermediate School 90 on West 168th Street. During these
20 years, I matured. I learned how to present myself in a positive way: taking off my hat inside buildings, judging when it was appropriate to make jokes (I had to learn this lesson a few times) and knowing how to speak in certain situations.

At one tournament I learned an important lesson from Chia. It was the last round of the U.S. Amateur Team East. I was playing for a top prize and was nervous. In the middle of the game I found a winning combination and I began to slam the pieces out of happiness. Then a big hand stopped the game clock and pulled me away. It was Chia. I could tell that he was angry, but I did not realize what I had done wrong. We
30 talked about the meaning of sportsmanship. I apologized for my rudeness to my opponent and forfeited the game. I didn't win a prize.

With Chia's <u>mentorship</u>, I learned from my mistake. As a coach at I.S. 90, I've had to teach the same lesson to others. It makes me feel good about myself because I like helping the younger kids learn the game Chia taught me to love.

Chia left I.S. 90 the year I became an eleventh-grader. He recommended me as an assistant chess coach, for which I am paid. This is my second year at I.S. 90 as an assistant coach. My responsibilities

include teaching chess strategies and tactics three days a week. I also
40 chaperone the team at tournaments almost every weekend.

All of this would not have been possible if not for Mr. Chiappetta. He
turned me to chess and kept me involved. He gave me the opportunity to
earn money doing something I love. Chess has kept me off the streets. It
has challenged me and taught me to think in new ways. Because of
chess, I was recently honored by the Daily News as one of the "21 New
Yorkers to Watch in the 21st Century." Chess has made me a mentor to
younger students, giving me the chance to become their Chia.

EVALUATE
How would you evaluate the impact Chia had on Carlos's life? Explain your thinking.

_____
_____
_____
_____
_____
_____
_____

Feeding Frenzy
from *People*, June 2, 1997

Peter Ames Carlin and Don Sider

When 15-year-old David Levitt makes his weekly appearance at the
Haven of Rest food bank in Pinellas Park, Florida, he is greeted as a
Good Samaritan.[1]

No one knows better than Levitt how to get food to the hungry.
Since 1994 the surplus food-sharing program he designed as an 11-year-
old for the Pinellas County public schools has sent more than a quarter-
million pounds of cafeteria leftovers to the county's shelters and food
banks. Singled out for praise last year by President Clinton, Levitt, a
freshman at Seminole High, is currently backing state legislation to
10 protect donors of surplus food from liability lawsuits.[2] "It's a no-brainer,"
says State Representative Dennis Jones, who is shepherding Levitt's bill
toward certain passage when the state legislature meets next spring.
"You wonder why it's taken so long for someone to do it."

The same question crossed Levitt's mind in 1993, when he first read
about Kentucky Harvest, a nonprofit organization that funnels leftover
food from restaurants and other businesses to charities. He was only
a sixth-grader, but Levitt understood that a nation that regularly sends
30 million people to bed hungry shouldn't toss nearly 20 percent of its
edible food into the garbage. Buttonholing[3] Osceola Middle School
20 principal Fred Ulrich outside class one day, he asked if he could start a
Harvest program using cafeteria leftovers. "I figured he didn't know me,"
says Levitt, "so he couldn't be mean."

WORDS TO OWN
legislation (lej′is·lā′shən) *n.*:
law or body of laws.

IDENTIFY
List David's goals.

_____
_____
_____
_____

INTERPRET
Underline the statistic in the paragraph you have just read. What do these numbers say about hunger in the United States?

_____
_____
_____
_____
_____

1. **Good Samaritan:** person who unselfishly helps others. The term comes from a Bible
   parable in Luke 10:30–37.
2. **liability lawsuits:** legal actions brought against a person or group to make up for loss or
   damage that has occurred.
3. **buttonholing** *v. used as adj.*: speaking intently with another person in an attempt to
   persuade him or her to do something.

WORDS TO OWN
bureaucratic (byoor′ə·krat′ik)
adj.: referring to rigid
governmental routine.
undaunted (un·dôn′tid) *adj.:*
not discouraged by a difficulty
or setback.

IDENTIFY

Circle the problems David
faced in setting up a Harvest
program. Then underline the
steps he took to solve each
problem.

EVALUATE

David's mother says that he is
a "typical teenager." Do you
agree or disagree with her
statement? Give your reasons.

Ulrich wasn't mean. He was merely realistic, pointing out that district health regulations prohibited using previously served food. ("Red tape, red tape,"[4] Levitt sighs.) But, encouraged by his mother, Sandy, Levitt attended a Pinellas County school-board meeting and made his case for a local Harvest program. He not only won the board's approval but a spontaneous ovation to boot.

The board's approval, alas, merely gained him entrance to the
30 bureaucratic maze. Next he had to contend with state health-department rules governing the handling of secondhand food. For a time it seemed that packaging requirements would doom the program—the state demanded specific containers, and the schools had no money to pay for them. Undaunted, Levitt wrote to the First Brands Corporation, which promptly shipped eight cases of plastic bags to his doorstep, and on November 8, 1994, Levitt helped make the school's first delivery: cartons of milk and bags of salad for Haven of Rest. *"That,"* he says, "was satisfaction."

The younger child (sister Jamie is 18) of Sandy Levitt, a bookkeeper,
40 and her husband, Rich, vice president of a medical-supply company, Levitt grew up in Seminole, a suburb of St. Petersburg, earning A's and B's in school and playing volleyball and a handful of musical instruments. "David's a typical teenager," notes his mother. Eventually he would like to attend the U.S. Air Force Academy and learn to fly. "That's today," he says. "Call me tomorrow—I might change."

What doesn't change is his ability to make things happen. And while he's fortunate to have a mother who helps push his projects along (Sandy is "the silent driving force," according to her husband), Levitt's energy has won him plenty of fans. "David has drawn attention to
50 hunger and the availability of food in the community," says Mary Dowdell, director of Tampa Bay Harvest. Adds Stan Curtis, the Kentucky stockbroker who started the first Harvest program: "Any parent in America would be glad to have him as a son."

Including the First Dad,[5] who invited Levitt to the White House last spring as part of a Points of Light ceremony.[6] Taking his medal from Hillary Rodham Clinton, Levitt wasn't shy about pushing his agenda. "What," he asked the First Lady, "do you do with the White House leftovers?"

---

4. **red tape** *n.:* complicated official forms and regulations.
5. **First Dad:** the president, if he has children; in this case, President Clinton.
6. **Points of Light ceremony:** awards ceremony sponsored by the Points of Light Foundation to honor people who have performed outstanding community service. The foundation, begun in 1990, took its name from a phrase used by former president George Herbert Walker Bush to describe private acts of goodwill: "a thousand points of light."

Resource Source Chart

Supporting a Main Idea with Primary and Secondary Sources

Use the **primary** and the **secondary** sources in this lesson to support the **main idea** for a research paper on volunteering. A **main idea** is a message, an opinion, or an idea that the writer wants to communicate to the reader. What details, facts, quotations, descriptions, or statements from the two articles you have just read support the main idea below?

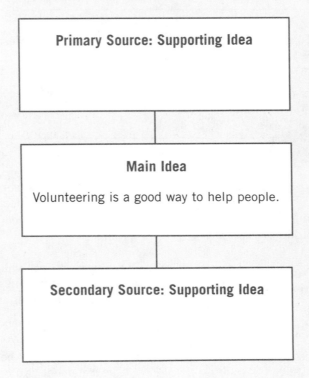

Primary Source: Supporting Idea

Main Idea

Volunteering is a good way to help people.

Secondary Source: Supporting Idea

Analyzing Informational Materials

Reading Check

1. In "Teaching Chess, and Life," what lesson did Carlos Capellan learn after he slammed his chess pieces down during a tournament? _____
_____
_____

2. What motivated David Levitt to develop his food-sharing program, as described in "Feeding Frenzy"? _____
_____

Test Practice

Circle the letter of the correct answer.

1. Which of the following statements is the *most* accurate **evaluation** of "Teaching Chess, and Life?"

   A The author uses both fact and opinion to make his point.

   B The author includes only opinions in his article.

   C The author includes facts that can't be checked for accuracy.

   D Because he does not support his point, the author fails to show why Chia has been so influential.

2. Which sentence *best* expresses the **main idea** of "Feeding Frenzy"?

   F Good deeds should be given public recognition.

   G Many government regulations serve no purpose.

   H A good cause is worth pursuing, even in the face of difficulties.

   J Millions of people in America go to bed hungry.

3. Of the two articles, which gives the *best* picture of the difficulties faced by those who wish to do community service?

   A "Teaching Chess, and Life," because it tells about at-risk young people.

   B "Feeding Frenzy," because it includes the statement "No one knows better than David how to get food to the hungry."

   C "Feeding Frenzy," because it describes the obstacles to starting a food-sharing program.

   D "Teaching Chess, and Life," because the author needed Chia's help and guidance.

Vocabulary: How to Own a Word

Mapping an Unfamiliar Word

A word map, like the one below, can help you get to know a new word
better by organizing ideas related to the word. Fill out the map for
legislation. Remember that you can always make a word map of your own
when you encounter an unfamiliar word.

Word Bank

mentorship

legislation

bureaucratic

undaunted

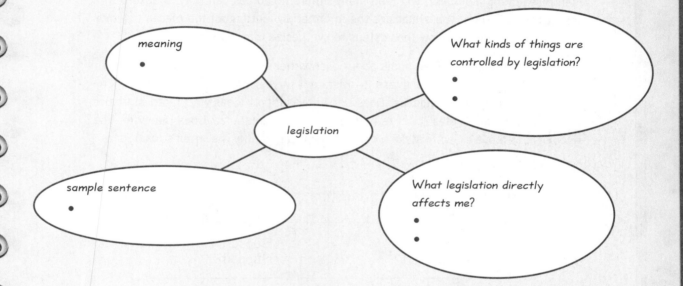

On a separate sheet of paper, make word maps like the one above for the remaining Word Bank
words.

Edgar A. Poe: Mournful and Never-Ending Remembrance
Poe's Death Is Rewritten as Case of Rabies, Not Telltale Alcohol
If Only Poe Had Succeeded When He Said Nevermore to Drink
Rabies Death Theory

Make the Connection

Synthesizing: Seeing the Big Picture

When researching a subject, you read many different sources carefully to absorb what each has to say. Then, you **synthesize** the information, putting all the pieces together to see the big picture. Follow these steps to synthesize information:

- **Find the main idea.** Take notes about each writer's main idea. To work through a difficult passage, **paraphrase** it—restate it in your own words.
- **Look for supporting evidence.** Does the writer support ideas with facts, statistics, examples, anecdotes (brief real-life stories), or quotations? Does the writer use logic to prove a point? Make a chart to help you identify the writer's main ideas and support.

Main Idea 1	Main Idea 2
Support 1 Support 2	Support 1 Support 2

- **Compare and contrast.** Look for similarities and differences between sources. Compare and contrast the main ideas and support the authors use.
- **Make connections.** Does the information in your sources remind you of ideas that you've read about before in articles, books, stories, or poems?
- **Put it all together.** Once you've completed these steps, you're ready to **synthesize** what you've learned in a research report, an editorial, a speech, or a letter to help an audience see the big picture. When you present research information, be sure to credit sources properly.

Edgar A. Poe: Mournful and Never-Ending Remembrance

Kenneth Silverman

Poe's Death Is Rewritten as Case of Rabies, Not Telltale Alcohol

FROM *The New York Times,* September 15, 1996

If Only Poe Had Succeeded When He Said Nevermore to Drink

FROM *The New York Times,* September 23, 1996

Burton R. Pollin
Robert E. Benedetto

Rabies Death Theory

FROM *The New York Times,* September 30, 1996

R. Michael Benitez M.D.

IDENTIFY

Underline the fact that you must keep in mind while reading the rest of this excerpt.

_____
_____
_____
_____
_____
_____
_____
_____

EVALUATE

Was Snodgrass's conclusion logical? Explain why or why not.

_____
_____
_____
_____
_____
_____
_____
_____
_____

WORDS TO OWN

insensible (in·sen′sə·bəl) _adj._: not fully conscious or aware.
imposing (im·pō′ziŋ) _adj._: large and impressive-looking.

_____
_____
_____
_____
_____
_____

Edgar A. Poe: Mournful and Never-Ending Remembrance

Kenneth Silverman

In the early morning of September 27, a Thursday, Poe began the first leg of his return to the North, setting out from Richmond for Baltimore on the 4 A.M. steamer,[1] with a trunk containing some clothing, books, and manuscripts.

No reliable evidence exists about what happened to or within Poe between that time and October 3, a week later, when a printer named Joseph Walker saw him at Gunner's Hall, a Baltimore tavern, strangely dressed and semiconscious.

It was Election Day for members of Congress, and like other local watering holes[2] the tavern served as a polling place. Poe seemed to Walker "rather the worse for wear" and "in great distress." Apparently flooded with drink, he may also have been ill from exposure. Winds and soaking rains the day before had sent Baltimoreans prematurely hunting up overcoats and seeking charcoal fires for warmth. Poe managed to tell Walker that he knew Joseph Evans Snodgrass, the Baltimore editor and physician with whom he had often corresponded while living in Philadelphia. As it happened, Walker had worked as a typesetter for Snodgrass's _Saturday Visitor._ He sent Snodgrass a dire note, warning that Poe needed "immediate assistance."

When Snodgrass arrived at Gunner's Hall, he found Poe sitting in an armchair, surrounded by onlookers. Poe had a look of "vacant stupidity." He wore neither vest nor tie, his dingy trousers fit badly, his shirt was crumpled, his cheap hat soiled. Snodgrass thought he must be wearing castoff clothing, having been robbed or cheated of his own. He ordered a room for Poe at the tavern, where he might stay comfortably until his relatives in Baltimore could be notified. Just then, however, one of them arrived—Henry Herring, Poe's uncle by marriage, who somehow had also learned of his condition. A lumber dealer now nearly sixty years old, he had wed Muddy's[3] sister, and spent time with Poe during his early days in Baltimore and later when both families lived in Philadelphia. But he refused now to take over his care, saying that on former occasions, when drunk, Poe had been abusive and ungrateful. Instead, he suggested sending Poe to a hospital. A carriage was called for. Poe had to be carried into it, Snodgrass said—insensible, muttering.

Through the chilly wet streets Poe was driven to the hospital of Washington Medical College, set on the highest ground of Baltimore. An imposing five-story building with vaulted gothic windows, it afforded both public wards and private rooms, advertised as being spacious, well

---

1. **steamer** (stēm′ər) _n._: steamship, or ship driven by steam power.
2. **watering holes:** informal term for bars or taverns.
3. **Muddy's:** Muddy was Poe's nickname for Maria Clemm, his aunt and mother-in-law. Poe had married his cousin, Virginia Clemm.

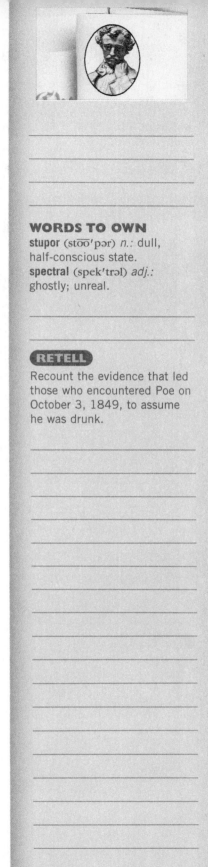

ventilated, and directed by an experienced medical staff. Admitted at five
in the afternoon, Poe was given a private room, reportedly in a section
reserved for cases involving drunkenness. He was attended by the
resident physician, Dr. John J. Moran, who apparently had living
quarters in the hospital together with his wife. Moran had received his
medical degree from the University of Maryland four years earlier and
was now only about twenty-six years old. But he knew the identity of his
patient—a "*great* man," he wrote of Poe, to whose "rarely gifted mind
are we indebted for many of the brightest thoughts that adorn our
literature." He as well as the medical students, nurses, and other
physicians—all considered Poe, he said, "an object of unusual regard."

According to Moran and his wife, Poe reached the hospital in a
stupor, unaware of who or what had brought him there. He remained
thus "unconscious" until three o'clock the next morning, when he
developed a tremor[4] of the limbs and what Moran called "a busy, but not
violent or active delirium."[5] His face was pale and he was drenched in
sweat. He talked constantly, Moran said, addressing "spectral and
imaginary objects on the walls." Apparently during Poe's delirium, his
cousin Neilson Poe came to the hospital, having been contacted by Dr.
Moran. A lawyer and journalist involved in Whig politics,[6] Neilson was
just Poe's age. In happier circumstances Poe would not have welcomed
the visit. Not only had Neilson offered Virginia[7] and Muddy a home
apart from him; his cousin also, he believed, envied his literary
reputation. Years before he had remarked that he considered "the little
dog," as he called Neilson, the "bitterest enemy I have in the world."
The physicians anyway thought it inadvisable for Neilson to see Poe at
the moment, when "very excitable." Neilson sent some changes of linen
and called again the next day, to find Poe's condition improved.

Poe being quieted, Moran began questioning him about his family
and about where he lived, but found his answers mostly incoherent.
Poe did not know what had become of his trunk or when he had left
Richmond, but said he had a wife there, as Moran soon learned was
untrue. He said that his "degradation," as Moran characterized it, made
him feel like sinking into the ground. Trying to rouse Poe's spirits, Moran
told him he wished to contribute in every way to his comfort, and hoped
Poe would soon be enjoying the company of his friends.

Then Poe seemed to doze, and Moran left him briefly. On returning
he found Poe violently delirious, resisting the efforts of two nurses to keep
him in bed. From Moran's description, Poe seems to have raved a full
day or more, through Saturday evening, October 6, when he began
repeatedly calling out someone's name. It may have been that of a

40

50

60

70

---

4. **tremor** (trem′ər) *n.*: involuntary trembling, especially from a physical illness.
5. **delirium** (di·lir′ē·əm) *n.*: irrational, raving behavior, often caused by high fever.
6. **Whig politics:** The Whigs were one of the two major American political parties of the time,
   the other being the Democrats.
7. **Virginia:** Poe's wife, Virginia Clemm. She died of tuberculosis in 1847.

WORDS TO OWN
stupor (stoo′pər) *n.*: dull,
half-conscious state.
spectral (spek′trəl) *adj.*:
ghostly; unreal.

RETELL
Recount the evidence that led
those who encountered Poe on
October 3, 1849, to assume
he was drunk.

IDENTIFY

Re-read the paragraph that most completely **synthesizes** the available **evidence** about Poe's death. What two explanations are given?

_____

_____

_____

_____

_____

_____

_____

_____

_____

_____

_____

_____

_____

_____

_____

_____

IDENTIFY

Underline the **main idea** of the article.

_____

_____

_____

_____

_____

_____

_____

_____

_____

80 Baltimore family named Reynolds or, more likely, the name of his uncle-in-law Henry Herring. Moran later said that he sent for the Herring family, but that only one of Herring's two daughters came to the hospital. Poe continued deliriously calling the name until three o'clock on Sunday morning. Then his condition changed. Feeble from his exertions he seemed to rest a short time and then, Moran reported, "quietly moving his head he said '*Lord help my poor Soul*' and expired!"

The cause of Poe's death remains in doubt. Moran's account of his profuse perspiration, trembling, and hallucinations indicates delirium tremens, *mania à potu*.[8] Many others who had known Poe, including the

90 professionally trained Dr. Snodgrass, also attributed his death to a lethal amount of alcohol. Moran later vigorously disputed this explanation, however, and some Baltimore newspapers gave the cause of death as "congestion of the brain" or "cerebral inflammation."[9] Although the terms were sometimes used euphemistically[10] in public announcements of deaths from disgraceful causes, such as alcoholism, they may in this case have come from the hospital staff itself. According to Moran, one of its senior physicians diagnosed Poe's condition as encephalitis, a brain inflammation, brought on by "exposure." This explanation is consistent with the prematurely wintry weather at the time, with Snodgrass's

100 account of Poe's partly clad[11] condition, and with Elmira Shelton's recollection that on leaving Richmond Poe already had a fever. Both explanations may have been correct: Poe may have become too drunk to care about protecting himself against the wind and rain.

Poe's Death Is Rewritten as Case of Rabies, Not Telltale Alcohol
from *The New York Times*, September 15, 1996

The following news article announced a new theory about Poe's death, developed by Dr. R. Michael Benitez. In response to this article, Burton R. Pollin and Robert E. Benedetto wrote a letter disputing Dr. Benitez's theory. Dr. Benitez replied by writing a letter defending his ideas.

Edgar Allan Poe did not die drunk in a gutter in Baltimore but rather had rabies, a new study suggests.

The researcher, Dr. R. Michael Benitez, a cardiologist[1] who practices a block from Poe's grave, says it is true that the writer was seen in a bar

---

8. **delirium tremens, *mania à potu*:** Delirium tremens refers to an alcoholic state in which the victim behaves irrationally and sometimes violently, hallucinates (sees imaginary things), and trembles. *Mania à potu* is a Latin phrase meaning "madness from drinking."
9. **"congestion of the brain" or "cerebral inflammation":** These are terms for conditions of the brain caused by injury or infection.
10. **euphemistically** (yōo′fə·miz′ti·kali) *adv.*: in a manner meant to mask or substitute for something unpleasant or offensive.
11. **clad** (klad) *adj.*: dressed.

1. **cardiologist** (kär′dē·äl′ə·jist) *n.*: doctor who specializes in diseases of the heart.

on Lombard Street in October 1849, delirious and possibly wearing somebody else's soiled clothes.

But Poe was not drunk, said Dr. Benitez, an assistant professor of medicine at the University of Maryland Medical Center. "I think Poe is much <u>maligned</u> in that respect," he added.

10　　The writer entered Washington College Hospital comatose,[2] Dr. Benitez said, but by the next day was perspiring heavily, hallucinating, and shouting at imaginary companions. The next day, he seemed better but could not remember falling ill.

On his fourth day at the hospital, Poe again grew confused and <u>belligerent</u>, then quieted down and died.

That is a classic case of rabies, the doctor said. His study is in the September issue of *The Maryland Medical Journal*.

In the brief period when he was calm and awake, Poe refused alcohol and could drink water only with great difficulty. Rabies victims frequently

20　exhibit hydrophobia, or fear of water, because it is painful to swallow.

There is no evidence that a rabid animal had bitten Poe. About one-fourth of rabies victims reportedly cannot remember being bitten. After an infection, the symptoms can take up to a year to appear. But when the symptoms do appear, the disease is a swift and brutal killer. Most patients die in a few days.

Poe "had all the features of encephalitic[3] rabies," said Dr. Henry Wilde, who frequently treats rabies at Chulalongkorn University Hospital in Bangkok, Thailand.

Although it has been well established that Poe died in the hospital, legend

30　has it that he succumbed in the gutter, a victim of his debauched[4] ways.

The legend may have been fostered by his doctor, who in later years became a temperance advocate[5] and changed the details to make an object lesson of Poe's death.

The curator of the Edgar Allan Poe House and Museum in Baltimore, Jeff Jerome, said that he had heard dozens of tales but that "almost everyone who has come forth with a theory has offered no proof."

Some versions have Poe unconscious under the steps of the Baltimore Museum before being taken to the hospital. Other accounts place him on planks between two barrels outside a tavern on Lombard

40　Street. In most versions, Poe is wearing someone else's clothes, having been robbed of his suit.

Poe almost surely did not die of alcohol poisoning or withdrawal, Mr. Jerome said. The writer was so sensitive to alcohol that a glass of wine would make him violently ill for days. Poe may have had problems with

---

2. **comatose** (ko′mə·tōs) *adj.:* deeply unconscious and unable to be wakened.
3. **encephalitic** (en·sef′ə·lit′ik) *adj.:* related to encephalitis, which is an inflammation, or swelling, of the brain.
4. **debauched** (dē·bôchd′) *adj.:* characterized by extreme indulgence in pleasures.
5. **temperance advocate:** someone who believes that people should not drink alcohol.

WORDS TO OWN

maligned (mə·līnd′) *v.:* falsely accused of bad conduct; slandered.

belligerent (bə·lij′ər·ənt) *adj.:* angry and aggressive or ready to start a fight.

EVALUATE

Is the evidence offered in lines 16–27 persuasive? Explain your answer.

_____

_____

_____

_____

_____

_____

_____

_____

_____

_____

_____

_____

INTERPRET

Compare and contrast Jeff Jerome's claim in lines 42–46 with Henry Herring's opinion of Poe, as described in the previous selection.

_____

_____

_____

_____

_____

_____

_____

_____

_____

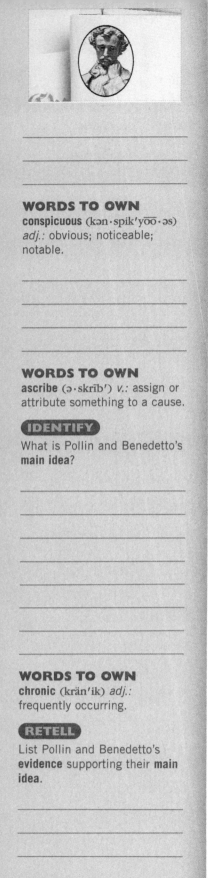

WORDS TO OWN
conspicuous (kən·spik′yōō·əs)
adj.: obvious; noticeable;
notable.

WORDS TO OWN
ascribe (ə·skrīb′) v.: assign or
attribute something to a cause.

IDENTIFY

What is Pollin and Benedetto's
main idea?

WORDS TO OWN
chronic (krän′ik) adj.:
frequently occurring.

RETELL

List Pollin and Benedetto's
evidence supporting their **main
idea.**

---

alcohol as a younger man, Mr. Jerome said, but by the time he died at forty he almost always avoided it.

Dr. Benitez worked on Poe's case as part of a clinical pathologic conference. Doctors are presented with a hypothetical[6] patient and a description of the symptoms and are asked to render a diagnosis.

50   Dr. Benitez said that at first he did not know that he had been assigned Poe, because his patient was described only as "E. P., a writer from Richmond." But by the time he was scheduled to present his findings a few weeks later, he had figured out the mystery.

"There was a conspicuous lack in this report of things like CT scans and M.R.I.'s," [7] the doctor said. "I started to say to myself, 'This doesn't look like it's from the 1990s.' Then it dawned on me that E. P. was Edgar Poe."

If Only Poe Had Succeeded When He Said Nevermore to Drink
from *The New York Times,* September 23, 1996

To the Editor:

Dr. R. Michael Benitez, an assistant professor of medicine at Maryland University Medical Center, is wrong to ascribe the death of Edgar Allan Poe to rabies through animal infection rather than to the traditionally maintained cause of alcoholism (news article, September 15).

Poe was found outside a Baltimore saloon in an alcoholic stupor on October 3, 1849, and died four days later. Dr. John J. Moran's account of his final days is given in a letter to Poe's aunt and mother-in-law, Maria Clemm; a *New York Herald* article in 1875, and a book by Moran in 1885.
10   Supplementary accounts of Poe's alcoholic condition came from Joseph Walker, a Baltimore printer who first found him; Dr. Joseph Snodgrass, an editor well known to Poe; and two of Poe's relatives. None of these confirm Dr. Benitez's statement that "Poe was not drunk." Evidence of Poe's chronic binges is strewn through his letters, in periodic admissions of "recoveries" and promises to his wife, Virginia, and her mother to "reform."

Dr. Benitez admits the primary weakness of his theory—lack of evidence of a bite or scratch. In those days, rabies was well known as to causes and symptoms, including itching and other sensations that could affect an entire limb or side of the body. How could Moran and his staff
20   ignore such symptoms in a patient?

And what of Poe's cat, dearly loved but left behind in the Bronx over three months earlier? Guiltless was the pet Caterina, who, uninfected and showing no sign of rabies, died of starvation when deserted by Clemm after Poe's death.

---

6. **hypothetical** (hī′pə·thet′i·kəl) *adj.:* in theory; not actual.
7. **CT scans and M.R.I.'s:** medical tests that use modern technology. Both tests produce an image of a cross-section of soft tissue such as the brain.

In short, there is no need to whitewash the self-destructive behavior of this literary genius and major American poet, critic, and teller of tales.

Burton R. Pollin
Robert E. Benedetto
Bronxville, New York
September 20, 1996

30

The writers are, respectively, professor emeritus of English, City University of New York, and an associate film professor at the University of South Carolina.

Rabies Death Theory
from *The New York Times,* September 30, 1996

To the Editor:

Contrary to a September 23 letter, I do not "admit" that the lack of bite or scratch is a weakness in my theory that Edgar Allan Poe may have died of rabies encephalitis.

Data published by the Centers for Disease Control and Prevention indicate that over the past 20 years in the United States there have been 33 reported cases of human rabies, yet only 24 percent of these victims could recall an appropriate history of animal exposure. Bat-related subtypes of rabies have been identified in 15 cases of human rabies since

10 1980, although patient contact of any sort with bats could be documented in only 7 of these patients.

A diagnosis is not always easy or straightforward. The incubation period[1] in humans may be as long as a year, if the inoculation[2] is small and occurs on the hand or foot. Thus the lack of evidence of a bite or scratch is not inconsistent with the diagnosis. Finally, although physicians knew how rabies was <u>transmitted</u> at the time of Poe's death, even at the time of Louis Pasteur's first use of a rabies "vaccine" in 1885 the causative agent, a rhabdovirus, was unknown.[3]

I was saddened to hear of the fate of Caterina, Poe's cat, yet nowhere

20 have I suggested that Poe contracted rabies from her, although it is worth noting that there was no available vaccine for pets at that time.

R. Michael Benitez, M.D.
Baltimore, Maryland
September 26, 1996

The writer is an assistant professor of medicine at the University of Maryland Medical Center.

---

1. **incubation period:** amount of time between a person's exposure to a disease and the appearance of symptoms.
2. **inoculation:** (i·näk′yə·lā′shən) *n.*: here, skin puncture from an animal bite or scratch through which a disease is passed on.
3. **even at the time of Louis Pasteur's . . . was unknown:** Louis Pasteur (1822–1895) was a French chemist who helped develop the important medical theory linking germs and disease. Pasteur developed a rabies vaccine using tissue from infected animals. Benitez is pointing out, however, that at the time of Poe's death, scientists had not isolated and identified the virus that causes rabies.

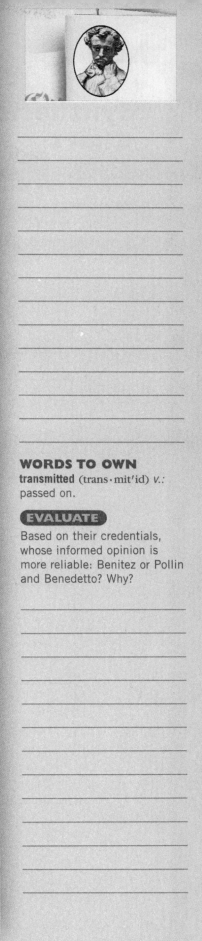

WORDS TO OWN
transmitted (trans·mit′id) *v.*: passed on.

EVALUATE

Based on their credentials, whose informed opinion is more reliable: Benitez or Pollin and Benedetto? Why?

Synthesizing: Seeing the Big Picture Chart

Create four **Main Idea** Webs like the one below. Complete one web for each of the four reading selections about Edgar Allan Poe's death. When you've finished all of the webs, compare and contrast the main ideas and supporting evidence of the book excerpt, the newspaper article, and the letters. Try making connections between the selections and your prior reading.

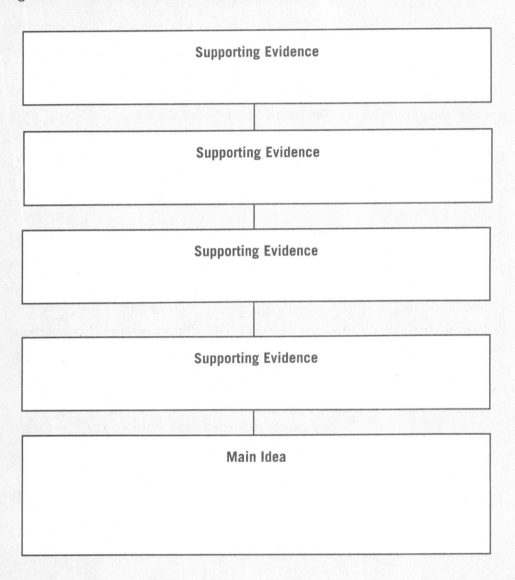

Supporting Evidence

Supporting Evidence

Supporting Evidence

Supporting Evidence

Main Idea

Analyzing Informational Materials

Reading Check

1. Make a time line of Poe's final days based on the information in the biography (*Edgar A. Poe: Mournful and Never-Ending Remembrance*). _____
_____
_____
_____
_____

2. Summarize the evidence cited to support Dr. Benitez's theory in the article ("Poe's Death Is Rewritten as Case of Rabies, Not Telltale Alcohol"). _____
_____
_____
_____
_____

3. According to Burton R. Pollin and Robert E. Benedetto, what is the major weakness of Dr. Benitez's theory? _____
_____
_____
_____
_____

Test Practice

Circle the letter of the correct answer.

1. What is the **main idea** in the letter by Pollin and Benedetto?

   A Poe has been unjustly accused of being and alcoholic.

   B There is a great deal of evidence that Poe's death was due to alcoholism.

   C Poe's cat could not have bitten him and given him rabies.

   D Poe was a great writer, but he had human faults.

2. What is the *strongest* **evidence** Dr. Benitez presents in his letter to defend his theory?

   F Rabies has a long incubation period, and many victims do not remember being attacked by an animal.

   G There was no available vaccine for pets at the time of Poe's death.

   H During Poe's lifetime doctors knew how rabies was passed on.

   J Louis Pasteur first used a rabies vaccine in 1885.

Analyzing Informational Materials
(continued)

3. What information in the biography could support Dr. Benitez's theory that rabies caused Poe's death?

  A It had been raining, and Poe may have suffered from exposure.

  B Dr. Moran stated that Poe sweated and addressed "imaginary objects on the walls."

  C Poe was so ill that he was taken to the hospital.

  D No one knows where Poe was the week before he appeared at the tavern.

4. Which of the following statements that **contrast** the biography with Pollin and Benedetto's letter is *not* true?

  F The biography states that Dr. Moran eventually claimed Poe didn't die from drinking too much, but the letter states that Dr. Moran provided evidence for this theory.

  G Pollin and Benedetto refer to Poe's letters as evidence, but the biography does not.

  H The biography does not discuss the rabies death theory, but the letter does.

  J The letter does not refer to Joseph Walker's description of Poe, but the biography does.

5. Which statement is the *most* important **similarity** between the article and Dr. Benitez's letter?

  A Both inform the reader that Dr. Benitez is an assistant professor of medicine.

  B Both use statistics to support a point.

  C Both point out that the lack of a bite or scratch does not weaken the rabies death theory.

  D Both state that only highly skilled doctors can diagnose rabies.

6. Which of the following statements is the *best* **synthesis** of the information in these four sources?

  F Poe was a tortured genius.

  G Poe's symptoms could point to several different causes of death.

  H All theories should take into account that Poe died drunk.

  J Poe's illness would have been correctly diagnosed by modern doctors.

Vocabulary: How to Own a Word

Understanding Word Derivations: Useful Roots to Know

A **root** is the part of a word that establishes its core meaning. Knowing what some common roots mean will help you figure out the definitions of new words.

Word Bank
insensible
imposing
stupor
spectral
expired
maligned
belligerent
conspicuous
ascribe
chronic
transmitted

Practice

Match each root in the chart below with a word from the Word Bank. Then, define the word, and write another word with the same root.

Word Roots

specere (Latin), "to see"
spirare (Latin), "to breathe"
ponere (Latin), "to place"
mittere (Latin), "to send"
male (Latin), "ill"
chronos (Greek), "time"

stupere (Latin), "to be stunned or amazed"
bellum (Latin), "war"
sentire (Latin), "to feel"
scribere (Latin), "to write"
spectare (Latin), "to behold"

Far-out Housekeeping on the ISS

Make the Connection

Using the Internet for Research

When you consult the World Wide Web for information on a particular topic, follow these steps:

1. Use a **search engine** to locate Web sites that are relevant to your topic. Enter a **search term,** a keyword. If the search produces too many sites, use a more specific term or try a different search engine.
2. If you know the **URL** (Uniform Resource Location), the site's Internet address, enter it in the location field on your browser screen.
3. Look for **hyperlinks** on the Web page that lead to other sources. You can reach a link by clicking on it. Some links may be underlined or appear in italics or in color. Other links may appear in a side column or at the conclusion of the article. Sometimes there are **audio** or **video** links. On some pages, symbols or pictures called **icons** provide links.

   Briefly respond to these questions:

   • What is the purpose of a search engine?

   _____

   _____

   • What keyword or keywords would you use to research living conditions in space?

   _____

   _____

   • How do hyperlinks assist you in research?

   _____

   _____

   The following article, which appeared on the Internet, deals with housekeeping on the International Space Station.

FAR-OUT HOUSEKEEPING ON THE ISS

Ron Koczor

IDENTIFY

List two reasons for considering space a hostile environment.

Inform Inspire Involve
science.nasa.gov

Far-out Housekeeping on the ISS

Life in space is a daring adventure, but somebody still has to cook dinner and take out the trash. Science@NASA interviews two astronauts about the thrill and routine of daily life in orbit.

NASA Science News home

🔊 Listen to this story

November 29, 2000—It's open for business! And even though the construction crews aren't done yet, the International Space Station's first occupants have moved in and set up housekeeping. If all goes as planned, the arrival of Expedition 1 in orbit earlier this month signaled the beginning of a new era. From now on, there will always be humans in space.

Living in space is a daunting adventure with plenty of derring-do and glamour. Hollywood spacefarers rarely have to take out the trash or clean the kitchen. But, what about real-life astronauts? Are there chores to do on the ISS? In a recent interview with Science@NASA, Dr. Edward Lu and Coast Guard Lieutenant Commander Daniel Burbank—two astronauts who helped build the space station—discussed the excitement and the day-to-day routine of life in orbit.

"Space really is the most hostile environment humans have ever tried to live in," said Burbank. "You depend on the Station and the people on the ground for everything you need to survive. It is complicated and everything has to work!" It's a risky adventure with very little margin for error, but, said the astronauts, the thrill of being there is something that neither would give up.

Hot Foods and Fresh Fruit

So what is it like being there for months or years at a time? For example, what does the ISS crew eat, and how is it cooked?

Right: The biggest challenge at mealtime for astronauts: catching your food! In this image Astronaut Loren Shriver (STS-46) demonstrates how objects act in free-fall while enjoying a snack of candy-coated peanuts. Residents of the ISS have more nutritious choices, too, including free fruits shuttled from Earth.

40   <u>All food</u> is delivered by the American space shuttle or Russian Progress vehicle. The crew helps select the foods they want from a wide-ranging menu.

    According to Vicki Kloeris, subsystem manager for shuttle and space station food at the Johnson Space Center, food aboard Space Station will come in several forms. "Most of the food will be processed and packaged in pouches or cans. Some will be dehydrated and the astronauts add hot water and eat. Some will be in pouches and cans and you simply heat and eat. A small amount will be fresh food delivered by the shuttle and Progress." The fresh food will include fruits and veggies, but nothing

50 that requires refrigeration. ISS will contain more than one oven when it is fully operational. In the early stages, food is being cooked using either a small food warmer built by the Russians or a U.S. built portable food warmer, about the size of a suitcase.

ISS, Phone Home.

Information gained from the experiences of the Russian MIR space station crews indicates that isolation is one of the biggest problems a long-duration crew will face. To prevent this on ISS, the crew members will be encouraged to phone home. And while working on ISS will not exactly be like spending a couple of weeks away from home on

60 business in the Big Apple or the Windy City, sailors traveling around the British Empire in the 17th and 18th centuries were more isolated than the ISS crew will be.

    "Each crew member will have a video telephone call from home each week," said Burbank. "And the crew will be receiving and sending daily e-mail messages to and from family and friends. No one should feel isolated from home and family."

Members of the STS-106 crew,
70 *including Lu and Burbank, snapped this picture of the ISS from the space shuttle* Atlantis *in September 2000.*
[more information]

Who Takes Out the Trash?

A recent Science@NASA story about <u>water recycling on the ISS</u> covered the great lengths that ISS designers are taking to minimize how much water and other consumables must be launched from Earth. Water recycling efficiencies of greater than 95% are the goal.

RETELL
Briefly tell how the space crews communicate with family and friends.

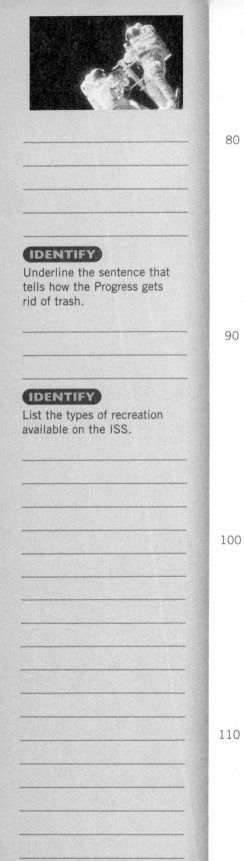

Back Forward Stop Reload Search

Location:

80 But other wastes cannot be recycled so efficiently, particularly solid waste from food containers, experiments, empty fuel containers, and other ISS activities. So: Who takes out the trash?

Again, Progress and Shuttle come to the rescue. Every arrival of Shuttle brings fresh supplies. And when it leaves, it becomes the world's most expensive trash hauler! Bags and containers of sealed trash will be brought back to Earth.

More exciting, perhaps, is how the Russian Progress disposes of trash. Again, when it arrives, it brings fresh supplies (but no crews, since it is just a supply vehicle). And when the fresh supplies are unloaded, the trash bags are piled in and Progress is sealed. After it

90 disconnects from ISS, it is placed into a lower orbit and makes a controlled reentry during which it and the trash are incinerated over the ocean.

R&R in Space

Crews will be busy during their tours of duty on ISS. But all work and no play . . . So what constitutes relaxation and recreation for the men and women living aboard ISS?

"Crew members will be allowed to take a certain amount of personal gear up with them," said Lu. "So things like checkers or chess sets, CDs and tape players, and the like are allowed. You can listen to your

100 favorite music if you like. DVD movies will also be available for viewing."

So it's not exactly like home! And you can't take an evening walk outside to watch the sunset. But the "sailors" on ISS will have it better than those intrepid explorers that left Europe in the 15th century looking for new lands, or the Polynesian sailors that charted and settled the vast Pacific Ocean, or the Asian explorers and settlers who walked the land bridge from Siberia into Alaska and opened two new continents for their people.

They do, however, share two important traits. First, they are the vanguard of their respective civilizations, doing what they believe will

110 improve the well-being of their people.

And second, they all had to forge ahead and ignore the shrill voices behind them warning that "beyond this point, there be dragons!"

Web Links

<u>Water on the Space Station</u>—The first Science@NASA article in this series about the practical challenges of extended living in space. This article looks at how water will be conserved and recycled on the space station—including the crew's own urine!

<u>Breathing easy on the Space Station</u>—The second Science@NASA article in this series about the practical challenges of extended living in space. The systems and methods used to ensure safe, breathable air for the crew are examined in this article.

<u>Microscopic stowaways on the Space Station</u>—The third Science@NASA article in this series about the practical challenges of extended living in space.

<u>International Space Station</u>—NASA's Web page for the International Space Station.

<u>Advanced Life Support Web Page</u>—from the Johnson Space Flight Center.

<u>Environmental Control and Life Support Systems</u>—describes the life-support systems being developed at Marshall Space Flight Center.

Join our growing list of subscribers—<u>sign up for our express news delivery</u> and you will receive a mail message every time we post a new story!!!

<u>More</u>   <u>Headlines</u>

| For lesson plans and educational activities related to breaking science news, please visit <u>Thursday's Classroom</u> | Author: <u>Ron Koczor</u>
Production Editor: <u>Dr. Tony Phillips</u>
Curator: <u>Bryan Walls</u>
Media Relations: <u>Steve Roy</u>
Responsible NASA official: <u>Ron Koczor</u> |

120

130

INFER

Write the title of the Web link you would use to research the existence of microorganisms in space.

Personal Gear Chart

Suppose you were to spend six months on the International Space Station. What possessions would you take with you? Fill in the chart and compare your answers with those of others in your group.

Personal Gear

Games	Music	Movies	Reading/Writing Material

Analyzing Informational Materials

Reading Check

1. Describe how food is brought to the International Space Station and how trash is removed.

_____

_____

2. List the traits that space travelers share with explorers who lived in earlier centuries.

_____

_____

Test Practice

Circle the letter of the correct answer.

1. If you wanted to learn more about living in space on a long-term basis, which search term would be the *most* useful?

A History of space exploration
B Space stations
C Astronauts
D Spacesuits

2. Which source would provide the *most* up-to-date information about extended living in space?

F An interview with astronauts who lived on the Mir space station
G A science textbook
H A history book about important space missions
J A Web page about new technology used on the ISS

3. If you wanted to learn about oxygen supplies for the ISS crew, which **link** on this Web page would be *least* likely to provide information?

A Breathing easy on the Space Station
B Advanced Life Support Web Page
C Environmental Control and Life Support Systems
D Water on the Space Station

Application

Generate a list of questions based on "Far-out Housekeeping on the ISS." Then, choose one question, and research it in a library and on the Internet. What sources did you use? What resources could you have used to answer the question?

Romeo and Juliet in Bosnia

Make the Connection

Connect and Compare

Whenever you read, you automatically look for connections with the world you know. You think about how the subject—a heartache, a family crisis, a societal wrong—connects with your own experience.

You should also **connect and compare** what you read to other works you have read. For example, you may remember a character in a novel who faces difficulties being with the one she loves and compare her responses with Juliet's. Each work you read on a subject thus adds to your overall understanding of the world.

One way to increase your understanding is to **synthesize**—or bring together into a whole—what you have learned from different sources on a topic. To do this, first **paraphrase** the ideas in each source—that is, restate them in your own words. Then, **connect** each source with the others—tell how they are similar and different. Finally, try to describe what all the works have added to your understanding of life.

A well-known literary creation like *Romeo and Juliet* often takes on a reality of its own in the mind or life of the reader. The left column of the box below states a few basic scenarios from Shakespeare's play. Fill in the right column with similar situations from your experience or from a story you've read or seen on film.

Romeo and Juliet	Your Connection
Two people meet and fall in love, but their families don't get along.	
Two young lovers must keep their relationship a secret.	
The love between two people brings warring families together.	

Romeo and Juliet in Bosnia

Bob Herbert

FROM *The New York Times,* May 8, 1994

PREDICT

Based solely on its title, guess what the editorial will be about.

_____

_____

_____

_____

_____

_____

WORDS TO OWN
carnage (kär′nij) _n._: slaughter; bloodshed.
reminiscing (rem′ə·nis′iŋ) _v._: thinking, talking, or writing about one's memories.
relentless (ri·lent′lis) _adj._: not letting up; persistent; harsh.
mundane (mun′dān′) _adj._: everyday; commonplace.

_____

_____

_____

WORDS TO OWN
compulsory (kəm·pul′sə·rē) _adj._: required by rule or law.

_____

_____

_____

_____

WORDS TO OWN
vulnerable (vul′nər·ə·bəl) _adj._: capable of being hurt.
primal (prī′məl) _adj._: original; primitive.

_____

_____

_____

If you watch _Frontline_ Tuesday night on PBS, you will see the story of two ordinary young people, Bosko Brkic, an Eastern Orthodox Serb, and Admira Ismic, a Muslim, who met at a New Year's Eve party in the mid-1980s, fell in love, tried to pursue the most conventional of dreams, and died together on a hellish bridge in Sarajevo.

The documentary, called "Romeo and Juliet in Sarajevo," achieves its power by focusing our attention on the thoroughly human individuals caught up in a horror that, from afar, can seem abstract and almost unimaginable. It's one thing to hear about the carnage caused by
10 incessant[1] sniper fire and the steady rain of mortar shells on a city; it's something quite different to actually witness a parent desperately groping for meaning while reminiscing about a lost daughter.

For viewers overwhelmed and desensitized by the relentless reports of mass killings and mass rapes, the shock of "Romeo and Juliet in Sarajevo" is that what we see is so real and utterly familiar. We become riveted by the mundane. Bosko and Admira could be a young couple from anywhere, from Queens, or Tokyo, or Barcelona.

We learn that they graduated from high school in June of 1986 and that both were crazy about movies and music. Admira had a cat named
20 Yellow that she loved, and Bosko liked to play practical jokes.

Admira's father, Zijo, speaking amid clouds of cigarette smoke, says, "Well, I knew from the first day about that relationship and I didn't have anything against it. I thought it was good because her guy was so likable, and after a time I started to love him and didn't regard him any differently than Admira."

Admira's grandmother, Sadika Ismic, was not so sanguine.[2] "Yes, I did have something against it," she says. "I thought, 'He is Serb, she is a Muslim, and how will it work?'"

For Admira and Bosko, of course, love was the answer to everything.
30 While Bosko was away on compulsory military service soon after high school, Admira wrote: "My dear love, Sarajevo at night is the most beautiful thing in the world. I guess I could live somewhere else but only if I must or if I am forced. Just a little beat of time is left until we are together. After that, absolutely nothing can separate us."

Sarajevo at the time was a cosmopolitan[3] city coming off the triumph of the 1984 Winter Olympics. With a population of Serbs, Croats, Muslims, Jews, and others, the city had become a symbol of ethnic and religious tolerance, a place where people were making a serious attempt to live together in peace.
40 But civilization is an exceedingly fragile enterprise, and it's especially vulnerable to the primal madness of ethnic and religious hatreds. Simple

---

1. incessant (in·ses′ənt) _adj._: never ceasing; continual.
2. sanguine (saŋ′gwin) _adj._: optimistic; hopeful; cheerful.
3. cosmopolitan (käz′mə·päl′ə·tən) _adj._: worldly; sophisticated.

tolerance is nothing in the face of the relentless, pathetic and near-universal need to bolster the <u>esteem</u> of the individual and the group by <u>eradicating</u> the rights, and even the existence, of others.

When the madness descended on Sarajevo, Bosko Brkic faced a cruel <u>dilemma</u>. He could not kill Serbs. And he could not go up into the hills and fire back down on his girlfriend's people. Says his mother, Rada: "He was simply a kid who was not for the war."

Bosko and Admira decided to flee Sarajevo. To escape, they had to
50 cross a bridge over the Miljacka River in a no man's land[4] between the Serb and Muslim lines. Snipers from both sides overlooked the bridge.

It has not been determined who shot the lovers. They were about two thirds of the way across the bridge when the gunfire erupted. Both sides blame the other. Witnesses said Bosko died instantly. Admira crawled to him. She died a few minutes later. The area in which they were shot was so dangerous that the bodies remained on the bridge, entwined, for six days before being removed.

Only the times and places change. Bosnia today, Rwanda and Burundi[5] tomorrow. Jews versus Arabs, Chinese versus Japanese,
60 blacks versus whites. There are various ostensible reasons for the endless conflicts—ideological[6] differences, border disputes, oil—but dig just a little and you will uncover the ruinous ethnic or religious origins of the clash.

The world stands helpless and sometimes depressed before the madness. Millions upon millions dead, millions more to die. It is not just the curse of our times. It seems to be the curse of all time.

---

4. **no man's land:** battle zone claimed by both sides in a war but controlled by neither, often where much of the fighting takes place.
5. **Rwanda and Burundi** (rə·wän′də, boo·roon′dē): African nations that have been the scene of ethnic warfare between the Tutsi and Hutu peoples.
6. **ideological** (ī′dē·ə·läj′i·kəl) *adj.:* based on political, social, or economic beliefs.

WORDS TO OWN
esteem (ə·stēm′) *n.:* respect.
eradicating (ē·rad′i·kāt′iŋ) *v.:* wiping out; destroying.
dilemma (di·lem′ə) *n.:* difficult choice; serious problem.

RETELL
Paraphrase the sentence in lines 41–44.

_____
_____
_____
_____
_____
_____

EVALUATE
Could what happened to Bosko and Admira happen in America? Explain.

_____
_____
_____
_____
_____
_____

EVALUATE
Someone once said that the death of one person is a tragedy, the deaths of a million people a statistic. How does Bosko and Admira's plight support this statement?

_____
_____
_____
_____

Connect and Compare Chart

Connect this informational piece to another work you have read or seen. It might be a love story, for example, or the portrayal of innocent victims. In the first two columns of the chart below, record parallel events and reactions that occur in "Romeo and Juliet in Bosnia" and in the work you have read or seen. In the third column, **synthesize** what the similarities and differences teach you about the overall situation.

"Romeo and Juliet in Bosnia"	Your Connecting Work	What You've Learned

Analyzing Informational Materials

Reading Check

1. Who are Admira and Bosko, the couple Bob Herbert writes about in "Romeo and Juliet in Bosnia"? _____

_____

2. What happened to Admira and Bosko? _____

_____

Test Practice

Circle the letter of the correct answer.

1. In both "Romeo and Juliet in Bosnia" and Shakespeare's *Romeo and Juliet* —

   A two characters named Romeo and Juliet die

   B two innocent lovers die because of a larger conflict

   C the destructiveness and pointlessness of war are described

   D young people are rejected by their families because of a feud

2. What is Bob Herbert's main **purpose** in "Romeo and Juliet in Bosnia"?

   F To point out parallels between the stories of Admira and Bosko and of Shakespeare's lovers

   G To show that love can triumph over death

   H To highlight the universal madness of conflicts like the one in Bosnia

   J To show that love is universal

3. Which of the following statements **synthesizes,** or brings together into a whole, themes from *Romeo and Juliet* and "Romeo and Juliet in Bosnia"?

   A Conflict can often destroy love.

   B People in love look to others for help.

   C Family conflicts can separate lovers.

   D People in love often face difficulties.

Vocabulary: How to Own a Word

Denotations and Connotations

Connotations are the emotions and associations suggested by a word, which go beyond the word's literal, dictionary meaning, or **denotation.** Often connotations show shades of meaning or intensity.

Practice

Compare the intensity of the words in each of the following pairs. If the word on the right seems stronger than the Word Bank word on the left, write "+" in the brackets between them. Use "−" if it seems weaker. Use a dictionary for help.

Word Bank
carnage
reminiscing
relentless
mundane
compulsory
vulnerable
primal
esteem
eradicating
dilemma

1. carnage   [   ] killing

2. reminiscing   [   ] remembering

3. relentless   [   ] persistent

4. mundane   [   ] common

5. compulsory   [   ] necessary

6. vulnerable   [   ] weak

7. primal   [   ] first

8. esteem   [   ] regard

9. eradicating   [   ] erasing

10. dilemma   [   ] choice

Selection: _____

Comparison and Contrast Chart

Issues/Characteristics	Topic/Item 1:	Topic/Item 2:

Summary statements: _____

_____

_____

Heroes with Solid Feet

Make the Connection

Evaluating an Argument: Intent and Tone

Writers make **appeals to reason,** or **logic,** by supporting their opinions with facts and statistics. By contrast, **emotional appeals** can win readers' hearts, even though they offer no objective evidence.

The author's **intent,** or **purpose,** determines the mix of **logical** and **emotional appeals**. In a largely objective argument, a reliance on **emotional appeals** would suggest that the writer was unable to back up the argument with hard evidence. However, a writer trying to make a more subjective argument—perhaps about honor or love—might not depend on using facts and statistics, which could seem cold and unfeeling.

Writers appeal to the reader's emotions with the following techniques:

- **Anecdotes.** Brief, colorful stories can personalize cold facts.
- **Loaded words.** Words like *hero, evil, love, hate, victim,* and *freedom* have strong **connotations,** or emotional associations; they work on our feelings.

The author's **intent** directly affects **tone,** which is created by the author's choice of words. In addition to **loaded language, sensory images** and **figurative language** also contribute to tone by painting vivid pictures in readers' minds.

Read the following sentences. Identify whether **loaded language, sensory images,** or **figurative language** is affecting each sentence's tone and mark the appropriate boxes. Each sentence may have more than one answer.

Sentence	Loaded Language	Sensory Images	Figurative Language
1. The turkey's aroma awakened the appetites of the dinner guests.	☐	☐	☐
2. The cruel indifference shown by the criminal sickened the judge.	☐	☐	☐
3. Frank ran toward Marie like a lovesick puppy.	☐	☐	☐

Heroes with Solid Feet

Kirk Douglas

IDENTIFY

Lines 9–12 contain several vivid sensory images. Circle each separate sensory image.

WORDS TO OWN

emaciated (ē·mā′shē·āt′id) adj.: extremely thin; wasted away.

annihilate (ə·nī′ə·lāt′) v.: completely destroy.

INFER

Earlier, the author said he was curious to visit Berlin again. What does his response to the reporter's question in lines 13–19 suggest about why he wanted to return?

EVALUATE

Seen as a whole, the essay is comprised of short anecdotes within a larger anecdote. How do the stories about the little heroes fit the argument of the essay?

Recently, I journeyed to Berlin to accept the Golden Bear, a lifetime achievement award, from the Berlin Film Festival. Those awards make me smile—lifetime achievement? Is this the end? Not long ago my son Michael received a lifetime achievement award. If you last long enough, you may get dozens.

I accepted the Golden Bear because I was curious to see Berlin again. During my earlier visits there, the city had been divided by a wall.[1]

In a press conference at the film festival, one journalist asked loudly, "As a Jew, how does it affect you to be in Berlin?" A montage of pictures we have all seen raced through my mind. Shattering glass windows, Hitler salutes, Jews being herded into freight cars, piles of <u>emaciated</u> Jews, ovens, dark smoke coming out of chimneys.

"The last century has been a disaster," I said. "My generation did not do a good job—so many wars, so much killing and of course, here in Germany, the Holocaust, perhaps the worst crime of all, the attempt to <u>annihilate</u> a people as a final solution."

They were all listening.

"But I don't think children should be punished for the sins of their fathers. We should do all we can to give our children that chance."

The questioner persisted. "So why did you come back to Berlin?" I ignored him. But the question bothered me. I didn't know a proper reason for a Jew to be in Berlin.

The audience at the awards ceremony gave me a standing ovation when I gave my speech in German, a language I learned when I made two movies in Germany. The papers were filled with my smiling face. The television reports were very complimentary. That night my wife and I had a wonderful Wiener schnitzel[2] with some friends and a Jewish friend of theirs, Inge Borck, who lived in Berlin throughout the war. She was such a happy person, smiling and laughing. But when I was told that her parents and grandparents had all been killed in the concentration camps, I blurted out, "So why do you stay in Berlin?"

Smiling, she gave me this answer: "I owe that to the little heroes."

"When the Gestapo[3] came to get them, my parents sent me to a small hotel to save my life. The owner was the first little hero. She kept me safe for a couple of nights. When it became dangerous, I met my second little hero. Or should I say heroine? She was our former housekeeper. She hid me for a while and endangered her own life. Then I lived in a cloister.[4] My little heroes were the nuns who took care of me when I was

---

1. divided by a wall: reference to the wall built by the Communists in 1961 that separated Communist East Berlin and democratic West Berlin. The Berlin Wall was taken down in 1989, when Germany was reunited under a democratic government.
2. Wiener schnitzel (vē′nər shnit′səl): German dish consisting of breaded veal cutlet.
3. Gestapo (gə·stä′pō): Nazi secret police.
4. cloister (klois′tər) n.: place where a religious group, such as a group of nuns or monks, lives apart from the rest of society.

very sick. They never asked questions. When the situation became
dangerous, my next little hero was a policeman who didn't agree with
the Nazis. All through the war, I was lucky to find little heroes who
helped me till the Russians came in."[5]

"So, why do you stay here?" I asked again. She looked at my
perplexed face and said, "I thought about it, but I feel I owe it to
the little heroes who helped me. Not everyone here was wicked."

Her story had a great impact on me. Of course, we are always
looking for a big hero to <u>emulate</u>, and very often we see them topple
from clay feet.[6] How much better to reach for the little heroes in life—
and to try to be one. It's not always as hard as it was for the people in
wartime Berlin. You aren't obligated to save a life—you only need to try
to help other people.

And if everyone tried—well, just think of the lifetime achievements.

---

5. **Russians came in:** In the spring of 1945, Germany was defeated by British, American, and
Russian troops. The war ended with the surrender of Japan.
6. **topple from clay feet:** "Clay feet" is a figurative expression that refers to heroes who are
discredited when their weaknesses are revealed. A statue in which the feet are made of
clay, which can crumble easily, will not stand for long.

WORDS TO OWN
emulate (em′yoo·lāt′) v.:
follow the example of; imitate.

IDENTIFY

Circle the loaded words in the
last sentence of the essay that
tie its ending to its beginning.

Intent and Tone Chart

Use the chart below to evaluate the author's argument. First, identify the writer's purpose, or intent. Then, list the best examples of the five types of support the author uses. Next, describe the tone of the piece. Finally, in your notebook comment on how successful the author was in convincing you of his opinion. Was your heart touched? your mind? both?

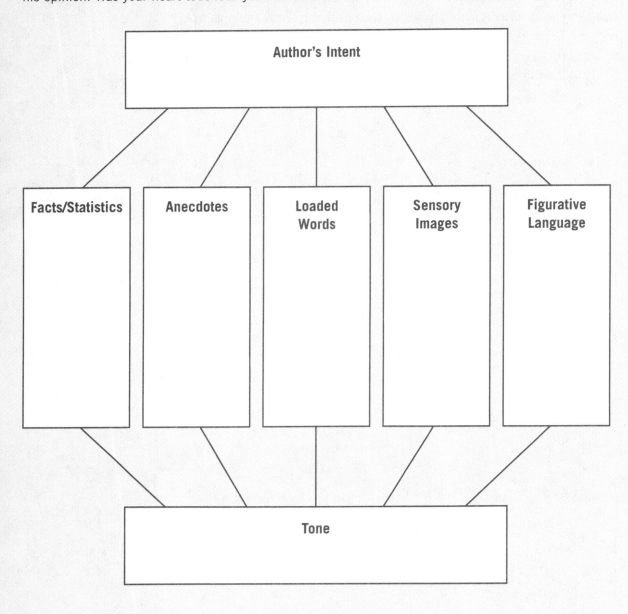

Author's Intent

Facts/Statistics	Anecdotes	Loaded Words	Sensory Images	Figurative Language

Tone

Analyzing Informational Materials

Reading Check

1. What question was Kirk Douglas asked when he appeared at the Berlin Film Festival?

   _____

   _____

2. Who is Inge Borck, and who are the "little heroes" she told Douglas about?

   _____

   _____

Test Practice

Circle the letter of the correct answer.

1. Kirk Douglas uses an anecdote when he—

   A describes what happened at the Berlin Film Festival

   B tells why he accepted the Golden Bear award

   C explains that he learned German while making movies in Germany

   D says everyone should try to be a "little hero"

2. Kirk Douglas uses loaded words in which of the following statements?

   F "If you last long enough, you may get dozens."

   G "Jews being herded into freight cars, piles of emaciated Jews, ovens, dark smoke coming out of chimneys."

   H "I didn't know a proper reason for a Jew to be in Berlin."

   J "'So, why do you stay here?' I asked again."

3. Which of the following is the most accurate statement of Kirk Douglas's purpose, or intent, in writing his op-ed article?

   A to persuade people never to forget the Holocaust

   B to prove that he was right to go to Berlin

   C to point out the importance of small acts of heroism

   D to explain how traditional heroes have clay feet

Vocabulary: How to Own a Word

Using Context; Understanding Idioms

> **Word Bank**
> advocate
> defers
> emaciated
> annihilate
> emulate

Word Knowledge: Using Context

Practice 1

Fill in each blank with the appropriate word from the Word Bank.

1. Years of poor nutrition made the refugees weak and _____ .

2. I always try to _____ people whom I admire, but I don't always succeed.

3. Sandra always _____ having fun after school until she has finished her homework.

4. When I was attacked by a swarm of bees, I wanted to _____ the entire hive.

5. Malcolm became an enthusiastic _____ for exercise after he started running and going to the gym regularly.

Understanding Idioms

An idiom is an expression peculiar to a particular language that means something different from the literal meaning of its words. Kirk Douglas uses the idiom *clay feet* to refer to a hero who is found to have less than heroic qualities. The expression comes from the notion that a statue with clay feet will topple, since clay can crack and crumble easily.

Other common idioms include *a fish out of water* ("out of one's element"), *to cry wolf* ("to give a false alarm," based on a fable of Aesop), and *long in the tooth* ("somewhat old," based on judging a horse's age by the length of its teeth).

Practice 2

Explain the meanings of the underlined idioms in the following sentences. Then explain where you think the expressions may have come from.

1. "Hold your horses," the teacher said. "The class hasn't been dismissed yet."

   _____

   _____

2. Sally is a couch potato who does nothing but watch television.

   _____

   _____

3. "Step on it!" called her mother. "You're going to be late to school!"

   _____

   _____

4. Natasha sent her letter to the editor by both e-mail and snail mail.

   _____

   _____

5. Pavel was star struck after meeting the best surfer on the beach.

   _____

   _____

Consumer Materials
for Computer Games

Make the Connection

Differentiating Computer Documents

Picture before you an unopened box containing the latest computer game console. In your hurry to get it out of its box, you let a sheaf of official-looking papers slide to the floor. There they lie, scattered among the packing litter, the **consumer documents**—the warranty, the product information, and the instruction manual. These documents can make a big difference in how you enjoy your new game, so before you put them away, it is important to read them carefully.

Here are some different types of consumer documents and the **elements** that such documents share:

- **product information**—descriptions of what the game console will do.
- **contract**—information on the legal uses of the game's software.
- **warranty**—details on what happens if the game console does not work as promised and what you must do to receive service.
- **instruction manual**—instructions on how to use the game console.
- **technical directions**—directions for installation and use.

All electronic equipment comes with these consumer documents, but the **features** of each document can affect your satisfaction with the product. All warranties specify what the manufacturer will do if the product fails, but one company might offer only repair, while another will give you a choice of getting your money back. Some contracts offer free technical support by phone around the clock; others offer none. Sometimes, when two products look nearly identical, the features of the consumer materials can tip your decision.

Consumer Materials *for* Computer Games

Flo Ota De Lange and Sheri Henderson

INTERPRET

If you bought this game system at a tag sale, would it still be covered by the warranty?

_____

_____

INTERPRET

What happens if you break the product within ninety days or a year of your purchase?

_____

_____

IDENTIFY

What does the consumer have to do first to ensure that he or she is covered under the warranty?

_____

_____

EVALUATE

For what purpose other than the warranty might a company use the consumer registration information?

_____

_____

IDENTIFY

When would a game system owner need the information on this page?

_____

_____

_____

_____

_____

Limited Warranty

WYSIWYGame Arts makes the following limited warranties. These limited warranties extend to the original consumer purchaser or any person receiving this product as a gift from the original consumer purchaser and to no other purchaser or transferee.

Limited Ninety [90] Day Warranty

WYSIWYGame Arts warrants this product and its parts against defect in materials and workmanship for a period of ninety [90] days after the date of original retail purchase. During this period, WYSIWYGame Arts 10 will replace any defective product or part, without charge to you. For replacement, you must deliver the entire product to the place of purchase.

Limited One [1] Year Warranty of Parts

WYSIWYGame Arts further warrants the parts of this product against defects in materials or workmanship for a period of one year after the date of original retail purchase. During this period, WYSIWYGame Arts will replace a defective part without charge to you, except that if a defective part is replaced after ninety [90] days from the date of the original retail purchase, you pay labor charges involved in the replacement. You must also deliver the entire product to an Authorized 20 WYSIWYGame Arts Service Station. You pay for all transportation and insurance charges for the product to and from the Service Station.

Owner's Manual and Warranty Registration

Read the owner's manual thoroughly before operating this product; WYSIWYGame Arts does not warrant any defect caused by improper installation or operation. Complete and mail the attached registration card; the warranty is effective only if your name and address are on file as owners of a WYSIWYGame Arts product.

Product Information Specifications

CPU	800 MHz
Video Card	250 MHz GPU
Resolution	1920 × 1080 maximum
Memory	128 MB
Storage	Memory Card
	Hard Drive
Sound Cord	64 Channels
DVD	Yes
Media	12X DVD-ROM 6.2 GB
Type	Capacity
Hard Drive	8 GB
Modem	Yes
Ethernet Port	Yes
Controllers	4

Safety Information

Please follow these important safeguards regarding the use and installation of your game console:

1. When installing your game console, please make sure that the unit receives proper ventilation. Vents in the console covering are provided for this purpose. Never block or cover these vents with any kind of object such as fabric, books, magazines, etc.
2. Do not install your game console in a bookcase or entertainment rack where it cannot receive proper ventilation.
3. Do not set the game console on a soft surface such as a bed, sofa, or rug, since doing so may result in damage to the appliance.
4. Do not place the game console in direct sunlight or near a heat source such as a radiator or hot air duct.
5. Unplug this appliance from the wall outlet and contact a qualified service person under the following conditions:
   - **A.** If the power-supply cord or plug is damaged.
   - **B.** If liquid has been spilled on, or objects have fallen into, the game console.
   - **C.** If the game console has been exposed to rain or water.
   - **D.** If the game console does not operate normally after following the operating instructions.
   - **E.** If the game console has been dropped or the cabinet has been damaged.
   - **F.** The game console exhibits a distinct change in performance.

Do not attempt to service this product yourself as opening or removing covers may expose you to dangerous voltage or other hazards. Refer all servicing to qualified service personnel.

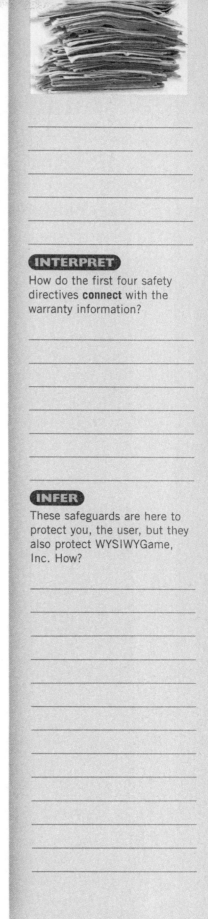

INTERPRET

How do the first four safety directives **connect** with the warranty information?

INFER

These safeguards are here to protect you, the user, but they also protect WYSIWYGame, Inc. How?

Consumer Materials for Computer Games

Consumer Materials Chart

Complete the following chart by checking off the appropriate situations in which each consumer document should be consulted. There can be more than one answer for each document.

Consumer Document	While Shopping	Right After Purchase	During Assembly	If It Malfunctions	When Buying Accessories
Warranty					
Product Specifications					
Safety Information					

Analyzing Informational Materials

Reading Check

1. What **features** are offered in the Limited Ninety [90] Day Warranty?

_____

_____

_____

_____

2. What are the differences between the features of the Ninety-Day and One-Year Warranties?

_____

_____

_____

_____

3. Where do you look to see if your computer game works with a modem?

_____

_____

_____

_____

4. If you dump an entire can of soda into your game console, what does the manufacturer suggest you do? Where do you find this advice?

_____

_____

_____

_____

Test Practice

Circle the letter of the correct answer.

1. If you wanted to tell a friend how powerful your game console is, you could look —

A in the Limited Warranty under "Registration"

B in the Instruction Manual under "Safety Information"

C in Product Information under "Specifications"

D in the Limited Warranty under "Limited One [1] Year Warranty of Parts"

2. Items 1 through 4 of the Safety Information are designed to protect the unit from —

F chilling

G overheating

H static electricity

J humidity

3. The Safety Information and the Limited Warranty are *similar* in that they both address —

A problems with the product

B how to avoid problems with the product

C how to buy the product

D how to set up the product

4. The Specifications and the Safety Information are *different* in that —

F Specifications describes elements but Safety Information describes features

G Specifications describes features but Safety Information describes elements

H Specifications describes use and installation but Safety Information describes features

J Specifications describes features but Safety Information describes use and installation

5. Consumer documents exist to protect —

A the user

B the manufacturer

C both of the above

D none of the above

Technical Directions for Customizing a Search Engine

Make the Connection

Following Technical Directions

How do you best use the Internet as a research tool? The first step is to choose a search engine you like and feel comfortable with. It is a good idea to customize your browser so that your favorite search engine is on your home page.

How do you do that? It is easy. You just follow the directions. The directions for computers as well as other scientific, mechanical, and electronic products and activities are called **technical directions.** You follow technical directions when you—

- do an experiment in the chemistry lab
- fix a flat on your bicycle for the first time
- program the remote control for your favorite radio stations
- learn how to operate your new microwave
- install a virus protection software on your computer

Technical directions sometimes seem complicated and difficult when you first look at them, but if you pay attention and follow each step carefully, they will help you to do the things you want to do.

When was the last time you followed technical directions? Use the graphic organizer below to make some notes about how easy or difficult it was and why. Refer to the list above or think of your own activity.

Activity: _____

What problems did you run into? _____

_____

_____

Did you solve the problem(s)? If so, how? _____

_____

_____

Technical Directions for Customizing a Search Engine

Flo Ota De Lange
and Sheri Henderson

Before you learn how to customize your browser, you will read a FAQ (Frequently Asked Questions) sheet about how search engines work and what they can do for you.

FAQs About Search Engines

Q: What does a search engine do?

A: A search engine helps you locate information available on the World Wide Web.

Q: How does a search engine do this?

A: A search engine matches the words of your search request against
10   the keywords of a Web site. It eliminates what doesn't match your request and tells you what does match.

Q: What is an example of a search request?

A: Say you wanted to know about computer games. You would choose a specific search engine and in the search box type in: computer games. The search engine would deliver to you the first ten most relevant listings of a possible 2,400,000 results.

Q: That's a lot of results. How do I narrow the search?

A: You narrow your search request to what you specifically want to know about computer games. For example, if you want to know
20   about the most popular ones, you could phrase your search request in this way: Computer games + most popular. The search engine would then give you the first ten most relevant listings of a possible 751,000 results.

Q: That's still too many. How can I narrow it further?

A: If you want to narrow your search further, you could do it by using quotation marks that search for phrases instead of individual words, in this way: "computer games" + "most popular." A search phrased in this way would return you the first ten most relevant listings of a possible 21,600 results.

30 **Q:** There are so many search engines. How do I decide which one to use?

A: The best way is to experiment with some prominent search engines. You might ask your computer-savvy friends which ones they use and then put these under your Favorites or Bookmarks list. When you decide which one works best for you, you could make that Web site your home page by customizing your browser.

Q: How do I customize my browser?

A: Customizing your browser involves following technical directions. You follow a sequence of steps. First, decide on a search engine
40   Web site and go there. Then find the directions for the browser you are using and follow them.

Q: Will the directions work with every browser in use today?

A: No, they will work only with the browser you chose to use.

Customizing Your Browser

The following are instructions for customizing your browser using a made-up search engine Web site: QuickFind. Reading QuickFind's instructions will make you familiar with following **technical directions** so that when you choose your own favorite search engine—and there are many out there to pick from—you'll have no trouble following the
50 instructions. You will be ready to move your favorite search engine Web page right onto your home page.

Technical Directions
QuickFind 1.0

1. Go to the "Address" window at the top of your screen and copy the URL.
2. Pull down the "Edit" menu from the tool bar at the top of your screen.
3. Click on "Options" or "Preferences" and wait for the window to open.
60 4. Select "Home Page" under the "Browser Options" category on the left.
5. Click the "Address" field on the "Home Page" and paste in the URL you copied in step 1.
6. Click "OK" at the bottom right.

Whichever search engine you choose, there is one last step to follow: Check your work. Quit your browser and then open it again. The browser should automatically open to the search engine you've selected. If it doesn't, repeat the process again, making sure to completely follow each step.

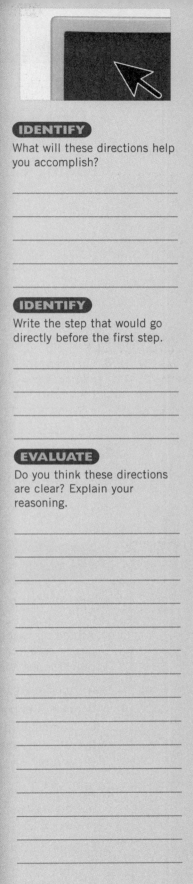

IDENTIFY

What will these directions help you accomplish?

_____

_____

_____

_____

IDENTIFY

Write the step that would go directly before the first step.

_____

_____

_____

_____

EVALUATE

Do you think these directions are clear? Explain your reasoning.

_____

_____

_____

_____

_____

_____

_____

_____

_____

_____

_____

Analyzing Informational Materials

Reading Check

1. What does a search engine do?

_____

_____

2. How should you choose a search engine?

_____

_____

3. If you want to customize your browser's home page, regardless of the browser you use, what is your first step?

_____

_____

4. What is the very last step in customizing your browser?

_____

_____

Test Practice

Circle the letter of the correct answer.

1. According to the FAQ sheet, you would phrase a search for the most popular computer games as —

  A mostpopularcomputergames

  B most + popular + computer + games

  C computer games + most popular

  D What are the most popular computer games?

2. According to the FAQ sheet, you can narrow a search by enclosing key phrases in —

  F question marks

  G quotation marks

  H plus signs

  J parentheses

3. In the QuickFind 1.0 browser instructions, the first thing you do is —

  A copy the URL

  B paste the URL

  C click on "Options"

  D go to the "Address" window

4. What is the last thing you do in order to activate the changes?

  F Paste the URL into the address box.

  G Pull down the "Edit" menu.

  H Click on "Address."

  J Click "OK."

Sequence Chart: Writing Technical Directions

How would you explain the process of setting an alarm clock? Fill in the sequence chart below with the required steps, using as many of the boxes as you can. Since clocks work differently, base your directions on an actual clock. Be as specific as possible: remember someone is going to use *your* directions to set the clock.

SEQUENCE CHART: SETTING AN ALARM CLOCK

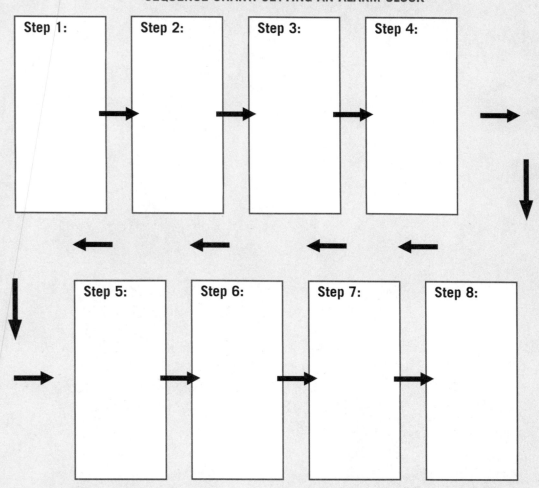

Now have someone use your directions to set the clock. Did you leave out any steps? Where could you have been clearer?

DIRECTIONS

Read the following short story. Then, read each multiple-choice question, and circle the letter of the best response.

Old Man at the Bridge

Ernest Hemingway

During the Spanish Civil War (1936–1939), the Loyalists, who supported the government of Spain, fought against the Fascists (or Nationalists), who were led by General Francisco Franco. "Old Man at the Bridge" is set during this conflict and shows its impact on the Spanish people.

An old man with steel rimmed spectacles and very dusty clothes sat by the side of the road. There was a pontoon bridge across the river and carts, trucks, and men, women and children were crossing it. The mule-drawn carts staggered up the steep bank from the bridge with soldiers helping push against the spokes of the wheels. The trucks ground up and away heading out of it all and the peasants plodded along in the ankle deep dust. But the old man sat there without moving. He was too tired to go any farther.

It was my business to cross the bridge, explore the bridgehead beyond and find out to what point the enemy had advanced. I did this and returned over the bridge. There were not so many carts now and very few people on foot, but the old man was still there.

"Where do you come from?" I asked him.

"From San Carlos," he said, and smiled.

That was his native town and so it gave him pleasure to mention it and he smiled.

"I was taking care of animals," he explained.

"Oh," I said, not quite understanding.

"Yes," he said, "I stayed, you see, taking care of animals. I was the last one to leave the town of San Carlos."

He did not look like a shepherd nor a herdsman and I looked at his black dusty clothes and his gray dusty face and his steel rimmed spectacles and said, "What animals were they?"

"Various animals," he said, and shook his head. "I had to leave them."

I was watching the bridge and the African looking country of the Ebro Delta[1] and wondering how long now it would be before we would see the enemy, and listening all the while for the first noises that would signal that ever mysterious event called contact, and the old man still sat there.

"What animals were they?" I asked.

"There were three animals altogether," he explained. "There were two goats and a cat and then there were four pairs of pigeons."

"And you had to leave them?" I asked.

"Yes. Because of the artillery.[2] The captain told me to go because of the artillery."

"And you have no family?" I asked, watching the far end of the bridge where a few last carts were hurrying down the slope of the bank.

"No," he said, "only the animals I stated. The cat, of course, will be all right. A cat can

---

1. **Ebro Delta:** the land at the mouth of the Ebro, the longest river in Spain.
2. **artillery** (är·til′ər·ē) *n.:* mounted guns, such as cannons.

look out for itself, but I cannot think what will become of the others."

"What politics have you?" I asked.

"I am without politics," he said. "I am seventy-six years old. I have come twelve kilometers now and I think now I can go no further."

"This is not a good place to stop," I said. "If you can make it, there are trucks up the road where it forks for Tortosa."

"I will wait a while," he said, "and then I will go. Where do the trucks go?"

"Towards Barcelona," I told him.

"I know no one in that direction," he said, "but thank you very much. Thank you again very much."

He looked at me very blankly and tiredly, then said, having to share his worry with some one, "The cat will be all right, I am sure. There is no need to be unquiet about the cat. But the others. Now what do you think about the others?"

"Why they'll probably come through it all right."

"You think so?

"Why not," I said, watching the far bank where now there were no carts.

"But what will they do under the artillery when I was told to leave because of the artillery?"

"Did you leave the dove cage unlocked?" I asked.

"Yes."

"Then they'll fly."

"Yes, certainly they'll fly. But the others. It's better not to think about the others," he said.

"If you are rested I would go," I urged. "Get up and try to walk now."

"Thank you," he said and got to his feet, swayed from side to side and then sat down backwards in the dust.

"I was taking care of animals," he said dully, but no longer to me. "I was only taking care of animals."

There was nothing to do about him. It was Easter Sunday and the Fascists were advancing toward the Ebro. It was a gray overcast day with a low ceiling so their planes were not up. That and the fact that cats know how to look after themselves was all the good luck that old man would ever have.

---

1. Why did the old man at the bridge leave his home in San Carlos?

   A   He was taken prisoner by the enemy.
   B   He was fleeing an artillery attack.
   C   He needed medical attention.
   D   He wanted to get help for his animals.

2. The story's most serious **external conflict** is between —

   F   the old man and the narrator
   G   the two main characters and the war
   H   the old man and the soldiers at the bridge
   J   the narrator and the captain

3. The old man faces an **internal conflict** between —

A rescuing the cat and saving the goats and pigeons

B his loyalty to the government and his belief in the enemy's cause

C his desire to take care of his animals and the need to leave his home

D crossing the bridge to seek shelter and fleeing to Barcelona

4. What is the narrator's **motivation** for urging the old man to move on?

F Concern for the old man's safety

G The need to carry out his orders

H Anger at the old man

J A desire to reunite the old man with his family in Barcelona

5. Several times the narrator says that he was "watching" the bridge or the far bank of the river. What **character trait** does the narrator reveal through this description?

A Curiosity

B Bravery

C Carelessness

D Alertness

6. What does the old man reveal about himself when he says in his **dialogue** with the narrator, "I am without politics"?

F He does not care about his native town.

G He has not taken sides during the war.

H He is rebelling against the leaders of his country.

J He is trying to hide his beliefs from the narrator.

7. Which of the following words *best* describes the **relationship** between the narrator and the old man?

A Protective

B Hostile

C Indifferent

D Loving

8. From what the narrator says in the last paragraph about the old man's luck, we can infer that the **narrator** feels—

F sympathetic and optimistic

G relieved and carefree

H powerless and pessimistic

J superstitious and frightened

DIRECTIONS

Read the following selection. Then, read each multiple-choice question, and circle the letter of the best response.

Snow

Julia Alvarez

Our first year in New York we rented a small apartment with a Catholic school nearby, taught by the Sisters of Charity, hefty women in long black gowns and bonnets that made them look peculiar, like dolls in mourning. I liked them a lot, especially my grandmotherly fourth-grade teacher, Sister Zoe. I had a lovely name, she said, and she had me teach the whole class how to pronounce it. *Yo-lan-da.* As the only immigrant in my class, I was put in a special seat in the first row by the window, apart from the other children, so that Sister Zoe could tutor me without disturbing them. Slowly, she enunciated the new words I was to repeat: *laundromat, cornflakes, subway, snow.*

Soon I picked up enough English to understand holocaust[1] was in the air. Sister Zoe explained to a wide-eyed classroom what was happening in Cuba. Russian missiles were being assembled, trained supposedly on New York City. President Kennedy, looking worried too, was on the television at home, explaining we might have to go to war against the Communists. At school, we had air-raid drills: An ominous bell would go off and we'd file into the hall, fall to the floor, cover our heads with our coats, and imagine our hair falling out, the bones in our arms going soft. At home, Mami and my sisters and I said a rosary[2] for world peace. I heard new vocabulary: *nuclear bomb, radioactive fallout, bomb shelter.* Sister Zoe explained how it would happen. She drew a picture of a mushroom on the blackboard and dotted a flurry of chalk marks for the dusty fallout that would kill us all.

The months grew cold, November, December. It was dark when I got up in the morning, frosty when I followed my breath to school. One morning, as I sat at my desk daydreaming out the window, I saw dots in the air like the ones Sister Zoe had drawn—random at first, then lots and lots. I shrieked, "Bomb! Bomb!" Sister Zoe jerked around, her full black skirt ballooning as she hurried to my side. A few girls began to cry.

But then Sister Zoe's shocked look faded. "Why, Yolanda dear, that's snow!" She laughed. "Snow."

"Snow," I repeated. I looked out the window warily. All my life I had heard about the white crystals that fell out of American skies in the winter. From my desk I watched the fine powder dust the sidewalk and parked cars below. Each flake was different, Sister Zoe had said, like a person, irreplaceable and beautiful.

---

1. **holocaust** *n.:* (hä′lə·käst′) great or total destruction of life.
2. **rosary** (rō′zər·ē) *n.:* in the Roman Catholic religion, series of prayers counted off on a special set of beads.

1. Why does Yolanda yell, "Bomb! Bomb!" when when she sees snow?

   A The winter landscape is bare, as if a bomb had destroyed everything.

   B The snowflakes look like her teacher's pictures of the fallout from a bomb.

   C New in school, she wants to gain her classmates' attention.

   D She wants to show that she has understood her teacher's lessons.

2. How does the use of a **first-person narrator** affect the telling of the story?

   F The reader sees events through the eyes of several characters.

   G The description of events is unbiased.

   H The reader is presented with Yolanda's personal view of events.

   J Yolanda lies in the story.

3. Why is it important that the story is told from the **point of view** of a recent immigrant to the United States?

   A Yolanda is unfamiliar with some aspects of life in the United States.

   B Living in the United States makes Yolanda frightened and insecure.

   C Yolanda's classmates don't explain things to her.

   D Yolanda's teacher treats her unfairly.

4. What is the *best* description of the narrator's **voice** in this passage: "I saw dots in the air like the ones Sister Zoe had drawn—random at first, then lots and lots"?

   F Sophisticated

   G Childlike

   H Hopeful

   J Playful

5. What is the **tone** of the story?

   A Sarcastic and superior

   B Angry and suspicious

   C Homesick and sad

   D Innocent and sincere

6. What impression does the narrator create of Sister Zoe?

   F Sister Zoe has knowingly exaggerated the danger in order to scare the children.

   G Sister Zoe is a nervous, easily frightened person.

   H Sister Zoe mocks Yolanda and doesn't think she's intelligent.

   J A caring teacher, Sister Zoe helps her students learn.

7. What is the point of Sister Zoe's comparison of snowflakes to people?

   A Every person is special.

   B Snowflakes are as important as people.

   C Snowflakes, like people, can't be described.

   D Yolanda is the same as everyone else.

DIRECTIONS

Read the following fable. Then, read each multiple-choice question, and circle the letter of the best response.

The Princess and the Tin Box

James Thurber

Once upon a time, in a far country, there lived a King whose daughter was the prettiest princess in the world. Her eyes were like the cornflower, her hair was sweeter than the hyacinth, and her throat made the swan look dusty.

From the time she was a year old, the Princess had been showered with presents. Her nursery looked like Cartier's[1] window. Her toys were all made of gold or platinum or diamonds or emeralds. She was not permitted to have wooden blocks or china dolls or rubber dogs or linen books, because such materials were considered cheap for the daughter of a king.

When she was seven, she was allowed to attend the wedding of her brother and throw real pearls at the bride instead of rice. Only the nightingale, with his lyre[2] of gold, was permitted to sing for the Princess. The common blackbird, with his boxwood flute, was kept out of the palace grounds. She walked in silver-and-samite[3] slippers to a sapphire-and-topaz bathroom and slept in an ivory bed inlaid with rubies.

On the day the Princess was eighteen, the King sent a royal ambassador to the courts of five neighboring kingdoms to announce that he would give his daughter's hand in marriage to the prince who brought her the gift she liked the most.

The first prince to arrive at the palace rode a swift white stallion and laid at the feet of the Princess an enormous apple made of solid gold which he had taken from a dragon who had guarded it for a thousand years. It was placed on a long ebony table set up to hold the gifts of the Princess' suitors. The second prince, who came on a gray charger, brought her a nightingale made of a thousand diamonds, and it was placed beside the golden apple. The third prince, riding on a black horse, carried a great jewel box made of platinum and sapphires, and it was placed next to the diamond nightingale. The fourth prince, astride a fiery yellow horse, gave the Princess a gigantic heart made of rubies and pierced by an emerald arrow. It was placed next to the platinum-and-sapphire jewel box.

Now the fifth prince was the strongest and handsomest of all the five suitors, but he was the son of a poor king whose realm had been overrun by mice and locusts and wizards and mining engineers so that there was nothing much of value left in it. He came plodding up to the palace of the Princess on a plow horse, and he brought her a small tin box filled with mica and feldspar and hornblende[4] which he had picked up on the way.

The other princes roared with disdainful laughter when they saw the tawdry gift the fifth

---

1. **Cartier's** (kär′tē·āz): store selling expensive jewelry in New York City.
2. **lyre** (līr) *n.:* small stringed instrument.
3. **samite** (sam′īt) *n.* used as *adj.:* heavy silk fabric.
4. **mica . . . hornblende:** types of ordinary rocks.

prince had brought to the Princess. But she examined it with great interest and squealed with delight, for all her life she had been glutted with precious stones and priceless metals, but she had never seen tin before or mica or feldspar or hornblende. The tin box was placed next to the ruby heart pierced with an emerald arrow.

"Now," the King said to his daughter, "you must select the gift you like best and marry the prince that brought it."

The Princess smiled and walked up to the table and picked up the present she liked the most. It was the platinum-and-sapphire jewel box, the gift of the third prince.

"The way I figure it," she said, "is this. It is a very large and expensive box, and when I am married, I will meet many admirers who will give me precious gems with which to fill it to the top. Therefore, it is the most valuable of all the gifts my suitors have brought me, and I like it the best."

The Princess married the third prince that very day in the midst of great merriment and high revelry. More than a hundred thousand pearls were thrown at her and she loved it.

Moral: All those who thought that the Princess was going to select the tin box filled with worthless stones instead of one of the other gifts will kindly stay after class and write one hundred times on the blackboard, "I would rather have a hunk of aluminum silicate than a diamond necklace."

Drawing for "The Princess and the Tin Box" (1948) by James Thurber.

Copyright © 1948 James Thurber. Copyright © 1976 Rosemary A. Thurber. From *The Beast in Me and Other Animals*, published by Harcourt Brace.

---

1. The details about the princess's life before her eighteenth birthday imply that she was—

   A raised to value only material goods
   B indifferent to the feelings of others
   C easily bored
   D not interested in getting married

2. Which adjective *best* describes the princess's **character**?

   F Materialistic
   G Curious
   H Indecisive
   J Modest

3. How are the gifts of the first four princes similar?

   A They are made from precious materials.
   B They are more valuable than anything the princess has ever been given.
   C They are useful objects.
   D They please the king more than the princess.

4. Which is the *most* important reason for expecting the princess to choose the fifth prince's gift?

   F The fifth prince is the strongest and handsomest of the suitors.
   G His gift is not valuable.
   H She seems most impressed by his gift.
   J She feels sorry for the fifth prince because he is poor.

5. The princess's choice of the third prince's gift is an example of —

A verbal irony

B ambiguity

C dramatic irony

D situational irony

6. What **theme,** or insight about life, does the fable (and especially the moral) suggest?

F It's impossible to understand other people fully.

G Some people rush to judge others.

H Everyone really values material goods, and it is foolish to pretend otherwise.

J People value love more than wealth.

7. Why is the moral **ironic**?

A The reader expects the author to criticize the fifth prince for giving the princess a tin box.

B The reader expects the author to find fault with the princess's values.

C The reader expects the author to praise the king for thinking of his daughter's happiness.

D The reader expects the author to express admiration for the third prince's clever gift.

8. What is the **tone** of the fable?

F Ironic and grim

G Ironic and sorrowful

H Ironic and joyful

J Ironic and humorous

DIRECTIONS

Read the following poem carefully. Then, read each item, and circle the letter of the best response.

El Olvido

Judith Ortiz Cofer

It is a dangerous thing
to forget the climate of your birthplace,
to choke out the voices of dead relatives
when in dreams they call you
by your secret name.
It is dangerous
to spurn the clothes you were born to wear
for the sake of fashion; dangerous

to use weapons and sharp instruments
you are not familiar with; dangerous
to disdain the plaster saints
before which your mother kneels
praying with embarrassing fervor
that you survive in the place you have chosen
    to live:
a bare, cold room with no pictures on the walls,
a forgetting place where she fears you will die
of loneliness and exposure.
Jesús, María, y José, she says,
el olvido is a dangerous thing.

---

1. What does the term *el olvido* mean?

   A Danger
   B Forgetfulness
   C Mother
   D Birthplace

2. The speaker is warning against —

   F wearing new clothes
   G ignoring your heritage
   H embarrassing your mother
   J living in a cold, bare room

3. According to the speaker, it is dangerous to —

   A pray
   B wear traditional clothes
   C scorn religion
   D dream

4. What is meant by "to choke out" dead relatives' voices, in line 3?

   F To ignore what they taught
   G To smother them with love
   H To forget their ways
   J To become angry with them

5. Which of the following adjectives best describes the speaker's tone?

   A Playful
   B Ironic
   C Optimistic
   D Solemn

DIRECTIONS
Read the article. Then, read each question that follows, and circle the best response.

So You Want to Be an Astronaut?

Richard Knight

Richard Knight explains the problems that would-be space tourists will face.

All but the most hardened skeptics[1] now admit that, sooner or later, space tourism will become a reality. But the question is: when exactly?

The answer is: probably not for quite a while yet.

MirCorp, the company which has leased the Mir space station, is offering one place on its mission to the station in September—it announced the spare seat earlier this year. But the return fare will cost up to £20 million[2]—and costs are not the only problems facing future space cadets.

The Body
According to Royal Air Force space expert Derek Clark, our bodies are not built for spaceflight and any would-be tourist will have to accept certain health risks and discomforts.

Just getting to space is a physically demanding experience. Passengers will be pinned to the backs of their seats by a 3G force (increasing each tourist's apparent weight threefold) for 4 minutes 40 seconds from launch to orbit while being buffeted as they crash through the atmosphere.

However, since extreme forces beyond 3G (which might be experienced in an emergency) can either starve the brain of oxygen or cause it to hemorrhage,[3] each tourist will probably have to be fitted with a tailor-made G-suit.

In space, where there is almost no gravity, blood equalizes around the body, rather than being pulled into our legs. The effect is to give the brain more blood than usual. Our bodies cope with this by reducing blood mass through increased urination, reduced liquid intake, and nosebleeds. Passengers will take a day to get over this unpleasant process. Back on Earth, they will find their reduced blood mass is again drawn downwards, causing them to faint.

Before facing that challenge, however, 50 percent of space tourists will have spent most of their time feeling ill because of space sickness (an extreme form of travel sickness). This would contribute to weight loss: Each passenger will lose about 5 pounds on their first day in space and will continue to lose weight daily.

This is also because, with no gravity to fight against, muscles will deteriorate[4] fast, most seriously around the heart. In fact, tourists who stay in space long enough will find their hearts have become irreversibly weakened—which is the fate of some Mir astronauts. Each passenger would have to exercise for 6 hours a day to halt muscle deterioration.

---

1. **skeptics** (skep′tiks) *n.*: people who doubt something.
2. **£20 million:** sum approximately equal to $30 million.
3. **hemorrhage** (hem′ər·ij′) *v.*: bleed heavily.
4. **deteriorate** (dē·tir′ē·ə·rāt) *v.*: become weak or damaged.

Painful kidney stones are more likely to develop in space, and there is a need to protect would-be astronauts against infection. So tourists will either be isolated for a month prior to flight or given regular medicals during the lead-up. Having second thoughts, by any chance?

The Mind

Tourists will need to be quizzed by psychologists[5] in order to check whether they have the right mental stuff. This is because passengers may feel a profound sense of isolation as they look at Earth from space. Gazing out, they will be able to use the tips of their thumbs to blot the Earth from view, making everything they have ever known disappear.

---

5. **psychologists** (sī·kăl′ə·jists) *n.*: specialists who study the mind and emotions.
6. **claustrophobia** (klôs′trə·fō′bē·ə) *n.*: abnormal fear of being in an enclosed place.
7. **invincible** (in·vin′sə·bəl) *adj.*: all powerful; unbeatable.
8. **For now . . . phew!:** After the publication of this article, Dennis A. Tito, an American, became the first space tourist, blasting off into space on April 28, 2001. Paying $20 million for the trip, he joined a Russian crew on an eight-day journey to the International Space Station.

As the sun rises and sets 16 times a day in space, sleep patterns will also be disrupted, possibly unhinging passengers. Some will suffer claustrophobia[6] from being confined to a narrow capsule in which one cannot walk, open a window or—of course—get out!

Another problem is that former astronauts are statistically more likely to suffer serious accidents when they return to Earth. This might be because, having flown to space and taken such a huge risk, they feel invincible[7] and take greater chances than normal. *Still* feel like going?

Enough Demand?

Do sufficient numbers of people really want to travel to destination space? It is likely to be enormously expensive: Will enough people be able to find the money? Once the market is proved, the money required to fuel passenger space planes should be more forthcoming than it is at present. For now, however, we can only guess when the first scheduled flight beyond the atmosphere will take off . . . phew![8]

—*from* The Times *(London), April 22, 2000*

---

1. Which of the following questions is answered in the article?

   A What causes heart damage during prolonged space travel?

   B Why might space travelers develop kidney stones?

   C What can space travelers do to avoid becoming depressed?

   D What will the interior of a passenger space plane look like?

2. Which of the following research questions about space tourism is the *most* narrow and focused?

   F What types of people want to be astronauts?

   G In the future, will space tourism become as routine as international airplane flights are now?

   H How does a G-suit prevent a person from being injured during liftoff?

   J How effective are the U.S. government's current plans for the space program budget?

3. Assume your initial research question is "How do people feel once they return to earth after traveling in space?" Which follow-up question will *best* help you narrow your research?

   A Do people visit doctors frequently after space flights?

   B Are people satisfied with their lives once they are back on earth?

   C Do people ever regret traveling in space?

   D What specific physical effects do people experience after a space flight, and how long do the effects last?

4. If you wanted to do further research on the effects of space travel on the mind, which question would give you the *most* relevant information?

   F Will space tourists returning to earth be tested by psychologists?

   G Is there a cure for claustrophobia?

   H How do disrupted sleep patterns affect the human mind?

   J Which former astronauts have had serious accidents?

5. Which research question about the effects of space travel on the body follows *most* directly from the information in this article?

   A When will doctors and nurses be trained to work in space?

   B Does gravity have harmful effects on our bodies when we are on earth?

   C What are the symptoms of space sickness, and how long does it last?

   D What kinds of circulation problems do people face on earth?

6. If you wanted to use a search engine to learn how tourists will be transported to space, which would be the *most* helpful search term?

   F Mir space station

   G Space planes

   H Space missions

   J Royal Air Force

7. If you wanted to find out about recent discoveries concerning living conditions in space, which resource would be the *most* useful?

   A Web site sponsored by NASA or another space agency

   B History book about space exploration

   C Magazine article about the funding of space programs

   D Biographical dictionary

DIRECTIONS

The following passage is from the true story of a year the writer spent observing a fifth-grade classroom in Holyoke, Massachusetts. Read the passage carefully. Then, read each item, and circle the letter of the best response.

from Among Schoolchildren

Tracy Kidder

*M*rs. Zajac wasn't born yesterday. She knows you didn't do your best work on this paper, Clarence. Don't you remember Mrs. Zajac saying that if you didn't do your best, she'd make you do it over? As for you, Claude, God forbid that you should ever need brain surgery. But Mrs. Zajac hopes that if you do, the doctor won't open up your head and walk off saying he's almost done, as you just said when Mrs. Zajac asked you for your penmanship, which, by the way, looks like you did it and ran. Felipe, the reason you have hiccups is, your mouth is always open and the wind rushes in. You're in fifth grade now. So, Felipe, put a lock on it. Zip it up. Then go get a drink of water. Mrs. Zajac means business, Robert. The sooner you realize she never said everybody in the room has to do the work except for Robert, the sooner you'll get along with her. And . . . Clarence. Mrs. Zajac knows you didn't try. You don't just hand in junk to Mrs. Zajac. She's been teaching an awful lot of years. She didn't fall off the turnip cart yesterday. She told you she was an old-lady teacher.*

She was thirty-four. She wore a white skirt and yellow sweater and a thin gold necklace, which she held in her fingers, as if holding her own reins, while waiting for children to answer. Her hair was black with a hint of Irish red.

It was cut short to the tops of her ears, and swept back like a pair of folded wings. She had a delicately cleft chin, and she was short—the children's chairs would have fit her. Although her voice sounded conversational, it had projection.[1] She had never acted. She had found this voice in classrooms.

Mrs. Zajac seemed to have a frightening amount of energy. She strode across the room, her arms swinging high and her hands in small fists. Taking her stand in front of the green chalkboard, discussing the rules with her new class, she repeated sentences, and her lips held the shapes of certain words, such as "homework," after she had said them. Her hands kept very busy. They sliced the air and made karate chops to mark off boundaries. They extended straight out like a traffic cop's, halting illegal maneuvers yet to be perpetrated. When they rested momentarily on her hips, her hands looked as if they were in holsters. She told the children, "One thing Mrs. Zajac expects from each of you is that you do your best." She said, "Mrs. Zajac gives homework. I'm sure you've all heard. The old meanie gives homework." Mrs. Zajac. It was in part a role. She worked her way into it every September.

At home on late summer days like these, Chris Zajac wore shorts or blue jeans. Although there was no dress code for teachers here at Kelly School, she always went to work in skirts or dresses. She dressed as if she were applying for a job, and hoped in the back of her mind that someday, heading for job interviews, her students would remember her example. Outside

---

1. **projection** (prō·jek′shən): carrying power.

school, she wept easily over small and large catastrophes and at sentimental movies, but she never cried in front of students, except once a few years ago when the news came over the intercom that the Space Shuttle had exploded and Christa McAuliffe had died—and then she saw in her students' faces that the sight of Mrs. Zajac crying had frightened them, and she made herself stop and then explained.

At home, Chris laughed at the antics of her infant daughter and egged the child on. She and her first-grade son would sneak up to the radio when her husband wasn't looking and change the station from classical to rock-and-roll music. "You're regressing,[2] Chris," her husband would say. But especially on the first few days of school, she didn't let her students get away with much. She was not amused when, for instance,

---

2. **regressing:** here, acting childish.

on the first day, two of the boys started dueling with their rulers. On nights before the school year started, Chris used to have bad dreams: her principal would come to observe her, and her students would choose that moment to climb up on their desks . . . or they would simply wander out the door. But a child in her classroom would never know that Mrs. Zajac had the slightest doubt that students would obey her.

The first day, after going over all the school rules, Chris spoke to them about effort. "If you put your name on a paper, you should be proud of it," she said. "You should think, 'This is the best I can do and I'm proud of it and I want to hand this in.'" Then she asked, "If it isn't your best, what's Mrs. Zajac going to do?"

Many voices, most of them female, answered softly in unison, "Make us do it over."

"Make you do it over," Chris repeated. It sounded like a chant.

---

1. Which of the following descriptions of Mrs. Zajac's movements does **not** use figurative language?

   A Making karate chops to mark off boundaries

   B Extending her hands as if to halt illegal maneuvers

   C Swinging her arms, with her hands in small fists

   D Placing her hands on her hips as if her hands were in holsters

2. Tracy Kidder's tone, or attitude, toward Mrs. Zajac could be described as —

   F amused

   G scornful

   H pitying

   J admiring

3. Which of the following details about Mrs. Zajac is the most subjective?

   A She wore a skirt and sweater.

   B She had a frightening amount of energy.

   C She wore a gold necklace.

   D She had black hair.

4. Who is speaking in the first paragraph?

   F Tracy Kidder

   G A student

   H Mrs. Zajac

   J The principal

5. Mrs. Zajac tries to set a good example for her students by —

   A wearing a skirt or dress to class every day

   B being easy on the students the first day

   C showing all emotions in front of her students

   D letting them know her dreams

DIRECTIONS

Read the following selection. Then, read each question, and circle the letter of the best response.

Justice for All

Imagine this scenario: Someone has stolen an audiotape player that you brought to school for a special program. You know that the tape player was stolen and not lost because you distinctly remember putting it in your locker before going to class. During lunch that same day, you see another student with a tape player that looks exactly like the one taken from your locker. You watch the student put the tape player in his backpack. Later, you manage to sneak into the student's backpack to retrieve your tape player, but a teacher catches you removing the tape player from the backpack. You are accused of stealing. "But it's *my* tape player!" you protest. The student who owns the backpack claims that the tape player belongs to *him.* The teacher escorts you to the principal's office. After hearing the teacher describe what she saw, the principal decides to suspend your school privileges for a month.

I ask you: Is this fair? It's a *raw deal,* if you ask me.

An incident similar to this one happened at our school recently. Someone who was retrieving an item stolen from a friend got in a great deal of trouble. This person had no recourse. There was no court of law, no jury. Fortunately, the student who took the item that didn't belong to him confessed. The item was returned to its rightful owner.

I am proposing a formal hearing process at our school for students who are suspected of breaking the rules. It is dangerous business for students to be punished without the right to a hearing.

Part of this process would include forming a hearing committee composed of teachers and students. We could also include the principal or assistant principal. This committee would act as a jury. It would create written guidelines for a formal hearing procedure. The committee members would also decide on an appeals process for students who are unhappy with the committee's decision.

No one wants to be falsely accused or wrongly punished. We all want to be treated fairly and justly. After all, isn't that one of the pillars on which our nation was established?

1. Which sentence *best* states the writer's main proposition?

   A We need a hearing process for students accused of breaking school rules.

   B Students accused of breaking rules should not be punished at school.

   C Students unfairly accused of breaking rules deserve an apology.

   D We need to create a committee to review our school's rules.

2. Paragraph 2 suggests strong feeling because the sentences are —

   F short and direct
   G written as dialect
   H punctuated heavily
   J parallel in structure

3. In this selection, the writer engages the reader's attention by —

   A using repetition to make a point
   B telling a humorous story
   C using dialect to tell a story
   D asking direct questions of the reader

4. In a summary of the selection, which of these should be placed in quotation marks?

   F Falsely accused or wrongly punished
   G The notion of justice
   H Due process of law
   J Rights and responsibilities

5. Which of the following is a critical detail that should be included in a summary of the selection?

   A The writer wants only teachers on the hearing committee.

   B The writer wants only students on the hearing committee.

   C The writer wants both students and teachers on the hearing committee.

   D The writer does not want the principal on the hearing committee.

6. Which detail could be omitted in a summary of the selection?

   F A student was unfairly punished.
   G The committee could act as a jury.
   H The item was returned to its owner.
   J Students deserve the right to a hearing.

7. In paragraph 2, the expression *raw deal* refers to —

   A an unsettled matter
   B a point of argument
   C an inexpensive item
   D unfair treatment

DIRECTIONS

Read the selection. Then, read each question that follows, and circle the best response.

Preparation and Operation of Sounds-Right Compact Disc Player

Flo Ota De Lange and Sheri Henderson

Introduction

Welcome to CD technology! This compact disc player uses a laser to "read" the music on a disc. Your new Sounds-Right Compact Disc Player will give you many hours of listening pleasure if you take the time to read and follow the instructions below for connecting and operating the CD player and amplifier. Do not be discouraged by the number of steps involved. Just take one step at a time, and you will soon be listening to your favorite music.

Connecting the Compact Disc Player to the Amplifier

- Turn off and unplug the CD player and amplifier.
- Connect the ends of the Stereo Connection Cable to the unit's L (left) and R (right) LINE OUT jacks. Match the red plug to the red R jack and the white plug to the white L jack.
- Connect the other end of the Stereo Connection Cable to the amplifier's corresponding left and right CD INPUT jacks.

- Plug the AC power cord into the back of the CD player, and then plug the other end into one of the AC outlets on the back of the amplifier.

Playing a Disc

- You may load up to five compact discs into your CD player.
- Turn on the amplifier, and select "CD" on the input selector.
- Press the POWER button on the CD player.
- Press the OPEN/CLOSE button on the CD player to open the disc tray. The disc tray will slide out.
- Place a disc (with the label facing upward) in one of the disc holders. Place only one disc in each holder.
- To load another disc, press the DISC SKIP button to turn the rotary tray to the next disc holder.
- Press the OPEN/CLOSE button again to close the disc tray.
- Select disc No. 1 with the DISC SKIP button.
- Press the PLAY/PAUSE button. The display will show the disc and track number in play.
- To stop play, press the STOP button.
- To stop play temporarily, press the PLAY/PAUSE button. To start play from the PAUSE or STOP mode, press the PLAY/PAUSE button again.

1. Which sentence *best* states the writer's *main* proposition in the paragraph under "Introduction"?

   A   The laser on a CD player "reads" the music on a disc.

   B   A Sound-Right CD player will give hours of listening pleasure.

   C   You will soon be listening to your favorite music.

   D   Connecting and operating a CD player is not difficult.

2. In a summary of the steps for preparing and operating a CD player, which detail is *most* important to include?

   F   Turn off the power to the CD player and amplifier while connecting these units.

   G   Up to five compact discs can be loaded into the CD player.

   H   A display will show the disc and track number in play.

   J   Press the STOP button to stop play.

3. These instructions are organized in —

   A   cause-and-effect order

   B   order of importance

   C   step-by-step order

   D   order of difficulty

4. What information from the instructions might you also expect to see in an advertisement for the CD player?

   F   Do not be discouraged by the steps involved.

   G   The Sounds-Right CD Player can load up to 5 CDs.

   H   Select "CD" on the input selector of the amplifier.

   J   To stop, press the STOP button on the CD player.

5. Which button would you push to temporarily stop disc play on the CD player?

   A   POWER

   B   OPEN/CLOSE

   C   PLAY/PAUSE

   D   STOP

6. Which button allows you to turn the rotary tray?

   F   DISC SKIP

   G   POWER

   H   PLAY/PAUSE

   J   OPEN/CLOSE

For permission to reprint copyrighted material, grateful acknowledgment is made to the following sources:

Gillon Aitken Associates Ltd.: "So you want to be an astronaut?" by Richard Knight. Copyright © 2000 by Richard Knight. Originally appeared in *The Times*, London, April 22, 2000.

Arte Público Press: "El Olvido" from *Terms of Survival* by Judith Otiz Cofer. Copyright © 1987 by Judith Ortiz Cofer. Published by Arte Público Press–University of Houston.

The Associated Press: "Poe's Death Is Rewritten as Case of Rabies, Not Telltale Alcohol" from *The New York Times*, September 15, 1996. Copyright © 1996 by The Associated Press.

R. Michael Benitez: "Rabies Death Theory" by R. Michael Benitez from "Editorial Desk" from *The New York Times*, September 30, 1996. Copyright © 1996 by R. Michael Benitez.

Susan Bergholz Literary Services, New York: "Snow" from *How the García Girls Lost Their Accents* by Julia Alvarez. Copyright © 1991 by Julia Alvarez. Published by Plume, an imprint of Dutton Signet, a division of Penguin Putnam Inc., and originally in hardcover by Algonquin Books of Chapel Hill. All rights reserved.

Brandt & Hochman Literary Agents, Inc.: "The Most Dangerous Game" by Richard Connell. Copyright © 1924 by Richard Connell; copyright renewed © 1952 by Louise Fox Connell.

Carlos Capellan and Chess in the Schools: "Teaching Chess, and Life" by Carlos Capellan from *The New York Times*, September 3, 2000. Copyright © 2000 by Carlos Capellan.

Eugenia W. Collier: Slightly adapted from "Marigolds" by Eugenia W. Collier from *Negro Digest*, November 1969. Copyright © 1969 by Johnson Publishing Company, Inc.

Dell Publishing, a division of Random House, Inc.: "Harrison Bergeron" from *Welcome to the Monkey House* by Kurt Vonnegut, Jr. Copyright © 1961 by Kurt Vonnegut, Jr.

Doubleday, a division of Random House, Inc.: "My Papa's Waltz" from *The Collected Poems of Theodore Roethke*. Copyright 1942 by Hearst Magazines, Inc.

Dutton Signet, a division of Penguin Putnam Inc.: Adapted footnotes by J. A. Bryant, Jr., from *Romeo and Juliet* by William Shakespeare, edited by J. A. Bryant, Jr. Copyright © 1964, 1986, and renewed © 1992 by J. A. Bryant, Jr.

Dutton, a division of Penguin Putnam Inc.: "Can Animals Think?" edited and adapted from *The Parrot's Lament* by Eugene Linden. Copyright © 1999 by Eugene Linden. Originally published in *Time*, 1999.

Farrar, Straus & Giroux, LLC: From *The Odyssey* by Homer, translated by Robert Fitzgerald. Copyright © 1961, 1963 by Robert Fitzgerald; copyright renewed © 1989 by Benedict R. C. Fitzgerald.

Harcourt, Inc.: "The Necklace" by Guy de Maupassant from *Adventures in Reading*, Laureate Edition. Copyright © 1963 by Harcourt, Inc., copyright renewed © 1991 by Deborah Jean Lodge, Alice Lodge, Jeanne M. Shutes, Jessica Sand, Lydia Winderman, Florence F. Potell, and Mary Rives Bowman.

HarperCollins Publishers, Inc.: From *Edgar A. Poe: Mournful and Never-ending Remembrance* by Kenneth Silverman. Copyright © 1991 by Kenneth Silverman.

Hill and Wang, a division of Farrar, Straus & Giroux, LLC: "Thank You, M'am" from *Short Stories* by Langston Hughes. Copyright © 1996 by Ramona Bass and Arnold Rampersad.

Henry Holt and Company, LLC: "Fire and Ice" from *The Poetry of Robert Frost*, edited by Edward Connery Lathem. Copyright © 1951 by Robert Frost; copyright © 1923, 1969 by Henry Holt and Company, Inc.

Houghton Mifflin Company: From *Among Schoolchildren* by Tracy Kidder. Copyright © 1989 by John Tracy Kidder. Published by Houghton Mifflin Co., Boston, 1989. All rights reserved. From *One Belfast Boy* by Patricia McMahon. Copyright © 1999 by Patricia McMahon. All rights reserved.

James R. Hurst: "The Scarlet Ibis" by James R. Hurst from *The Atlantic Monthly*, July 1960. Copyright © 1960 by The Atlantic Monthly.

Sharon Ingram: From the diary of Sharon Ingram from *Children of "The Troubles": Our Lives in the Crossfire of Northern Ireland*, edited by Laurel Holliday. Copyright © 1997 by Sharon Ingram.

Alfred A. Knopf, a division of Random House, Inc.: "Dream Deferred" ("Harlem") from *Collected Poems* by Langston Hughes. Copyright © 1994 by the Estate of Langston Hughes.

The New York Times Company: From "In America: Romeo and Juliet in Bosnia" by Bob Herbert from *The New York Times*, May 8, 1994. Copyright © 1994 by The New York Times Company. "Heroes with Solid Feet" by Kirk Douglas from *The New York Times*, April 23, 2001. Copyright © 2001 by The New York Times Company.

Naomi Shihab Nye: "Daily" from *Hugging the Jukebox* by Naomi Shihab Nye. Copyright © 1982 by Naomi Shihab Nye.

ACKNOWLEDGMENTS

People Weekly: From "Feeding Frenzy" by Peter Ames Carlin and Don Sider from *People Magazine*, June 2, 1997, pg.101–102. Copyright © 1997 by People Weekly. All rights reserved.

Peters Fraser and Dunlop Group Limited on behalf of The Estate of Liam O'Flaherty: "The Sniper" from *The Martyr* by Liam O'Flaherty. Copyright © 1933 by Liam O'Flaherty.

Pocket Books, a Division of Simon & Schuster, Inc.: From Introduction from *Children of "The Troubles": Our Lives in the Crossfire of Northern Ireland,* edited by Laurel Holliday. Copyright © 1997 by Laurel Holliday.

Burton R. Pollin: "If Only Poe Had Succeeded When He Said Nevermore to Drink" by Burton R. Pollin from "Editorial Desk" from *The New York Times,* September 23, 1996. Copyright © 1996 by Burton R. Pollin.

Random House, Inc.: "The Round Walls of Home" from *A Natural History of the Senses* by Diane Ackerman. Copyright © 1990 by Diane Ackerman.

Science@NASA: From "Far-out Housekeeping on the ISS" by Ron Koczor from *Science@NASA website,* accessed on March 13, 2001, at http://science.nasa.gov/headlines/y2000/ast29nov_1.htm. Copyright © 2000 by NASA.

Scribner, a division of Simon & Schuster, Inc.: "Old Man at the Bridge" from *The Short Stories of Ernest Hemingway.* Copyright 1938 by Ernest Hemingway; copyright renewed © 1966 by Mary Hemingway.

Gary Soto: "The Talk" from *A Summer Life* by Gary Soto. Copyright © 1990 Gary Soto.

The Literary Estate of May Swenson: "Southbound on the Freeway" from *The Complete Poems to Solve* by May Swenson. Copyright © 1963 and renewed © 1991 by May Swenson.

Rosemary A. Thurber and Barbara Hogenson Agency: "The Princess and the Tin Box" from *The Beast in Me and Other Animals* by James Thurber. Copyright © 1948 by James Thurber; copyright renewed © 1976 by Helen Thurber and Rosemary A. Thurber. All rights reserved.

The University of Georgia Press: Slight adaptation of "American History" from *The Latin Deli: Prose and Poetry* by Judith Ortiz Cofer. Copyright © 1993 by Judith Ortiz Cofer.

University Press of New England: "The Talk" from *A Summer Life* by Gary Soto. Copyright © 1990 by University Press of New England.

PHOTO CREDITS

Abbreviations used: (tl) top left, (tc) top center, (tr) top right, (l) left, (lc) left center, (c) center, (rc) right center, (r) right, (bl) bottom left, (bc) bottom center, (br) bottom right, (bkgd) background.

Page 3, (bl), © Charlie Traub, (bkgd), Karin Daher/Gamma Liaison; 11, Superstock, Inc.; 33, Image Copyright ©2003 Photodisc Inc.; 43, Image Copyright ©2003 Digital Vision; 49, Image Copyright ©2003 Photodisc Inc.; 59, Image Copyright ©2003 Digital Vision; 69, © Ken Karp; 81, Francisco Hidalgo/The Image Bank; 91, Image Copyright ©2003 Photodisc Inc.; 103, Image Copyright ©2003 Photodisc Inc.; 115, (br), Margarette Mead/The Image Bank, (bkgd), Eastcott/Momatiuk/Woodfin Camp & Associates; 131, Courtesy of the Illinois State Historical Library; 137, Image Copyright ©2003 Photodisc Inc.; 143, NASA; 149, (bl), CORBIS, (bkgd), © John Smart; 155, 163, 167, Image Copyright ©2003 Photodisc Inc.; 175, P. Briel/The Image Bank; 181, 191, 202, Everett Collection; 209, (br), Erich Lessing/Art Resource, New York, (bkgd), Getty Images/Stone; 222, (rc), Eric Lessing/Art Resource, New York, (bkgd), Getty Images/Stone; 228, (rc), Antikensammlung Staatliche Museen zu Berlin Preussischer Kulturbesitz. photo: Christa Begall, (bkgd), Getty Images/Stone; 234, (c), The De Morgan Foundation, London/The Bridgeman Art Library, London/New York, (bkgd), Getty Images/Stone; 243, (tl), HRW Illustration, (bkgd), Jack Fields/CORBIS; 253, 261, Image Copyright ©2003 Photodisc Inc.; 269, (tl), Art Today, (bl), Image Copyright ©2003 Photodisc Inc.; 281, Image Copyright ©2003 Photodisc Inc.; 289, (bl), Courtesy FRONTLINE, (bkgd), Everett Collection; 297, 305, 311, Image Copyright ©2003 Photodisc Inc.